CHINA'S DRUG PRACTICES AND POLICIES

China's Drug Practices and Policies

Regulating Controlled Substances in a Global Context

HONG LU
TERANCE D. MIETHE
University of Nevada, USA

BIN LIANG
Oklahoma State University-Tulsa, USA

ASHGATE

Published by
Ashgate Publishing Limited
Wey Court East
Union Road
Farnham
Surrey, GU9 7PT
England

Ashgate Publishing Company
Suite 420
101 Cherry Street
Burlington
VT 05401-4405
USA

www.ashgate.com

British Library Cataloguing in Publication Data
Lu, Hong, 1966-
    China's drug practices and policies : regulating controlled
    substances in a global context.
    1. Opium abuse--China--History--20th century. 2. Opium
    trade--China--History--20th century. 3. Drug control--China-
    -History--20th century. 4. Narcotic laws--China--History--
    20th century.
    I. Title II. Miethe, Terance D. III. Liang, Bin, 1972-
    363.4'5'0951-dc22

Library of Congress Cataloging-in-Publication Data
Lu, Hong, 1966-
    China's drug practices and policies : regulating controlled substances in a global context
/ by Hong Lu, Terance D. Miethe, and Bin Liang.
    p. cm.
    Includes bibliographical references and index.
    ISBN 978-0-7546-7694-2
    1. Narcotic laws--China. 2. Narcotic laws--China--History. I. Miethe, Terance D. II.
Liang, Bin, 1972- III. Title.

    KNQ3092.L8 2009
    344.5105'45--dc22

2009008828

ISBN 9780754676942 (hbk)
ISBN 9780754693932 (ebk)

Mixed Sources
Product group from well-managed
forests and other controlled sources
www.fsc.org Cert no. SA-COC-1565
© 1996 Forest Stewardship Council

Printed and bound in Great Britain by
MPG Books Group, UK

Contents

List of Figures

List of Boxes

List of Tables

List of Abbreviations

ACCORD	ASEAN and China Cooperative Operations in Response to Dangerous Drugs
ASEAN	Association of Southeast Asian Nations
BJS	Bureau of Justice Statistics
CCP	Chinese Communist Party
DEA	Drug Enforcement Administration
FDI	Foreign Direct Investment
FIE	Foreign Invested Enterprise
GDP	Gross Domestic Product
GNP	Gross National Product
ICPO	International Criminal Police Organization
INCB	International Narcotics Control Board
INCSR	International Narcotics Control Strategy Report
MOU	Memorandum of Understanding on Narcotic Drugs Control
NAOA	National Anti-Opium Association
NBSC	National Bureau of Statistics of China
NNCC	National Narcotics Control Commission
NPC	National People's Congress
PRC	People's Republic of China
SEZ	Special Economic Zone
SOE	State-owned Enterprise
SPC	Supreme People's Court
UK	United Kingdom
UN	United Nations
UNCND	United Nations Commission on Narcotic Drugs
UNDCP	United Nations International Drug Control Programme
UNGASS	Special Session of the United Nations General Assembly
UNODC	United Nations Office on Drugs and Crime
US	United States
WTO	World Trade Organization

Preface and Acknowledgments

The global war on drugs that began with the International Opium Commission in 1909 in Shanghai has marked its 100-year anniversary. These prohibition efforts will seemingly carry on and probably intensify in the years to come. China's drug control efforts, as part of the global system, witnessed many "ups and downs" over its own history, but it also greatly influenced the nature of the various global movements in drug control.

China was the very first nation to regulate opium activities. Its history of legal regulation of narcotics spans over 160 years, beginning in 1792 when Emperor Yongzheng issued the first royal opium regulation edict and beyond 1952 when the Chinese Communist government declared its anti-drug campaign victory. From 1792 to the present, over 500 opium and other narcotics laws, regulations, legal documents, and local rules had and have been enacted and published, making China the country with the most narcotics regulations in the world. The transition of China from the largest opium importer, consumer, and producer in the nineteenth and twentieth centuries to a drug-free nation by the 1950s is often considered a significant feat in the war on drugs.

In addition to its legal regulation over time, opium and other narcotic drugs have also played a major role in the social, political, and economic history of China. During the early Imperial era, opium served as a medicine for various health problems and became a foreign luxury item for consumption by the royal court and the wealthy. Similar to the social and symbolic values of tea drinking, social customs and rituals were developed around opium smoking. By the mid-nineteenth century, a culture of opium smoking had become fully entrenched within all segments of Chinese society.

During this same period, however, opium and its regulation emerged as one primary cause of the growing political and economic conflict that derived from the clash of Western imperialism and China's national sovereignty. Opium continued to be a major political and economic force in the Republic Era. Examples of these practices include the use of forced opium cultivation by warlords to finance their military expenses, the Nationalist's plan to establish an official government monopoly on opium sales/distribution, and the narco-chemical policies adopted by the Japanese to immobilize Chinese resistance in Japanese-occupied areas. Similarly, the drug eradication movement that followed the establishment of the People's Republic of China (PRC) was a major political and social milestone for the new government. Most recently over the last two decades, drug-related activities have reemerged as both a local and global social problem in contemporary China.

The major purpose of the current book is to explore the nature of China's history of narcotic drug use and regulations. Three major historical periods are examined: Imperial China (pre-1911), the Republic Era (1911–1949), and the PRC era (1949–present). Given the significance of opium over China's long history, most of our attention focuses on patterns of opium consumption, trade, and importation. By identifying the prevailing social, political, and economic conditions in these historical periods, our analyses examine how these conditions shaped the nature of opium-related activities and its legal regulations. Theories of law and society are also applied to further enhance our understanding of China's legal responses to these drug-related activities over time.

The authors would like to acknowledge the assistance of a number of people in this project. First of all, we are indebted to our editor, Eric Levy, at Ashgate Publishing for his encouragement and support. Throughout the course of this project, our graduate assistants, Melanie Taylor, Sarah Prather, and Brittnie Watkins provided valuable library and editorial assistance. We would also like to acknowledge the comments of previous reviewers who provided critical feedback on this book. Financial support for travel and faculty research given to the first author by the University of Nevada, Las Vegas is also greatly appreciated. We would also like to thank the East Asian Library at University of Southern California, the Asian Reading Room at the Library of Congress, and the library at East Asian Institute of National University of Singapore for their invaluable collections on East Asian, particularly Chinese, literature and their online resources. Finally, we would like to thank our family members, Jason, Shannon, Selina, Nancy, Alex, Zachary, and Ying for their unwavering love and support. Without them, this project would not have been possible.

Chapter 1
The Consumption and Control of Illegal Substances

People have consumed herbal and chemical substances for medical or recreational use throughout much of human history. The nature of the legal regulation and control of these substances, however, varies cross-culturally, over time, and by the particular type of substance. For example, alcohol and tobacco have a long history of recreational use in most countries, but the public consumption of these substances in the U.S. has come increasingly under greater legal regulation in the past decade (e.g., through the passage and stricter enforcement of drunk driving laws, public smoking bans). In other countries, religious doctrines (e.g., the Quran's prohibitions against alcohol use) and cultural values (e.g., the Confucianist views of ritual propriety) have served as a relatively stable force in limiting the use of alcohol and other spirits for recreational purposes.

Similar to alcohol and tobacco, the regulation of narcotic drugs (e.g., opium and its derivates [morphine, heroin]) and other controlled substances (e.g., marijuana) has also varied considerably over time and from place to place. Opium and morphine, for example, have been used for centuries for medicinal purposes (e.g., pain relief, treating diarrhea), but the legal status of these drugs as controlled substances has changed dramatically over time in most countries (e.g., legal and widely accepted in some time periods but vilified and demonized in other historical times). Although the passage of "medical marijuana" laws in several U.S. states represents an emerging view about its medical benefits, the recreational use of marijuana and its legal regulation follows a similar pattern of volatility over time and from place to place.

Using a comparative and historical approach, the current study examines patterns of drug consumption and its regulation in China over time. It focuses on China's history of opium use, importation, and cultivation before the twentieth century and other drugs (e.g., morphine, heroin, and methamphetamines) in contemporary China. The primary purpose of this study is to explore how various political, economic, and social conditions at particular historical periods affect the nature of drug use and its regulation. Major theories of law and society will also be evaluated in terms of their relative abilities to explain both historical changes and stability in patterns of narcotic drug use and its social control. These theories and the rationale for using China as a case study for this comparative and historical analysis are described below.

Theories of Law and Society

Laws serve various purposes and functions in society. From a functionalist perspective, laws are designed to regulate and coordinate social relations (e.g., contracts), maintain stability in a society, and to reinforce shared values and beliefs. A conflict perspective, in contrast, views law as a more dynamic force to enhance or preserve special interests. Both of these general perspectives on law and society have generated particular theories that identify the political, economic, and social conditions that enable and constrain the ability of law to achieve various goals. The written works of Emile Durkheim, Donald Black, labeling theorists and social constructionists, and William Chambliss are specific examples of these general perspectives that are relevant to the historical study of the legal regulation and social control of drugs.

Durkheim's functional theory contends that the nature of law and legal sanctions is a reflection of the type of social solidarity in a society (Durkheim 1964). In relatively simple and homogenous societies, social order is maintained through mutual dependencies and a shared normative structure. As an affront to this collective conscience, acts of crime and deviance in these types of societies evoke repressive sanctions (e.g., imprisonment, corporal punishment, and other types of public degradation) that function to preserve and protect social solidarity. In more diverse and complex societies, social order is maintained through contracts and the use of restitutive sanctions (e.g., compensation, reparation). This presumed transition from repressive to restitutive law as societies become more complex is a basic premise in many other theories of law and society.[1]

According to Black's theory of the behavior of law, the quantity, direction, and style of law vary in relationship to several basic aspects of social life. These social correlates include *stratification* (i.e., inequality of wealth and/or social mobility), *morphology* (e.g., the degree of social integration), *culture* (e.g., the complexity/ diversity of ideas, degree of conformity), *organization* (i.e., the centralization of political and economic action), and *social control* (i.e., the amount of non-legal or informal control) (Black 1976). Empirical evaluations of Black's theory find some support for the idea that the quantity of law varies directly with the degree of stratification, integration, culture, and organization (i.e., societies that are more stratified and integrated, culturally diverse, and more centralized in their organization structures have a greater quantity of law than their respective counterparts) (See, for example, Lu and Miethe 2007b, 25–39). Confirmatory evidence is also found for Black's claim of an inverse relationship between informal and formal social control and variation in the style of law by stratification (e.g., law having a penal style when directed toward lower-ranking people but a compensatory style when it is directed toward higher-ranking individuals or groups).

---

1 For related theories that also suggest the transition from repressive to restitutive law in more diverse and complex societies see Nonet and Selznick 1978.

The labeling perspective within the sociological study of crime and deviance offers a distinct viewpoint for examining the nature of law and social control (For reviews of labeling theory, see Becker 1963). From this perspective, no particular act is inherently or innately criminal. Instead, the criminality of an act, and by extension the offender, is socially constructed by those who have the power or wealth to get their particular wishes and desires codified in law. Labeling theories examine the nature of societal reaction to particular behavior (e.g., public denunciation and degradation ceremonies), assess whether the state's response is commensurate with the gravity of the particular problem, and explore the process and means by which claim makers construct an image of their own righteousness by demonizing those activities that may harm their vested interests.

Among the various conflict theories of law and society, Chambliss' theory of structural contradictions is of particular interest because of its emphasis on the dynamic nature of law creation (see, for instance, Chambliss 1979, 149–171; Chambliss and Zatz 1993). In particular, this theory contends that the struggle to resolve fundamental contradictions in political, economic, and social relations is the basis of law creation. These legal resolutions, in turn, create other dilemmas and contradictions that lead to further conflicts and changes in existing laws. It is this dynamic process of attempting to resolve these structural contradictions that explains the nature and content of law.

When applied to the historical study of drug use and its social control, these different theories of law and society provide a strong foundation for exploring the nature of change and stability in drug consumption and its regulation over time. For example, Durkheim's theory suggests that efforts to control illicit drug activity would represent a movement from repressive to restitutive sanctions as a society becomes more diverse and complex. However, most functionalist theory would also allow for particular periods of legal repression in more developed countries, especially when a particular drug represents a serious threat to the collective consciousness. Labeling theory offers a similar expectation about the presence of sporadic times of severe legal punishments for illicit drug activities, but the prime objective of legal repression under this perspective is the promotion of self-interests and not necessarily to preserve and protect the wider society. Similarly, social forces (e.g., political, economic, and cultural factors) are considered important causal agents in all types of law making under both Blacks' and Chambliss' theories.

Although both perspectives share a concern about the relationship between law and society, it is important to emphasize that the basic assumptions underlying functionalist and conflict approaches to drug regulation are qualitatively different. In particular, functionalists view societies as integrated through shared values and in a state of dynamic equilibrium where adjustments affecting the social system are made with minimal change within this system (for a review of the basic assumptions underlying functionalism, see Van Den Berge 1967, 294–310). Changes in legal prohibitions against illicit drug activity over time under this functionalist model would involve slow, piecemeal reforms that maintain the status quo. The conflict perspective, in contrast, assumes that legal regulations of drugs and other behaviors may be more susceptible to dramatic changes over time because they often represent the intense and ongoing power struggles and tensions between different groups (e.g., rulers and the ruled, competing interest groups). A primary goal of the current study is to explore the relative value of functional and conflict perspectives in explaining the nature of stability and change over time in narcotic drug consumption and its legal control in China.

Legal Impact Studies and the Effectiveness of Law

Socio-legal studies are widely applied to assess the impact and effectiveness of particular laws in achieving both instrumental and symbolic goals. The particular types of laws covered within these legal impact studies are virtually unlimited, including any and all types of administrative and regulatory codes, state and federal criminal laws, and civil disputes among individuals and organizations.

Legal impact studies typically involve a comparison of attitudes or behavioral patterns before the passage of legal action and after its implementation. Unfortunately, this before/after design is problematic for making clear inferences about the particular legal impact because it often fails to account for a variety of other factors that may also explain changes over time.[2] These problems are compounded when other issues are also considered. For example, legal changes may not be easily observed when the change is long-term rather than short-term, is more symbolic than behaviorally based, involves a subsequent change in both attitudes and legal behavior, and when the impact of the change is indirect (i.e., mediated through other mechanisms) rather than direct. Unintended and collateral consequences that may minimize the positive impact of legal reforms must also be considered in any judgments about legal effectiveness.

Another problem with legal impact studies is that law is not a distinct moment in social life that can be isolated for study and separated from other social processes. Instead, law is an integral part of society, a part of the interactions among individuals and institutions, and a unique product of a particular political and economic system. Under these conditions, measuring the impact of a single law on its intended target often offers an incomplete picture at best.

A related challenge faced in legal impact research is that contrary to the general, widely accepted assumption that law has clear intention, studies often find that the motive behind a particular piece of legislation may be rather complicated, has a hidden agenda, or results from a compromise among various competing interests

---

2   Within the area of research methodology, these problems with the before/after design involve what are called threats to the internal and external validity of the research findings. These threats are produced by the lack of control for other factors that may influence the apparent changes attributed to changes in the law.

and goals (Platt 1969). As a consequence, it is difficult to conduct a straightforward analysis of the before and after effects.

Even with these limitations, however, conducting an examination of the impact of specific legislation within a particular historical period is a valuable and informative endeavor. Based on a wide array of past research, the following conditions are often found to be conducive to bringing about the intended legal changes (Carter 1988, 25–39; Evan 1965, 288–291):

- The law derives from a legitimate, authoritative, and prestigious source.
- The law embodies values understandable and compatible with existing social norms.
- The proposed changes have successful precedents in other communities or nations.
- The changes are intended to be made in a relatively short time.
- Those who are responsible for enforcing the law must be committed to the change intended by law.
- The new law has positive and negative sanctions that are precise enough to be enforced.
- The new law is widely known by the general public through widespread publicity.

Previous research has also found that laws are likely to produce an uneven impact. For example, studies have demonstrated that the U.S. Supreme Court ban of prayer in the public schools resulted in "any response imaginable" ranging from strict compliance, symbolic compliance, or indifference, to utter defiance (Kidder 1983, 117; Patric 1957, 455). Previous research also suggests that the legal impact of particular practices is often unpredictable, resulting in situations in which laws passed to produce one outcome have unintended side effects or opposite effects. Labeling theory, for example, often recognizes that an intended goal of criminal laws is to reform offenders through punishment, but the stigmatizing process of punishment and labeling may unintentionally propel the offender further into criminal activities.

Besides the broader social and cultural conditions in which legal change takes place, previous research on legal impact has more closely examined the social world of law enforcers (i.e., the police, prosecutors), law interpreters (i.e., judges), and the populations directly targeted in the specific laws. Collectively, these three groups are labeled as filtering agents and they are believed to have a great impact on mediating and moderating the impact of law. For example, numerous studies find that law enforcers are likely to selectively enforce laws depending on their judgment about the laws' severity and fairness, the prevailing norms, and/or the enforcers' personal beliefs.[3] The same is true for judges, whose decisions are

---

3 The punitive laws of the eighteenth-century England that subjected pick-pockets and petty thieves to the death penalty resulted in a drastic decline in prosecutions for

influenced by the social environments surrounding them and judicial rulings are reflective of these environments.[4]

National and international evidence also reveals that groups affected by legal changes (i.e., the target population) may alter the law or invent ways to take advantage of the law. In the international context, for example, colonial laws and indigenous ways were often in conflict and resulted in semi-colonial and semi-indigenous legal orders in British colonies such as India and South Africa. Similarly, domestic laws in the U.S. that regulate various public order offenses such as narcotics, prostitution, gambling, and pornography had unintentionally resulted in "crime tariffs", increasing the personal risks associated with doing business in these illegal market, driving the price up for the service or product, and leading to the formation of criminal organizations (Packer 1968, 277–282).

When legal reforms are designed to invoke dramatic changes over previous practices, it is widely recognized that these legal changes will inevitably face resistance on many levels, including resistance based on social factors (e.g., vested interests, social class, ideological resistance, organized opposition), psychological factors (e.g., habit, motivation, ignorance, selective perception, moral development), cultural factors (e.g., fatalism, ethnocentrism, incompatibility, superstition), and economic factors (e.g., limited economic resources).

Given these issues surrounding legal impact research, it should be clear that a systematic study of law and legal change requires the examination of the particular content of the legal rules and the wider social context in which they are implemented. In the current study, we are mindful of these limitations of legal impact research when we seek to understand the wider social context in which particular drug-related activities come under legal control throughout various times in China's history.

Historical Data Sources on Drug-Related Activities in China

In an attempt to portray an objective and accurate pattern of drug-related activities in China, we will rely on available historical records, official accounts, and scholarly works. Unfortunately, comprehensive and accurate historical data on drug activities in China are limited for several basic reasons:

---

those crimes (Tobias 1968, 199). Police officers in Connecticut altered their procedures in stopping and arresting speeders after the stiff speeding law passed in this U.S. state (Campbell and Ross 1968). Local police officers continued to enforce the "laws" against homosexuals even after the laws were repealed in 1972 (Ross 1976, 411).

4   For detailed discussions on how extra-legal factors played a role in judges' decisions, see Becker 1966; Giles and Walker 1975; and Kritzer 1979. Critical legal theorists argued that the "haves" are usually the beneficiaries of the filtering process, not the "have nots", as courtroom routines favor landlords, businesses, and large corporations over tenants, consumers and individual citizens (Galanter 1974, 95).

- First, official efforts at data collection of any sort (e.g., population census) have not been an established practice within the Chinese government throughout its long history. This data is especially likely to be absent or not collected in a systematic manner for drug-related offenses because these activities often occur outside public view and may warrant severe punishment upon detection.
- Second, the legal status of opium-related activities has changed over time (e.g., from legal, acceptable medicine to regulated illicit drugs, to de facto legal drugs, and again to heavily regulated drugs), decreasing the likelihood that uniform data would be collected on these practices over different time periods.
- Third, the operation of vested interests by government officials and other organizations (e.g., foreign governments, hospitals, missionary/religious groups, anti-opium associations) may distort the nature and gravity of drug problems that are revealed in existing historical records. Depending upon the particular context, these organizations may either underestimate or overestimate the prevalence of particular drug problems.

These problems with the availability of historical data are not unique to the study of drug-related activities in China. In fact, historical studies of virtually any topic and in any geographical location face similar problems with data availability and comparability over long historical periods. To deal with these problems, most historians will compile records from all available sources, compare and contrast the patterns within them, and then arrive at general conclusions about the extent and nature of the particular trends over time. A similar methodological process of triangulation will be used in the current study.

The primary data sources for estimating the prevalence of China's opium-related activities involve national and foreign documents (e.g., surveys and other reports on consumption, cultivation, and importation; customs/trade ledgers; arrest and sentencing records), local and regional counts of the number of drug facilities and paraphernalia (i.e., opium dens, opium pipes, opium shops), and various ethnographic accounts. Any gross discrepancies in these estimates across different sources will be noted before identifying particular historical patterns.

Among various types of drug-related activities, data on consumption patterns are the most problematic for determining historical trends. To provide average estimates of consumption, previous studies of China's drug history have often combined information on the dosage level of the average drug user with national importation and cultivation data. For example, it has been estimated that there were about 2.1 million opium smokers in China between 1838 and 1839 (Hsu 2000, 171–172). This number was derived from the amount of opium imported (40,000 chests), the amount of catties of extract from the raw opium (2.4 million catties of opium can be extracted from 40,000 chests), and the average amount of opium extract consumed daily by an average opium smoker (estimated at .05

Chinese ounce[5]) (Hsu 2000, 171–172). Other estimates of opium use among the adult population in the nineteenth century range from less than 1% to 60% or higher (Dikotter, Laamann and Xun 2002, 52). Obviously, the utility of these types of consumption estimates depends on the accuracy of the data, the average dosage level, and the supply of opium. Unfortunately, given the absence of any other systematic data, these types of derived measures represent the only available estimates of consumption patterns for most of China's history.[6]

International Drug-Related Activities in the Twenty-first Century

Drug-related activities (i.e., consumption, cultivation/manufacturing, and trade) have been a national and international problem in many countries over the last two centuries. Specific regions of the world have been the primary sources of opiates and other controlled substances. For example, the "Golden Crescent" (i.e., Afghanistan, Pakistan, and Iran) has been the primary opiates producer and distributor of opiates (especially heroin) in the last century. The principal source countries for cocaine have been Columbia, Bolivia, and Peru (for discussions of the international drug trade see Arnold, 2005; Inciardi 1986, 2002). The U.S. has been the world's largest market for all types of drugs. It has also been the most active country in its efforts to combat international drug trade by establishing Drug Enforcement Administrative (DEA) offices in more than 70 overseas locations (Arnold 2005, 1).

Since the late 1990s, the United Nations' Office on Drug and Crime (UNODC) has made a concerted effort to publish "comprehensive and balanced information about the world drug problem." Their publications, "*World Drug Trade Reports*", provide estimates of contemporary world patterns of consumption, production, and seizures by law enforcement agencies of various illicit drugs. Some of these worldwide estimates of illicit drug activities over the last several decades are summarized in Table 1.1 and Figure 1.1.

Given problems of reporting illicit behaviors and especially variability across different countries in their reporting practices, it is reasonable to question the accuracy of these estimates of illicit drug consumption and production. Nonetheless, these United Nations' reports suggest that illicit drug activities are clearly a global enterprise in the twenty-first century. This is especially true for illicit substances like opium and cocaine that have a global market but whose production is limited to specific regions of the world.

---

5   One Chinese ounce equals approximately 31 grams.

6   Drug consumption had also been estimated by agencies specializing in drug treatment and control throughout different historical periods. However, the methods of their data collection are largely unknown and these types of data are also susceptible to political manipulation and distortion.

Table 1.1 Annual Global Prevalence Estimates of Drug Use in 2005–2006

Drug Type	User population (in millions)	Percentage of users in age group 16–64
Cannabis	158.8	3.8%
Amphetamines	24.9	0.6%
Opiates	15.6	0.4%
Cocaine	14.3	0.3%

Source: United Nations (2007) *World Drug Reports*.

National and international enforcement policies regarding drug interdiction have often resulted in large seizures of illegal drugs. For example, according to the United Nations' (2007) reports, about 42% of the global cocaine production and 26% of the global heroin production were intercepted by the authorities. However, there is no direct evidence that these enforcement activities have affected consumption patterns. In fact, these supply-side suppression practices have more often than not simply increased the price of drugs for consumers and have been associated with adverse collateral consequences (e.g., civil rights violations, illegal/unethical police practices, increased criminal activity to support drug habits). In addition, little empirical support is also found for the presumed deterrent effect of increased criminal punishments for the use, possession, and/or sale of illegal substances.

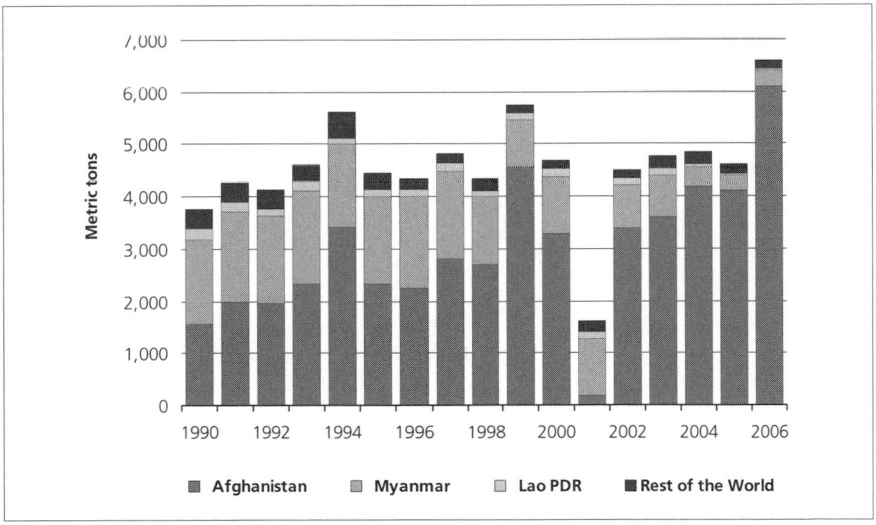

Figure 1.1a Global Opium Production (metric tons), 1990–2006
Source: United Nations (2007) *World Drug Reports*.

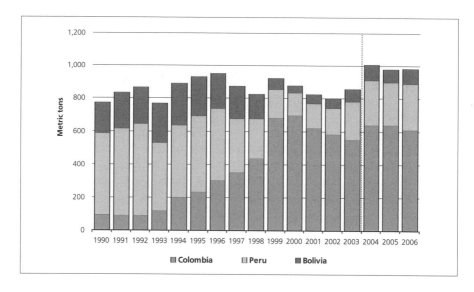

Figure 1.1b Global Cocaine Production (metric tons), 1990–2006
Source: United Nations (2007) *World Drug Reports*.

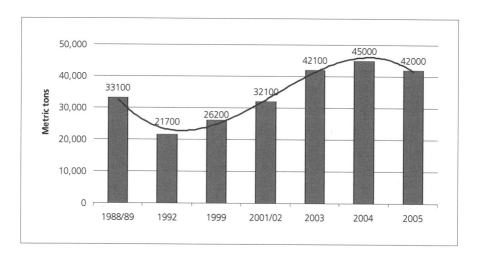

Figure 1.1c Global Cannabis Herb Production (metric tons), 1988–2005
Source: United Nations (2007) *World Drug Reports*.

	Abuse of opiates ...		... of which abuse of heroin	
	population in million	in % of population 15-64 years	population in million	in % of population 15-64 years
EUROPE	3,860,000	0.7	3,250,000	0.6
West & Central Europe	1,420,000	0.5	1,370,000	0.4
South-East Europe	184,000	0.2	130,000	0.2
Eastern Europe	2,300,000	1.6	1,750,000	1.2
AMERICAS	2,130,000	0.4	1,480,000	0.3
North America	1,310,000	0.5	1,245,000	0.4
South America	830,000	0.3	230,000	0.1
ASIA	8,480,000	0.3	5,350,000	0.2
OCEANIA	90,000	0.4	30,000	0.1
AFRICA	980,000	0.2	980,000	0.2
GLOBAL	15,550,000	0.4	11,090,000	0.3

■ Above global average   ■ Around global average   ☐ Below global average

Figure 1.1d Annual Prevalence of Opiates Abuse, 2005
Source: United Nations (2007) *World Drug Reports*.

The international community has long recognized the global nature of the drug problem and been dealing with this problem through the establishment of special commissions and advisory committees, and calling for agreements and conventions on this issue. Within this international context, China's extensive history of the legal control over narcotics serves as an important case study for exploring the national and global efforts in drug regulation and control. In Chapter 6 we will demonstrate how and to what extent China's drug activities and legal responses have both shaped, and been shaped by, international efforts in regulating and controlling illicit drugs for the past century.

Previous Studies of Drug Consumption and Legal Regulation

Since the last quarter of the twentieth century, an enormous amount of research literature has evolved on patterns of drug consumption and its legal regulation (for reviews of the literature on various types of drug consumption and drug laws see Arnold 2005; McAllister 2000). National agencies in the U.S. and other Western countries fund numerous drug surveys, compile trends in particular types of drug use, document the legal penalties for drug use and distribution, and provide the latest information on drug abuse prevention. Theories of the etiology of drug use (e.g., why people use drugs) are also plentiful in this research literature (for a review of current theories of drug consumption, see Mosher and Akins 2007).

Comprehensive studies on the nature of legal regulation of particular controlled substances and its effectiveness have been conducted in several comparative and historical contexts. Some of the most widely cited case studies of the legal regulation of controlled substances include the following:

- Gusfield's study of the U.S. temperance movement focused on the symbolic value of law as a source of prestige and status for those groups that support it (Gusfield 1963). In the case of prohibition of alcohol, the "symbolic crusade" served to affirm and legitimate the dominance of groups that supported abstinence. Aside from its symbolic value, however, the claims by these moral reformers that the legal prohibition against selling alcohol would be effective in reducing crime and improving public health proved to be wishful thinking. In fact, the Volstead Act of 1919 has been most commonly linked to several adverse consequences, including increased alcohol poisoning due to the low quality control of illegal alcohol and the creation of a black market for alcohol that contributed to the rise of organized crime (for studies of prohibition and its consequences see: Asbury 1950; Blocker 1989; Lee 1963; Timberlake 1963).
- McCoy's study of the politics of heroin focuses on the use, production, and trafficking of heroin throughout Indochina in the twentieth century (McCoy 1973; 2004). McCoy pays particular attention to the complicit role of American diplomats and the Central Intelligence Agency (CIA) in narcotic trafficking in this region by its alliance with groups actively engaged in the drug industry, covering up the involvement of known heroin traffickers, and actively engaging in the transport of opium and heroin. Subsequent revisions of his original book have expanded the coverage to the CIA's involvement in the global drug trade.
- Becker's study of the enactment of the Marijuana Tax Act of 1937 describes how enterprising individuals or groups (i.e., moral entrepreneurs) were able to redefine marijuana use as a dangerous drug (Becker 1963). Legal efforts to deter marijuana use have been common throughout various countries over time. However, arrest practices and penalties for the use or possession of this controlled substance vary widely across jurisdictions and the actual deterrent effect of the legal sanctions for marijuana use is largely unknown.
- Numerous descriptive accounts exist on the social, political, and economic factors associated with the Opium Wars between China and Great Britain in the nineteenth century (see, for examples, Beeching 1976; Hanes and Sanello 2004). Depending upon their particular focus, these studies have examined the contributory roles of such factors as the trade deficits, conflicts of culture and ethnocentrism, and the superiority of British military technology and weaponry in the onset of these wars and their resolution.

As suggested in many of these studies, efforts to control the consumption of illegal substances through legal regulation have met with only limited success.

What these studies of law and society also indicate is that legal regulation and its effectiveness are affected by social, political, and economic forces in particular places at particular times. Our study of the consumption and social control of narcotic drugs in China will augment this previous research and address how well existing theories of law and society explain patterns of stability and change in drug consumption and its legal regulation over distinct historical periods.

The Current Study

Using a comparative and historical approach, the current study examines patterns of narcotic drug consumption and its legal control in China. It focuses primarily on opium and its derivatives (i.e., morphine, heroin) because these drugs have been most widely associated with China's culture. Drawing upon historical records and previous descriptive accounts, the current study addresses the following research questions:

- What are the major political, economic, and social factors associated with the legal regulation of opium's use, importation, and cultivation in China over time? Have particular political, economic, and social factors been more or less important in the legal control of narcotics over particular historical periods?
- What is the nature and prevalence of China's narcotic drug activities (i.e., consumption, importation, and cultivation) and the legal and extra-legal controls of these activities over time?
- What existing theories of law and society best explain the nature and prevalence of change and stability in China's legal regulation of opium and other narcotic drugs over time? How well do the basic tenets of functionalist and conflict theories of law and society conform to the historical patterns of legal regulation and how well does existing research on laws' symbolic and instrumental value apply to the Chinese experience? What are the theoretical implications of our analysis of legal regulation in China for cross-national studies of the interrelationships between law and society in other socio-political contexts?

As a case study for comparative analysis, China's socio-political and legal regulation of narcotics provides an important context for studying the interrelationship between law and society for several reasons. First, China has a long and rich written history involving over 2,000 years of available documents for studying its laws and social history. Second, Chinese society has experienced both long periods of stability as well as dramatic changes in its political, economic, and social structure over time. For example, China was under an imperial, dynastic rule for thousands of years throughout most of its history, followed by a brief Republic Era led mostly by the Nationalist Party (1911–1949), and then the People's Republic of China, led by the Communist Party, was founded in 1949. This temporal pattern of stability and change offers an ideal setting for the contextual analysis of law and society. Third, opium has occupied a central place in much of China's history, being the primary catalyst for two wars with Great Britain, a major social custom (i.e., smoking in opium dens), and also considered a national "epidemic" at some points in time. Under these conditions, a comprehensive study of China's narcotic history provides an ideal setting for the sociological investigation of the dynamic interplay between political and economic conditions, social and cultural forces, and legal regulations.

Organization of the Book

The remaining chapters of this book are organized in the following manner. Chapter 2 describes the political, economic, social, and cultural conditions of Imperial China (pre-1911), and patterns of drug consumption, trade, and cultivation within this historical era. This chapter also identifies the legal and administrative procedures used to combat and control opium-related activities. It is this historical pattern of stability and change in drug activity and laws that is to be explained by the political, economic, and social factors that underlie existing theories of law and society.

Chapter 3 describes political, social, and economic conditions in the Republic Era (1911–1949) and the impact of these factors on the passage and enforcement of drug laws. It focuses on how the drug trade, cultivation, and usage were affected by the Nationalist government and the warlords in gaining political and economic advantage in an effort to achieve political and military control. The complex and dramatic transformation of the political, social, and cultural conditions during this brief Republic Era provides an important context for studying drug consumption and its control because this historical period involved multi-level interests, conflicts, dilemmas, and contradictions.[7]

Chapter 4 examines characteristics and patterns of drug-related activities in the People's Republic of China (PRC). It explores patterns of change and stability in social, political, and economic conditions over distinct periods of the PRC's history and their impact on legal efforts to control drug consumption, cultivation, and trade. The first 30 years (1949–1978) represented the Mao era when strict state control in political, economic, social, and cultural arenas was widely practiced. The second phase of the PRC history occurs after 1978 and is marked by its "Open Door" policy and economic reforms. Our analysis in this chapter focuses on the social context of these two stages of the PRC history in which illicit drug activity

---

7   These contradictions and competing interests include national interests vs. local protectionism, political sovereignty, national identity, and unity vs. warlordism and the emergence of diverse ideologies, international norms vs. ethnic minority customs, and short-term economic profits vs. long-term adverse effects on national health and the economy.

was virtually eradicated from the 1950s until the 1970s but reemerged upon economic reforms made after 1978.

Chapter 5 applies existing functionalist and conflict theories to explain change and stability in patterns of drug-related activities across the different periods of Chinese history. It focuses on the ability of these theories to identify the major social, political, and economic forces that account for the nature of legal regulation and control of drug-related activities in specific historical periods. Guided by past research on the effectiveness of law, this chapter also examines the impact of the Chinese drug laws from several perspectives, including the extent to which the enforcement of the new drug laws in the reform era is met with resistance (i.e., social, psychological, economic, cultural), and filtered by law enforcers, law interpreters, and the target population.

The final chapter summarizes the results of this study and describes their implications for current global efforts to regulate and control illicit drug activities. In particular, we link China's drug prohibition efforts to the global context and pay special attention to how China struggled with its drug control in the eighteenth and nineteenth centuries when the "free trade" policy was practiced and imposed onto China by foreign powers, and then how China tried to cooperate and catch up with international drug control efforts in the twentieth century when the world entered into a drug prohibition era, and finally how China actively reached out and sought cooperation with other nations in fighting its arising domestic drug problems by the end of the twentieth century and now in the twenty-first century. Future prospects of the continued quest for drug eradication in China and elsewhere are also explored within the context of the efficacy of legal controls in periods of transition. Appendices are provided on selected major Chinese laws, administrative regulations, and judicial interpretations pertinent to narcotic drug laws passed after 1978 to acquaint readers with regulatory and control efforts on narcotic drugs in contemporary China.

Chapter 2
Social Conditions and Opium in Imperial China (Pre-1911)

This chapter examines the historical development of opium laws in Imperial China. It covers the earliest documented history up until the collapse of the last dynastic power – the Qing Dynasty in 1911. After providing a general overview of the social conditions of Imperial China (i.e., its basic political, economic, and cultural characteristics), we describe patterns of legal regulation of opium-related activities (i.e., consumption, trade, and domestic cultivation) over this historical period. Specific political, economic, and cultural factors are identified as facilitators and constraints that may account for patterns of change and stability in opium-related activities within this era. Particular emphasis is placed on the social context of opium-related activities in the eighteenth and nineteenth centuries, a time at which opium became the focus of national and international attention.

An Overview of the Social Conditions of Imperial China

China's Imperial history covers over 2,000 years. It began with the Qin dynasty of 221 BC and ended with the demise of the Qing Dynasty in 1911. During this long historical period, Chinese civilization gradually evolved into a system with a united political system, a homogeneous culture, an intensive agriculture, close-knit and highly-structured family and village life, and hierarchical and bureaucratic administration that combined administrative and judicial functions into one.[1] General features of these social conditions in Imperial China are described below.

The Political Structure of Imperial China

China experienced a long, continuous history of dynastic rule by its majority ethnicity, Han. Only two times during this history was China ruled by different ethnic groups, first by the Mongols during the Yuan Dynasty (1279–1368) and then by the Manchus during the Qing Dynasty (1644–1911). Even though it was

---

1   Similar to beliefs about China's political unity over time, Fairbank (1978a, 1–34) argues that the claims of cultural unity and homogeneity evolving around the Confucian teachings in China was a great social myth.

considered a "foreign" dynasty, the Qing government continued the basic political structure and institutions established by the Han rulers.

Box 2.1 Political Structure in Imperial China

Central Government
- Emperor
- Principle offices
- Coordinate offices
- Imperial departments

Local Government
- Provincial governments managed by the governor and royal commissioners representing the interest of the central government
- Circuit intendants and prefects
- District level governments governed by the magistrate

The central feature of the political structure of Imperial China is the concentration of power in the emperor and little separation of power among the Western conception of the three branches of the government – executive, legislative, and judicial.[2] Depending on the particular emperor, the political system of this era could be highly effective and efficient but at the same time extremely conducive to corruption and abuse.

The political structure of the Qing Dynasty had two main layers: the central government and the local government. On the top of the central government's hierarchy was the emperor, followed by the Principle Offices, Coordinate Offices, and Imperial Departments. The local political structure consisted of three main levels:

- the provincial level superseded by the governor with the assistance of commissioners (i.e., in charge of finance, judiciary, and education, and

---

2   For example, the emperor decided all state policies, commanded the army, ratified treaties with foreign nations, enacted and amended laws by decrees and edicts, and served as the highest court of appeal by granting pardons and reprieves. Although granted the supreme power of all three functions of government, the emperor was still bound by certain restrictions including family and clan law, opinions of the appointed high ranking officials (e.g., ministers served on the Six Boards who advised the emperor on major issues of the country), and the public's sentiments as may be manifested in the form of rebellion (Hsu 2000, 45–46).

special commissioners in charge of salt, grain transport, customs, rivers, waterways, and postroads) appointed by the emperor;
- the intermediary offices of the circuit intendants and prefects; and
- the district under the governance of the magistrate (for a detailed treatment of the functions of each of these central government offices see Hsu 2000, 55–57).

The district magistrate was responsible for collecting taxes, settling disputes, and maintaining public order in the local community. Official posts allocated by the central government only reached to the district magistrate level. Within each of the districts were villages, cities, towns, countryside settlements, and rural markets. These smaller local rural units were largely operated and managed by local residents, not by the central government's appointed officials.

Box 2.2 District Magistrates in China

- Lowest-level appointed governmental officials
- Appointed for three-year terms
- Holding positions outside their home provinces
- Little kinship ties and personal obligations
- Corruption and callousness highlighted as common traits

As the lowest level royal appointed officials, the magistrates were typically appointed for three-year terms and always to provinces outside their homes to avoid nepotism. Because of this arrangement, magistrates commonly had no kinship ties in the local community and had little personal obligations to serve the people. Often, the magistrates treated their deployment as a type of career development instead of serving the people. Corruption and callousness were often viewed as the common traits shared by these governmental officials (Fairbank 1987, 39–40).

Two neighborhood organization systems developed within the district level – *baojia* and *lijia* – were created to fill the void of governmental control at the local neighborhood level. These types of neighborhood organization systems will become especially important when we examine and attempt to understand the nature of China's drug use, cultivation, trade, and its control.

Baojia was developed in 1644 to facilitate census registration and police control. Under this system, every 10 households formed a *pai* (with a headman called the *paizhang*) and every 10 *pai* constituted a *jia* (with its headman called *jiazhang*). Every 10 *jia* made up a *bao*, so the *Baozhang* was in charge of 1,000 households. The *baojia* provided the police a central figure to watch for and report crimes and criminals in neighborhoods. Failure to perform the registration and crime control duties of the *baojia* was a punishable offense. In fact, all households within the unit would be subject to collective punishment if a crime occurred without appropriate intervention by residents in the *baojia* system.

Box 2.3 Neighborhood Organization

baojia
- designed to facilitate police control through self-control
- main functions including census registration and crime watch
- collective responsibility system

lijia
- primary function including assessing and collecting taxes

Lijia was a similar system to the *baojia* even though its function was primarily for assessing and collecting the land and poll taxes (Hsu 2000, 57–59). These two neighborhood level mechanisms – *baojia* and *lijia* – were designed for self-governance and control by the local people in the absence of control exerted by the central government (Fairbank 1987, 39).

The peasants occupied the lowest position at the bottom of Qing's political institutional hierarchy. This group was often characterized as docile, passive, and hard-working. Due to the relatively slow development of farming technology, peasants often worked all year round for a bare, hand-to-mouth subsistence. Most peasants were fatalistic and accepted the social circumstances they were in without much desire to change (Fairbank 1987). Nevertheless, peasant revolts became a relatively common scene in dynastic changes, particularly during hard times when taxation became too onerous and/or natural disasters occurred. This threat of peasants' revolt was their primary source of political power across all levels of government and helped them maintain a bare level of subsistence.

This structure of the political institutions under many Imperial dynasties, particularly in the Qing dynasty, had great significance in understanding how and why orders and wills of the emperor and the central government may not be fully carried out at the very bottom of the political institutional hierarchy. In particular, the local leaders were not political appointees of the emperor and were thus not directly accountable to the central government. To a greater extent, peasants were more responsive, willingly or unwillingly, to the order of the local leaders because these leaders either represented the local interest more closely than the central government, or they represented a much more immediate threat to the peasants' daily well-being than the central government.

Agrarian-Based Economy

Imperial China was predominantly an agrarian society, where soil and human labor constituted the economic foundations of the state (Hsu 2000, 59). Government revenue came from the land poll taxes, land rents, customs dues, salt tax, tea tax, license tax, and other sources (Hsu 2000, 61).

By the turn of the twentieth century, China was a highly populated country with approximately 400 million people.[3] Among them, four-fifths of the Chinese population lived in rural villages and relied on farming for daily survival. Deeply entrenched in a Confucian way of life, individuals were structurally bound to their village and family for everything: their livelihood, security, education, recreation, marriage, and other major social contacts. Ordinary peasants, despite being largely illiterate, were well-schooled in the Confucian beliefs about the bonds of kinship, the duties of status, and the forms of ritual propriety. Preoccupied with the maintenance of harmony, unity, and order among the village communities, technological advances in agricultural productivities were rarely emphasized.

The single-most-important economic policy in Imperial China was self-sufficiency in agricultural products. This self-sufficiency was fundamentally important for several basic reasons:

- China had a vast territory with a huge population;
- it had engaged in a closed-door trade policy with little commercial activities and trade exchanges with other nations; and
- agriculture output accounted for two-thirds of the entire gross national product (GNP) of Imperial China, according to an estimate in the 1880s.[4]

This self-reliance economic model certainly had its positive side. In particular, it helped China become financially independent from other nations, created community stability and unity, and the close-knit collectivities could potentially strengthen an individual's family and community ties and interdependency. It could also help the government and communities to utilize resources more efficiently and design an agricultural plan that fit the specific needs of the community. However, the self-sufficiency policy had several flaws.

---

3   There was no official demographic data in the late Qing Dynasty. The official estimate indicated an approximate 400 million people by the first decade of the twentieth century (see Feuerwerker 1980, 3).

4   The non-agriculture sectors included mining, manufacturing, construction, transportation, trade, finance, residential housing, government services, professional, gentry and other services, and net income from abroad. All of these products combined accounted for one-third of the GNP of China in the 1880s (Feuerwerker 1980, 2).

Box 2.4 Self-Sufficiency Economy

- Structural demand
  - Large population of over 400 million
  - Closed-door trade policy
  - Agricultural output as key to the national economy
- Positive impact
  - Financially independent nation
  - Community interdependency
- Negative impact
  - Reinforced geographic disparities
  - Overburdened farmers

First, it reinforced and perpetuated geographic disparities. Imperial China was comprised of vast and widely dispersed territories but some areas (e.g., eastern and southern coastal regions of China) had more productive land than others (e.g., western mountainous regions). The natural conditions in some areas were also more conducive to higher agricultural outputs than others. Because of this disparity in geography and natural resources, living standards varied dramatically in coastal areas and the remote south and western region of China.

Second, because agricultural output represented the majority of China's GNP, its central and local governments relied heavily on taxes from farmers to support their salaries, allowances, and operational budgets. Under these conditions, farmers shouldered the major burden of supporting not only their family, but also the operation of the local and the central government.[5] In times of trouble such as a natural disaster or a war, it was not unusual for farmers to owe more to the government even after a year's hard labor.

Third, the self-sufficiency policy could not meet the demand of the dramatic rise in China's population between the seventeenth and nineteenth centuries, an estimated increase from 150 million to 430 million (Jones and Kuhn 1978, 108–109). The rising population pressure on productive land became noticeable even in remote western regions such as Sichuan during that period of time (Jones and Kuhn 1978, 109).

A series of rebellions in the late Qing period (e.g., the Miao Rebellions, the rebellion of the secret societies of the south, the White Lotus Rebellion, the *Taiping* Rebellion) were triggered or facilitated in part by peasants' frustration

---

5   For example, the Qing government had a grain tribute administration policy in which the central government relied on various lower levels of the governments to collect grain taxes. At the bottom of this tax chain were the farmers. Thus, as the grain tribute administration bureaucracy grew, farmers would bear a greater burden to meet the quotas (Jones and Kuhn 1978, 119–128).

with their intolerable living conditions (Jones and Kuhn 1978, 132–144). These conditions included heavy taxation (i.e., while the basic quotas were fixed, the imposition of surtaxes for the local government had long been institutionalized), official corruption (i.e., the local officials' ability to control the price of the grain and the exchange rate from the grain to silver alone gave them the power to exploit the farmers), and famine (Jones and Kuhn 1978, 128–132). Taxation became even more of a problem after 1830 when the opium trade led to the Qing government's trade deficit and silver famine, and local officials were pressured to make up the silver shortage by levying heavier taxes on the local farmers.[6]

Foreign Trade, Restrictive Commercial Policies, and Ethnocentrism

Under the Confucian thought, commercial activities were regarded as beneath the dignity of the scholar-gentry, and the pursuit of profit was frowned upon as greedy and immoral. This view of merchants, along with the self-sufficiency mentality, inhibited the growth of business enterprises in Imperial China (Hsu 2000, 71–72).

Congruent with this traditional view of commerce, the Qing government maintained a policy that trade with foreign countries should be limited to one port area – Canton (translated as Guangdong in the PRC era) and needed to be far away from the center and the capital of the nation – Peking (translated as Beijing in the PRC era). No government officials were permitted to be involved in business dealings (Hao and Wang 1980, 153–156).

This restrictive commercial policy of the Qing government was also reflected in the treatment of foreign merchants as second-class citizens. In fact, it had long been considered a privilege, not a right, for foreigners to conduct business in China. Foreigners were required to observe and behave in accordance with the Chinese laws and customs, as well as some special rules set up just for them.[7] The

---

6 During the period of silver famine around the 1830s, the taxation system became desperate for peasants to meet the regular quotas and surtaxes. This was particularly devastating for peasants in the lower Yangtze region where it historically shouldered more tax burdens than any other regions in the nation because of its superior geographic location and natural resources. Nevertheless, the local government officials in the Yangtze region could not afford the heavy tax and had to falsely report natural disasters in order to secure tax remission from the central government (Jones and Kuhn 1978, 130–131).

7 Selected rules of code for foreign traders promulgated in 1759 included: (1) no foreign warships may sail inside the Bogue; (2) neither foreign women nor firearms may be brought into the factories; (3) pilots and compradors must register with the Chinese authorities; (4) foreign factories shall employ no maid and no more than eight Chinese male servants; (5) foreigners may not communicate with Chinese officials except through the proper channels; (6) foreigners are not allowed to row boats freely in the river but are allowed to visit the temple in groups of 10 or less three times a month on the 8th, 18th, and 28th; (7) foreigners may only ride in topless small boats; (8) foreign trade must be conducted through the Hong merchants; foreigners who live in the factories may walk

Chinese government also insisted that foreigners be subjected to the Chinese law when committing a crime in China, which often clashed with the foreign countries' demand of exemptions.[8]

This feeling of superiority among the Chinese emperors and high-ranking officials was largely attributable to the longstanding closed-door foreign policy that prevented the Chinese from having a better understanding of foreign countries. China's ethnocentrism was also derived from its self-sufficient agrarian economy, the sense of a mighty government and a prosperous economy, and grounded in its long history of surplus trade with foreign nations.[9]

Because of this Sino-centric mentality and closed-door foreign policy, however, the Qing government was ill-prepared for Western contact (see Fairbank 1978c). In the second half of the nineteenth century, foreign military actions resulted in the

---

freely within 100 yards of their factories; (9) foreign traders must not remain in Canton after the trading season; (10) foreigners may neither buy Chinese books nor learn Chinese (Hsu 2000, 150–151).

8   For the most part, civil disputes between foreigners and Chinese were rare; disputes between the Hong merchants and foreigners were often settled by negotiation and arbitration. Only in criminal cases where foreigners were either the criminal or the victim did the Chinese government insist on trying and executing the sentence according to the Chinese law. A criminal case involving a foreigner defendant or victim typically was resolved in one of the three ways: (1) the case was tried in China but the convicted offender was sent back to the native country for punishment; (2) the case was tried and sentence was executed in China; or (3) the case was tried in China in an absence of the defendant who fled from China, and the sentence was forwarded to the foreign country to be carried out (Hsu 2000, 153).

9   While foreign countries seemed to have an insatiable appetite for China's products, ranging from tea to silk and cotton, foreign products were not able to break into the Chinese market for most of the history of Imperial China. For example, in 1857, one year after the second Opium War, the British paid the Chinese 15 million pounds (GBP) for silk and tea. However, the Chinese gained a surplus of GBP 4.5 million by only spending GBP 1.5 million for cotton from India, GBP 2 million for British manufactures, and GBP 7 million on opium (Hanes and Sanello 2002, 164).

For thousands of years, China's major exception to its closed-door foreign policy involved diplomatic relationships with other nations in the surrounding areas of Asia that acknowledged Chinese sovereignty over them. For example, under several emperors' rules including Emperor Shunzhi (1644–1661), Kangxi (1662–1722), Yongzheng (1723–1735) and Qianlong (1736–1795) in the early Qing dynasty, China had numerous peripheral states coming to pay tribute, including Korea, Annam, Burma, Siam, Bhutan, Nepal, Gurkhas, Khokand, Bukhara, Burut, Badakshan, Afghanistan, and the Kazaks (Hsu 2000, 41).

To achieve political stability, the Qing government also permitted a limited trade with some distant countries. However, the government made it clear publicly that commercial interests should always be subordinate to political interests. Nevertheless, behind the official public policy, private individuals, local organizations, and even the central government profited from trade, particularly the enormous profits from the opium trade (Wakeman 1978, 163–212).

Qing government's defeat in a series of wars, including the two Opium Wars with Great Britain (1839–1842 and 1856–1860), the Sino-French War (1884–1885), and the Sino-Japanese War (1894–1895).[10] The Qing government's defeat in these wars resulted in the following activities:

- the emergence of a treaty system that led to the dramatic increase in the number of treaty ports from five in 1842 to 50 in 1911;
- the expansion of foreign extra-territorial consular jurisdictional rights over treaty-power nationals, their property, trade, and industry, along with foreign shipping privileges in Chinese waters;
- the employment of foreign administrators in various important posts such as customs, post office, and salt revenue administrations;
- the expansion of missionary work;
- the opening of Western schools, hospitals, and churches (Fairbank 1978a, 3–4).

This period of foreign invasion, exploitation, and aggression during the late nineteenth century and the early twentieth century has been collectively labeled as Western Imperialism. Among its consequences, Western Imperialism dramatically altered the Chinese society, exposed the inadequacies of the Qing government's ability to effectively address domestic problems, and precipitated the rise in anti-foreign sentiment and nationalism.[11]

---

10   The Opium War fought between the Qing government of China and Great Britain between 1839 and 1842 represents a "watershed event" in modern Chinese history (Xiao 2002, 42). Depending on the political and cultural perspectives, this war has been portrayed differently. For example, many popular and scholarly works in the Republic Era (1911–1949) and the early People's Republic of China (1949–1978) portrayed the war as caused by Western aggression and imperialism (Hu 1953; Yang 1981). This view was also held in some scholarly works published overseas (Fay 1975; Hsu 2000). In contrast, Western scholars and China observers tended to attribute the cause of the war to the Qing government's failure for not adopting an open trade policy, trade conflicts, and corruption by the Chinese governmental officials (Wakeman 1978, 163–212). However, most authors agree that the primary reasons for China's defeat in these wars include the following factors: (1) China's Sino-centric mentality and closed-door foreign policy, (2) Western military and technological superiority; and (3) the Qing government's official corruption, weakening military power, and declining public morality.

11   Anti-foreign sentiment and nationalism in China was manifested in two extremes. One is self-critical, modest, and preoccupied with modernity, whereas the other focuses on national culturalism, and reacts to foreign nations and cultures with disenchantment. While these two extreme perspectives on nationalism dominated political, economic and popular discourse from time to time, Xiao argued that for the most part, China's search for national identity was marked by a modest posture and openness toward the West. This is particularly the case in the contemporary era of economic reforms in the 1980s and onward (Xiao 2002, 41 and 50).

Social Stratification and the Culture of Consumption

Highly influenced by the Confucian doctrine of filial piety and ritual propriety, patriarchal and patrilineal principles of social hierarchy were firmly entrenched throughout the history of Imperial China. These structural arrangements were reinforced by various social conditions (e.g., agricultural self-sufficient production, limited physical mobility to other regions, and limited upward social mobility only through the rigorous education and examination system) (Jones and Kuhn 1978, 113–115). Under this stratification system, the interest of family, clan, and the local community often supersedes the interest of the individual.

Social scientists (especially sociologists and cultural anthropologists) have long noted that consumption is a way of communication, and certain goods carry a status symbol. This is especially true in a group-oriented society such as China, where pressures to conform to social conventions are tremendous. Collectivist societies are particularly likely to develop a culture of shame and guilt that encourages conformity to socio-cultural conventions and also affects consumers in their choices of goods.[12]

The Chinese words *ti-mian* best capture this conspicuous consumption culture in which consuming a good is not necessarily out of one's desire or needs but for the sake of being polite, fashionable, and/or face-saving.[13] For example, tea drinking and tobacco smoking became popular symbols of China's consumption culture for centuries before the introduction of opium. Due to its presumed health benefit and traditional Chinese preference and belief in herbal medicine, particular cultural symbols were developed from tea drinking and tobacco smoking.[14] Opium

---

12   According to Benedict, the shaming culture relies on external sanctions for good behavior, whereas the guilt culture relies on an internalized conviction of sin. Shame is a reaction to other people's criticism – it requires an audience or at least an imagined audience for the sanctions of shame to be potent. Shame serves as an external sanction for often unspoken but well-observed social-cultural conventions. Individuals in the shame culture fear or respect these conventions and are pressured to conform to pro-social conventions and customs. A guilt culture refers to self-discipline and self-perfection without the external pressure, a sense of honor and right from wrong that typically drives the individual to conform to social expectations (Benedict 1967).

13   Bourdieu (1984) pointed out that taste marks social classes, and consumption is predisposed to fulfill a social function of legitimating social differences. Certain goods and services are signs and symbols, which have an identity value. Similarly, Zheng (2005) argued that the consumption of opium should be viewed as fulfilling a social function of legitimating social differences, and suggested that opium smoking became a special culture and represented a status symbol when consumed by the wealthy and the powerful groups of the society.

14   Tea is considered one of the seven necessities of Chinese life, along with firewood, rice, oil, salt, sauce and vinegar. To the Chinese, tea not only has obvious health benefits such as assuaging thirst, killing bacteria, and preventing cancer, but it also has important social and cultural symbolism such as showing respect to guests. Certain rituals were associated

consumption exhibited a similar cultural status (e.g., as a foreign luxury item for conspicuous consumption) and social rituals emerged from its widespread use across a variety of social groups in Imperial China. These social rituals involved how opium was prepared, smoked, and where it was consumed (e.g., opium dens).

Patterns of Opium Consumption, Trade, and Cultivation

The rich social context of Imperial China provides the background for examining patterns of opium consumption, trade, and cultivation within this historical period. The best available evidence on the nature and prevalence of each of these types of opium-related activities is described below.

Opium Consumption

Opium did not originate from China. It was brought into China by Arab traders during the Tang Dynasty around 600 AD.[15] Opium was initially used for medicinal purposes for combating diarrhea, cholera, plague, headaches, inflammation, fever, dysentery, sunstroke, coughing, asthma, vomiting, and for helping people who were hungry to relieve their pain (Su and Zhao 1998, 113). Opium use was also found effective in controlling bodily fluids, and preserving vital energy for warming kidneys, muscles, and joints (Dikotter, Laamann, and Xun 2002, 317–336; Zheng 2005, 11–13).

There was a major transformation of opium from *yao* (medicine) to *chun yao* (spring drug or aphrodisiac) in the Ming Dynasty by 1483. During this period, opium was becoming "the art of alchemists, sex, and court ladies" and was used to help "induce sexual desire, vitalize intercourse, and control ejaculation or emission" (Zheng 2005, 12–13). Opium was administered in a variety of ways in the Ming era, such as powder, pellets, or syrup, or mixed with food and drink (Zheng 2005, 12).

---

with the tea culture. For example, tea means respect when offered to your guests and the elderly. Letting guests sit in the living room without serving tea is a humiliation to the guests. Tea may also serve as a means to apologize and to show submission and regret when offered by children to their parents, and as a mean for extended family members to meet and greet, or show gratitude, in wedding ceremonies. While tea customs and ceremonies were formed and preformed by different social (i.e., royal family, monks, gentry class) and religious (i.e., Buddhist, Daoist, Islamist) groups, and ethnicities/regions (i.e., Tibet, Mongol, Zhe-Jiang area), tea drinking for common people was popular simply for its pleasure and utility in social rituals (Wang 2000, 551–572).

15   Su and Zhao (1998, 111–112) claimed that opium was imported into China during the Tang Dynasty (618–907) by Arab traders via both sea and land. See also Dikotter, Laamann and Xun 2002, 317.

Box 2.5 Timeline for Opium Consumption

- Introduced into China from Arab traders in 600 AD
- Transformed from medical to more recreational use in late 1400s
- Opium smoking method introduced into China by the Dutch in the 1500s

Eating or drinking a raw form of opium was less lethal and addictive than the smokeable form of opium, which was first introduced into China during the 1500s (Booth 1998). In 1589, opium was first listed as a taxable commodity.

The method of opium smoking brought by the Dutch into India and the southeastern region (i.e., Guangdong and Fujian) of China was a major factor in the increased use of opium during the late Qing period.[16] The popularization of opium smoking was further enhanced by the brief prohibition of tobacco smoking in the 1630s and the 1640s of the late Ming Dynasty.[17] The banning of tobacco smoking encouraged millions of tobacco smokers to mix in increasing amounts of opium, and resulted in a growing number of tobacco smokers and opium users (See Candlin 1973; Su and Zhao 1998, 118–119; Wakeman 1978, 171; Yao and Xue 2004, 10–11).

No definitive records exist on the number of opium users in the eighteenth and nineteenth centuries in China. However, given that opium imports reached 1,000 chests[18] by 1767, it is reasonable to assert that an emerging opium market had developed (Su and Zhao 1998, 120). Consumption estimates derived from import figures suggest that an estimated 50,000 people in China were regular opium users in 1767. During the nineteenth century, the estimated number of opium users in China increased dramatically from 2 million in the 1830s to 20 million in the 1880s (Hsu 2000, 171–173; Su and Zhao 1998, 193–194). Estimates of the prevalence and proportion of the adult Chinese population that use opium for various purposes, different social groups, and particular time periods are summarized in Table 2.1.

---

16   It was recorded that in the late Ming period, opium smoking remained rare. Only the Fujianese people were witnessed smoking opium with a pipe (Su and Zhao 1998,118).

17   In 1637, Emperor Chongzhen banned tobacco smoking and sales and subjected violators to the punishment of decapitation. In 1640, the Emperor once again banned private planting of tobacco and subjected violators to severe punishment (Su and Zhao 1998, 117).

18   1,000 chests = 133,300 pounds.

Table 2.1 Estimates of Opium Use in Imperial China (up to 1911)

Opium User Group	Year	Opium Users/ Addicts		Data Source
National Users	1767	50,000 users		Hsu (2000)
	1830	1 million users		Hsu-based estimate
	1835	2 million addicts		Su and Zhao (1998: 146)
	1838–1839	2.1 million users		Hsu (2000: 171–172)
	1850	3 million users		Hsu-based estimate
	1880	20 million users		Su and Zhao (1998: 93–194)
	1890	15 million addicts		Spencer (1975: 154)
National Population Percent	1879	3.5% smokers		Hart (1879)
	1880	5% smokers		Su and Zhao (1998: 93–194)
	1890	3% addicts		Spencer (1975: 154)
Social Groups:				
Adult Male:	*1879–1906*	*1879*	*1906*	
Medical Use		50%	60%	Newman (1995, Tb 3 &4)
Festive Use		50%	70%	
Recreational Use:	1879–1906			
Light/occasional		15%	20%	
Moderate/regular		6%	12%	
Heavy/regular		1%	2%	
Adult Female:	*1894–1899*	*1879*	*1906*	
Medical Use		30%	40%	Newman (1995, Tb 3 &4)
Festive Use		25%	50%	
Recreational Use:				
Light/occasional		4%	8%	
Moderate/regular		1%	2%	
Heavy/regular		0%	0%	

Table 2.1 continued

Opium User Group	Year	Opium Users/ Addicts	Data Source
Work Groups:	1909	Percentage Addicted in High Production Regions	
Actors/Prostitutes/Thieves		95%	Spence cited in Zheng (2005: 154)
Officials and their staff		90%	
Merchants		80%	
Soldiers		30%	
Small shop keepers		20%	
Laborers/Small farmers		10%	
Work Groups:	1899	Percentage Use by Each Group	
Literiati		30%	
Soldier:		30%	
Officials		40–50%	Park (1899), RCO (1894) cited in Newman (1995: 780)
Merchants		20–30%	
Shopkeepers		10–20%	
Artesians		20–40%	
Coolies, boatmen		1–70%	
Select Areas/Provinces:	1909	Percentage Use by Adult Males	
Chefoo		33%	
Canton area		33%	International Opium Commission (1909)
Zhili		20–30%	
Hunan		20%	
Shanghai area		20%	
Manchuria		10%	

The data in Table 2.1 illustrate the wide variability in the estimates of opium users over time and among various groups. Nonetheless, several general observations can be derived from these data. First, opium use appears to have increased over this time period and the estimated proportion of users is considerably higher among men than women and among some work groups than others. Second, areas of high opium production and trade centers (e.g., Yunnan, Canton) also had higher levels of opium use. Third, the reported rates of opium addiction were estimated to be considerably higher among some groups (e.g., prostitutes, thieves, officials) than others (e.g., laborers, farmers).

It is important to note that the estimates of the number of heavy users of opium and opium addicts are wide and varied over the nineteenth century, depending upon the particular definition of addiction and the methods of calculating the number of users. For example, one source estimated the population of opium addicts to be at least 2 million by 1835 (Su and Zhao 1998, 146). By 1906, over 18 million adult males were estimated to be moderate to heavy users of opium, representing about 14% of the adult male population in China in this time period (Newman 1995, 787). Regardless of the actual number of opium addicts, the dominant image of China at this time was the "appearance of ubiquitous opium smoking", with addicts from virtually every social class – the wealthy members of the gentry, public officials who held high or low offices,[19] soldiers, laborers, housewives, and prostitutes all became heavily dependent on opium.

The Opium Trade

The opium problem in China's early history was a direct result of foreign importation because neither opium nor its derivatives were indigenous to China. The nature of both legal and illegal importation of opium from the Tang dynasty starting in 618 to the end of the Qing dynasty in 1911 is described below.

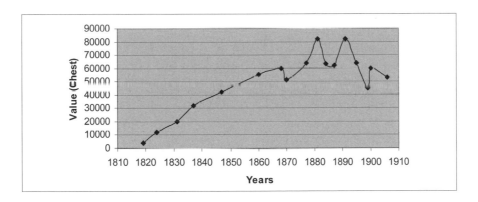

Figure 2.1 Legal Imports of Opium (1819–1907)
Source: Jiang and Zhu 1996, 25; Reins 1991, 11.

Opium imports were legal throughout the Tang, Song, Yuan, Ming, and the early years of the Qing dynasties. There was little mention in historical records of

---

19   According to Hsu (2000, 172), approximately 10–20% of central governmental officials and 20–30% of local officials smoked opium in the early nineteenth century. See also Su and Zhao 1998, 146, 363; Wakeman 1978, 178–179.

this time of the widespread use of opium or problems of opium addiction. Only a small quantity of opium was imported into China and taxes on this commodity were rather minimal.

As a response to the increasing use of opium, the Qing government nearly doubled the taxation on opium imports in 1688 (Su and Zhao 1998, 120). The increased taxes did not curtail its importation though. Concerns about increased opium use also formed the basis of a royal edict that banned opium imports between 1735 and 1796. Despite its illegality, opium continued to be smuggled into China by the Portuguese through Macao and into Guangdong (Canton). An estimated 200 chests of opium per year were smuggled into China via this route by 1736, and it increased to 1,000 chests (i.e., over 130,000 pounds) per year by 1767 (Su and Zhao 1998, 120). By 1773, the British had replaced the Portuguese as the major suppliers in the opium trade to China.

Once the British monopolized the opium trade to China through the East India Company, it attempted to change the Canton Trade System. This Canton Trade System worked toward the advantage of the Chinese government because of a huge trade surplus that arose from Western demands for large quantities of tea, silk, and rhubarb from China.[20] Several missions were launched to try to establish diplomatic representation in Beijing, to negotiate a commercial treaty to expand trade beyond Canton throughout China, and to end the abuse (e.g., unequal treatment of foreign and domestic merchants, official corruption) at Canton. All of these attempts failed.[21] Emperor Qianlong in two edicts rejected the proposal of establishing diplomatic residence in Beijing, calling it impractical, and stated that the dynastic tradition would not be changed to meet the needs of foreigners (Hsu 2000, 161–162).

Meanwhile, the Canton trade was undergoing dramatic changes due to the rapid growth of private and country-wide trade, especially the increases in opium smuggling from India to China.[22] All of these developments threatened the monopoly of the East India Company, and precipitated the clash between the British and the Chinese governments.

Within this context of changing trade conditions, opium importation continued to grow. In fact, even though opium use, cultivation, and trade were illegal in

---

20 To illustrate China's advantage in trade with the British in the eighteenth century, at times the cargo of the East India Company's ships from London to Canton consisted of 90% bullion to pay for the Chinese goods, and only 10% of goods to be bought by the Chinese (Hsu 2000, 150).

21 For example, the Macartney delegation of 84 members was sent to Beijing in 1792 to honor Emperor Qianlong's birthday with gifts valued at GBP 15,610, and to negotiate a treaty to expand trade with China. However, the "Ambassador was received with the utmost politeness, treated with the utmost hospitality, watched with the utmost vigilance (sic), and dismissed with the utmost civility" (Hsu 2000, 160–161).

22 For example, many private traders made transactions with outside anchorages such as Hong Kong and engaged in lucrative opium smuggling businesses without the East India Company's intervention (Hsu 2000, 166).

China at this time period, its importation skyrocketed from 1,000 chests in 1767 to an estimated 40,000 chests per year by 1838 and 1839.[23] Between 1800 and 1879, the total opium imported by the East India Company into China was 638,119 chests, at a cost of 602 million silver sycee to the Qing government (Su and Zhao 1998, 144).

Opium imports caused a continuous outflow of silver and stagnation in the demand for other commodities. Because of opium's illicit status, the opium trade was done on a cash basis (Hsu 2000, 169–171).

The Qing government had two types of payment systems: (1) the state-minted copper coins used in small daily market transactions and (2) the un-minted silver sycee used to the settlement of large accounts. With its primitive and inflexible monetary and financial system at the time, the Qing government relied on the maintenance of the stable exchange rates between the coins and the silver sycee. However, by the early 1830s, there was a serious decline in the availability of silver bullion, indicating a trend toward cheap coins and over-valued silver.[24] Recognizing this problem of a "silver famine", the Qing government decided to reexamine illegal drug imports as the trade deficit was mainly caused by the opium trade.[25]

To illustrate the impact of the opium trade on the Chinese fiscal deficit, the Chinese bought 18 million dollars (USD) worth of opium from the British in 1836 yet only sold USD 17 million worth of tea and silk to the British (Hsu 2000, 173). There is no doubt that the opium trade brought lucrative profits for the East India Company. For instance, opium sales totaled 10 million rupees in 1832, 20 million rupees in 1837, and 30 million rupees in 1838. Opium provided more than 5% of the company's revenue in India in 1826–1827, 9% in 1828–1829, and 12% in the 1850s (Hsu 2000, 172–173).

However, the East India Company's monopolistic rights in the trade with China came to a halt in 1834 as a result of the growing popularity of the *laissez-faire* doctrine and free trade in the eighteenth century in England. The final dissolution of the East India Company after it operated in China for more than a century resulted in several profound changes. One was the change of the Sino-British relations in which government relations had now replaced private arrangements in trade

---

23   It should be noted that for the large part, there were no official statistics on opium imports recorded by the Qing government (Hsu 2000, 169; Su and Zhao 1998, 143).

24   For example, while a tael of silver in 1740 exchanged for 800 copper coins, in 1828, it was worth 2,600 in Shandong province. As a way of dealing with this crisis, the government increased the annual minting (Hsu 2000, 172).

25   Besides drug trafficking, other factors also contributed to the silver famine, such as the lowering of government quality standards and a wave of counterfeiting, and allowing foreign silver coinage to circulate in China at an above-face-value premium to draw purer un-minted Chinese sycee out of the country (Polacheck 1992). Another ramification of the coin deflation and the rise in real tax rates was China's widespread popular tax-resistance movements, ranging from litigation, mass petitions, to mob violence, particularly in the 1840s and the 1850s (Jones and Kuhn 1978, 130–131).

dealings with China. Economic interests remained important in these agreements but national honor and prestige assumed a greater importance for the British than in the past and they would no longer play a subordinate role in trading with China. The halt of the East India Company's trade monopoly in China also caused great concerns among Chinese officials because the future control of foreign traders was now more difficult to manage when it involved numerous small, private traders. This concern was compounded by China's stereotypical image of foreign traders as being "greedy, violent, and unfathomable" (Hsu 2000, 173–174).

Subsequent diplomatic and trade negotiations between the British government (represented by various British officials/merchants such as Napier, Davis, Robinson) and the Qing government all ended up in failure. Upon taking office as the British Chief Superintendent of Trade in China in 1836, Elliot took a "middle of the road" position, and tried to show "confidence and strength combined with caution and conciliation" to gain the Guangdong authorities' trust (Hsu 2000, 176–177). At the same time, the Qing government was seriously debating its opium policy. The argument of legalizing opium trade seemed to be gaining momentum between May and September of 1836, and resulted in an oversupply of opium as foreign traders anticipated the legalization of opium.[26]

Ultimately, however, it was moralistic arguments about the threat of opium on society and family, and the need for strict enforcement of prohibition laws that won over Emperor Daoguang. The subsequent initiation of a sweeping enforcement campaign that punished domestic dealers and addicts and drove away foreign traders achieved some success, resulting in a sudden opium price drop.[27] What followed was the appointment of Lin Zexu as the Qing government's Imperial Commissioner and the subsequent stand-offs between Lin and Elliot before the onset of the first Opium War in 1839.

The causes of Opium War were multi-faceted. It involved the clashes between the Chinese and British governments over the opium trade policy and, more broadly, the general trade policy (e.g., the British requested a direct and equal dialog between the officials of the two countries) and extra-territoriality issues. The result of the war, however, was the passage of imbalanced treaties, first between the Qing government and the British government and followed by other Western nations such as France

---

26 The legalization arguments were made in two aspects: (1) the inability of the current prohibition law to regulate effectively; and (2) the drain of silver. The proponent of opium trade legalization argued that as long as scholars, officials, and soldiers are strictly prohibited from smoking, opium addiction by common people should not be a grave concern (Hsu 2000, 177–178).

27 It was reported that 2,000 opium dealers, brokers, and smokers were sentenced, imprisoned, and/or executed in 1838, smuggling boats virtually disappeared by the end of 1838, and the British traders suffered severe financial losses as a result of these enforcement campaigns in Canton (Hsu 2000, 178).

and the U.S.[28] For example, in 1858, the Qing government signed a treaty with the British, American, and French governments to allow taxation on opium imports and lifted the ban on opium trade.[29] These unequal treaties also resulted in a surge in opium imports because more ports were now forced open to foreign trade.

Based on the available data (see Figure 2.1), the number of opium chests increased steadily from 46,000 chests in 1848, peaked at 80,000 chests in 1880, started declining after that, and ultimately dropped to approximately 50,000 chests per year and continued that trend until 1905 (Blue 2000; Su and Zhao 1988, 161). Meanwhile, the Qing government had profited from taxes levied against opium imports. For example, the tax collected on opium imports reached 2 million *liang* in 1870, twice as much as taxes on all other imported commodities combined (Yao and Xue 2004; 90). Opium continued to be the largest single import in value terms in China until the mid-1880s. It was then replaced by cotton but still remained the second largest imported good.[30] The quantity of imported opium dropped considerably during the last decades of the nineteenth century because of the expanded domestic cultivation of poppies.[31]

Domestic Poppy Cultivation

Arab traders first brought opium to Iran, India, and China around the seventh and eighth centuries. By the beginning of the twentieth century, these three lands already became the global centers of opium production and consumption (Courtwright 2001, 32).

---

28   The first "unequal" treaty, the Treaty of Nanjing in 1842, marked the beginning of several treaties that the Qing government was forced to sign under the threat of military force with foreign countries including the U.K, France, the U.S., and Japan. Due to the coercive and unfair nature of these treaties, they are typically referred to as "unequal treaties" (Fairbank 1978b, 213–263).

29   Tax of 30 *liang* per *dan* was imposed on opium as a result of the treaty (Yao and Xue 2004, 86). Note: 1 *liang* = 50 grams; 1 *dan* = 50 kilograms.

30   Opium was mainly imported from India, colonized by the Great Britain at the time. In fact, opium and cotton combined made up approximately two-thirds of China's imports in the 1870s and the 1880s. By 1890, opium imports were surpassed by cotton and experienced a steady decline since then. For example, opium imports consisted of 43% of all imports in 1870, 39.3% in 1880, 19.5% in 1890, 14.8% in 1900, and only 12% in 1910 (Feuerwerker 1980, 8–9, 48–49). To further illustrate the importance of the opium trade for the economy, grain had been the most important commodity in domestic trade both in value and in volume in the eighteenth century. However, at the end of the nineteenth century, the value of the opium trade grew to 130 million taels, compared to 100 million taels for grain and 100 million taels for salt (Wong 2000, 203).

31   See Blue (2000) and Su and Zhao (1988, 161) for a discussion of this increase in domestic opium cultivation. Other authors have noted that opium planting produced a class of wealthy tenant-farmers in Sichuan province in the late Qing era (see Bastid-Bruguiere 1980).

Opium poppy is an annual. In full bloom, its flowers are arrayed in a rainbow of colors – red, purple, white, yellow, and pink. Its fruit is addictive and can be lethal. Several essential factors are required to have a sustained commercial cultivation of opium poppy: (1) ample water, (2) rich soil, (3) heavy fertilization (i.e., manure, night soil, soybean cakes, ammonium sulphate), and (4) access to ample, skilled farmers because cultivating opium is extremely labor-intensive. Opium is collected in small amounts by hand (with daily yields per worker measured in ounces), so the labor must be cheap as well as skillful (Courtwright 2001, 32; Slack 2001, 7–8). Given that South and East Asia had an ample supply of cheap labors who made a living in farming, the massive cultivation of poppy in these regions should not be a surprise.[32]

The diversity of climatic and topographic conditions in China led to dramatic regional differences in poppy planting and harvesting schedules. For example, Guizhou, a city in the southwestern region of China, typically had poppy planting in late November to early December and harvest in late March to early April. Northeastern and north central regions of China planted poppies in the spring and harvested it in the fall. Even though poppy cultivation is adaptive to a variety of weather conditions, drought, hailstorms, and rain storms, particularly during harvest season, may ruin the crop (Slack 2001, 7–9).

Box 2.6 Domestic Cultivation of Opium

- Domestic cultivation was not a major concern until 1796 when half of the provinces had opium cultivation activities.
- Annual harvest reached 10,000 chests, equivalent of the amount imported by 1830.
- Domestic cultivation gained popularity by 1860 due to enhanced technology and farming skills.
- Most provinces were involved with opium cultivation and annual output yielded 2-4 times more than that was imported by 1880.

Domestic cultivation of opium was rare in the Tang and Song dynasties when opium was initially brought into China. Even in the early Qing dynasty, when opium smoking became a concern in the Qing court, the royal edicts only banned

---

32   Two reasons may account for the popularity of opium in the East. One was religion. While Islam frowned upon alcohol, it tolerated opium. The other was opium's medicinal utility. Because of poverty, population density and a hot and humid climate, people in East and South East Asia suffered disproportionately more incidents of diarrhea and malarial fevers, particularly in India and southern region of China where these climatic conditions were more extreme (Courtwright, 2001, 32–34).

opium imports (the first edict banning opium import was issued in 1729) but not domestic cultivation. In 1796 and 1813, the edicts issued by Emperors Qianlong and Jiaqing, respectively, banned domestic cultivation of poppy.

No records exist on the extent or amount of domestic cultivation of opium in China until the 1830s. One source suggested that almost half of the Chinese provinces were involved in opium cultivation by 1830, particularly in the remote southwestern regions such as Sichuan, Guizhou, and Yunnan (Su and Zhao 1998, 144). Domestic opium cultivation took up 30,000 to 40,000 *mu*[33] of the productive land. The annual harvest reached 10,000 chests, an amount similar to the quantity of opium imported at this time (Su and Zhao 1998, 144–145).

Much of this opium production came from Sichuan and Yunnan provinces where the climate was ideal for opium poppy growth. Nevertheless, because of its poor quality, the market for domestically cultivated opium was weak for decades despite its cheaper prices compared with imported opium (Su and Zhao 1998, 186).

By 1860, domestically cultivated opium started to gain popularity among the Chinese. Due to technological innovations and enhanced farming skills in opium harvesting and processing, domestic cultivation dramatically increased. For example, the annual domestic harvest was estimated at 50,000 chests in 1866. It reached 70,000 chests by 1870, surpassing, for the first time, the amount of opium imported at that time. By 1880, almost all provinces in China had opium cultivation, and the amount was two to four times more than the amount imported from India.[34] By the turn of the twentieth century, poppy cultivation flourished in China and the annual harvest reached 300,000 piculs,[35] approximately six times more than that imported from India (Candlin 1973).

Based on the percentage of productive land used for opium cultivation, it can be established that domestic opium cultivation grew rapidly during the second half of the nineteenth century. For example, 1.8 million *mu* of productive land in 1866 was used for opium cultivation, representing .2% of the total productive land in China. By 1894, 12.3 million *mu* of productive land was used for opium cultivation, representing 1.5% of the total productive land in China. In other words, the percentage of productive land used for opium cultivation in China had increased more than sevenfold in about 30 years (see Table 2.2).

---

33   1 *mu* = .16 acre.

34   No details were available on the specific provinces that had or did not have opium cultivation at this particular time period. However, based on a report in the Republic era, with the exception of Tibet, Qinghai, and Mongolia, all other provinces had some degree of opium cultivation during the 1920s and the 1940s (Slack 2001, 7; Su and Zhao 1998, 189–190).

35   1 picul = 60.47898 kilograms.

Table 2.2 Estimates of Opium Production and Productive Lands

Year	Domestic Production	Land for Opium (*mu*)	Total Productive Land (*mu*)	%
1866	5,500,000	1,833,000	790,000,000	0.2
1870	7,700,000	2,566,000	801,000,000	0.3
1880	40,000,000	13,333,000	827,000,000	1.6
1894	40,000,000	13,333,000	866,000,000	1.5

Source: Xiyuan Huang 1986.

Laws prohibiting opium cultivation were passed in 1909 by the Qing government, resulting in several poppy eradication campaigns. Despite strong resistance, particularly revolts in regions where poppy growth was common and the main source of revenue (e.g., Zhejiang, Gansu, Shanxi, Guizhou, and Manchuria), these eradication campaigns brought "quick" and "impressive" results by early 1911 (Bastid-Bruguiere 1980, 598–599; Spence 1975, 173).

For example, poppy cultivation almost stopped in Sichuan and Shanxi, reduced by three-fourths in Yunnan and Guizhou, and more than 80% of all poppy farms were converted to food crops by early 1911 (Bianco 2000, 292–293; Wright 1968, 14). It appeared that the anti-opium war was on its way to achieve some success. However, the dynastic collapse of Qing and the takeover of the Nationalist Party in 1911 changed the political and legal order and had significant implications on the political and legal agenda to opium.

Table 2.3 Edicts, Decrees, and Laws on Drug Activities

Qing Dynasty

1729	Emperor Yongzheng (1722–1735) issued the first royal edict that penalized opium dealers and opium den keepers.
1735–1796	Emperor Qianlong (1735–1796) issued an edict that banned opium smuggling.
1796	Emperor Jiaqing (1796–1820) issued an edict banning opium imports and domestic cultivation.
1813	The Qing government issued a Decree on Punishing Officials, Soldiers and Civilians Who Smoke Opium. The same year, Emperor Jiaqing issued an edict banning domestic cultivation of poppy and extraction of its juice to make opium.
1815	The Qing government issued a regulation on the prohibition of opium.

Table 2.3 continued

Qing Dynasty

1818	Emperor Jiaqing issued another edict stressing that those who purchased and smoked opium and those customs officials who did not effectively deal with opium smuggling shall be punished severely.
1831	The Daoguang edict specified that: (1) opium planting, retailing, making, and preparing is the same crime as opium smuggling; (2) any local official taking bribery is as guilty as the opium smuggler; (3) opium plants, upon discovery, shall be eradicated and the land confiscated; (4) officials must go back to their locales to investigate crimes each spring; and (5) if opium smuggling was not eradicated, the official must be punished.
	In the same year, an edict prohibiting opium smoking was issued and specified that: (1) purchasing and smoking opium would be subject to 100 sticks; (2) officials who purchase and smoke opium shall be punished more severely (with one degree above the corresponding penalty); (3) eunuchs who purchase and smoke opium shall be exiled into a slave; and (4) parents and cohabitants shall be held responsible if their children and cohabitants smoke opium.
1833	The Qing government (Emperor Daoguang 1820–1850) issued an Act on the banning of domestic cultivation of opium.
1839	The Qing government (Emperor Daoguang 1820–1850) issued an Act of 39 Regulations on the Banning of Opium with severe punishment for opium import, opium cultivation, opium manufacture and processing, opium sale, opium use, operating opium dens, and manufacturing tools for opium smoking and subjected many such offenders to the death penalty of strangulation or decapitation.
1843	Emperor Daoguang issued another edict stating the importance of carrying out the law. However, in the same year, opium trade became de facto legal.
1854	Emperor Xianfeng (1850–1861) rejected a request of legalizing opium imports with taxation from the British government and stressed the resolution of banning opium
1858	Opium trade was legalized through the Beijing Treaty.
1860	The edicts banning the opium cultivation and trade were repealed.
1906 (September)	Emperor Guangxu (1875–1908) issued an edict that banned opium in order to eliminate bad customs.
1906 (November)	A Ten-Article Decree on Opium Prohibition was issued and covered key issues as follows: 1) elimination of the opium source (e.g., banning poppy cultivation; those issued with a license to cultivate poppy must reduce their output by 1/9th each year and rewards are given to those who give up poppy cultivation voluntarily; banning importation of opium and other narcotics drugs; banning importation and manufacture of morphine needles); 2) banning new smokers: those who were already opium addicts must receive a license to purchase opium; 3) detoxification plan (e.g., government officials must quit their habit in six months; those with a license to smoke opium must gradually reduce their daily allowed amount and quit the habit in accordance with the schedule based on age); and 4) closing opium dens: opium dens must be closed in six months.

Table 2.3 continued

Qing Dynasty	
1907	The Criminal Code of the Great Qing stipulated in Article 21 the offenses of opium, including manufacturing opium, selling opium, stocking opium with the intention of sale, smuggling opium, manufacturing tools for opium smoking, selling opium tools, stocking opium tools with the intention of selling them, smuggling opium tools, providing shelter for opium smoking, cultivating opium, and opium smoking.
1909	The Opium Smoking Prohibition Decree stipulated that those who cultivate, manufacture, and deal opium, as well as those who operate opium dens, were all subject to imprisonment. In the same year, Emperor Xuantong (1908–1911) issued an edict stressing that officials, soldiers, teachers and students must quit their smoking habits.
1911	The Qing government and the British government agreed to stop opium exportation from India by 1917.

Legal Regulations on Opium Activities

As a legal response to various problems associated with drug activities, Chinese governments throughout its Imperial history have made numerous attempts to regulate and control the use, importation, and cultivation of opium and other substances. Some of these royal edicts or decrees were primarily symbolic gestures that were not rigorously enforced, whereas other legal actions (e.g., the 1909 ban on opium cultivation) were taken seriously and apparently reduced drug activities. The full array of legal responses to drug-related activities in Imperial China is summarized in Table 2.3 and described above.

Strict governmental regulations on substances in China have been traced back to the early twelfth century. For example, citing fear of poisoning as a justification, the Mongol rulers, before and after their conquering of China and the establishment of the Yuan dynasty (1279–1368), imposed a strictly-regulated system of medical practice, banned the use of certain toxic drugs, and prohibited the sale of aconite and arsenic in 1268. Starting from 1272, anyone buying or selling prohibited drugs could be punished with death. A list of banned drugs publicized in 1311 included substances like laurel, euphorbia, and henbane.[36]

The first edict banning opium issued by an emperor was published in 1729. Historical accounts indicate that Emperor Yongzheng (1722–1735) was disturbed by opium smoking (mixed with tobacco at the time) and its deleterious effects on sexual desire and promiscuity, personal health, and the withdrawal from family and society (Su and Zhao 1998, 151). Concerned with the Confucian virtues and opium's potential destruction of family structure, Yongzheng issued a ban that penalized opium dealers and opium den keepers. According to this edict, opium dealers were subject to one month of *cangue* (i.e., a wooden collar that immobilizes the neck and

---

36   Hoizey 1993, 90–91.

hands) and exile into the military. Opium den keepers were subject to 100 sticks (i.e., one stick was equivalent to one beating) and exile (e.g., being sent 3,000 *li* [1 *li* = 0.31 mile] away from their homes), whereas local officials and neighbors of the drug dealers and opium den keepers would be subject to 100 sticks and penal servitude of two years. The punishment of local officials and neighbors was based on the *baojia* system of collective responsibility that required families and neighbors to monitor each other for illegal activities and other prohibitions.[37]

It is important to note that this initial royal edict penalized neither opium users nor opium imports. The use of opium for medicinal purposes was also exempted from this legal mandate. Given these omissions, it isn't surprising that both the importing of foreign opium and the smoking of pure opium became more popular in the eighteenth century.[38]

Box 2.7 Criminal Punishments in Early Edicts/Decrees

- Opium dealers (in 1729 edict)
  - one month of *cangue*
  - exile into the military
- Opium den keepers (in 1729 edict)
  - 100 sticks
  - exile
- Opium smugglers (edicts in 1735–1796)
  - one month of *cangue*, 100 sticks, and three years of military exile for domestic merchants
  - one month of *cangue*, 100 sticks, and exile for palace guards
- Opium smokers (in 1813 decree)
  - firing from their job posts, one month of *cangue* and 100 sticks for palace guards
  - one month of *cangue* and 100 lashes for soldiers and civilians
  - one month of *cangue* and exile to become a slave for eunuchs

---

37 For example, the edict specified that opium dealers were subject to military exile, and opium den keepers were subject to probation on the first offense and 100 lashes and exile on the second offense. For local officials and customs officers who neglected their duties and conspired with opium smugglers, the punishment would be severe (Su and Zhao 1998, 134–135).

38 It was recorded that the amount of imported opium doubled or even tripled from 200 chests to 500–600 chests in the subsequent years following the ban (Su and Zhao 1998, 134).

During the reign of Emperor Qianlong (1735–1796), another edict was issued to further ban opium smuggling. Domestic merchants who engaged in this practice were subject to one month of *cangue*, 100 sticks, and three years of military exile. Palace guards involved in smuggling were given one month of *cangue*, 100 sticks, and exile (e.g., being sent 1,000 *li* away from their homes and had their statuses turned into servants').

As an effort to completely ban the importation of opium, Emperor Jiaqing (1796–1820) issued an edict in 1796 to eliminate the tax on opium importation. By revoking this tax, the Qing government showed its resolution to completely ban the opium trade.[39] This edict also was directed at another source of the supply-side of opium by banning domestic cultivation of opium poppy.

The first major legal prohibition against the consumption of opium occurred in 1813 under the Qing government. Under this *Decree on Punishing Officials, Soldiers, and Civilians who Smoke Opium* (1813), palace guards who smoked opium were subject to termination from their job posts, one month of *cangue* and 100 stick lashings. Both soldiers and civilians who smoke opium were given similar punishments (i.e., one month of *cangue* and 100 lashes) but eunuchs who smoked opium were subject to harsher treatment by a month of *cangue* and exile to Heilongjian to become a slave. Given that two of the three orders in this decree involved palace personnel (i.e., the palace guard and eunuch), a reasonable inference is that opium smoking had become a great concern at least in the royal palace.

The concern about opium resulted in several additional royal edicts and decrees in this time period. For example, Emperor Jiaqing issued another edict against domestic cultivation of poppy and extraction of its juice to make opium in 1813 (Bello 2000, 127–141). This was followed by further regulations on opium in 1815. Emperor Jiaqing's edict in 1818 stressed severe punishment for those who purchased and smoked opium and those customs officials who did not effectively deal with opium smuggling. Most historical interpretations of the emergence of these early laws emphasized the deleterious effect of opium on basic Confucian principles of morality (e.g., filial piety, modesty in dietary habits, the pursuit of becoming *junzi* [a superior person] not *xiaoren* [an inferior person], *ren* [a man] not *shou* [a beast]) and on the well-being of the individual and society as the primary motivation for these legal prohibitions (Su and Zhao 1998, 536–541).

Beginning with Emperor Daoguang (1820–1850), the economic aspects of the opium trade became increasingly important as the basis for both the abolition and retention of legal controls over opium. During this time period, China experienced

---

39   As one example of Emperor Jiaqing's commitment to banning opium, an American opium ship in 1817 was confiscated in Guangdong and all of the opium on the ship was confiscated and burned. Nevertheless, the prohibition of opium did not achieve its intended effect because of several factors: (1) foreign merchants driven by huge profit were determined to smuggle opium into China; (2) Chinese local officials lacked resources and zeal to combat the smuggling; and (3) there was great demand from Chinese opium addicts (Su and Zhao 1998, 134–135).

a serious silver shortage and growing budget deficit due to the opium trade.[40] In response to these problems, the Qing government in 1833 banned opium imports and domestic cultivation.[41] This effort to ban opium imports, mainly from Guangdong, focused on arresting drug smugglers, whereas the eradication programs of domestic cultivation of opium were attempted through the *baojia* system (Su and Zhao 1998, 135). However, these strategies of strict enforcement of the laws were largely exercised in vain, given the huge profits generated by the drug trade that benefited both foreign merchants and Qing governmental officials from the lowest levels all the way to the emperor.[42]

In subsequent years, Emperor Daoguang solicited opinions on ways to deal with the opium trade. Two sides of the debate were ultimately presented to him: some officials argued for opium legalization under particular conditions and others argued for further criminalization of opium-related activities and stiff penalty.

Box 2.8 Opium Debate in the 1830s

- Legalization arguments
  - Unless willing to rule by terror, further enforcement of a drug ban would engender corruption
  - Gaining economic revenue through taxation upon legalization
  - Encouraging domestic cultivation of poppies to reduce dependence on foreign imports
- Criminalization arguments
  - Legalization would result in an epidemic of drug use
  - Legalization would erode public morality and family value
  - Opium represents a symbol of Western aggression

---

40   Opium traffic began to flourish in the 1820s and 1830s mainly in the southern and south-eastern coastal regions of China (Kuhn 1978, 264–265). Monetary imbalance caused by silver flowing out of the country to pay for illicit drug imports seriously disrupted taxation and commerce in the 1830s, resulting in tax-resistance, currency speculation, and popular hatred towards the Qing government (Jones and Kuhn 1978, 130–131).

41   Domestic cultivation of opium skyrocketed during the Daoguang reign, partly due to the increased skills on how to plant and cultivate opium and partly due to the arguments supported by some governmental officials that domestic cultivation would curtail foreign imports (Su and Zhao 1998, 142–143).

42   Because many of the official posts were purchased with silver, those officials' first job upon assuming their posts was to get back their investment. Ripping off opium smugglers seemed a perfect means to this end. Emperors were equally guilty of benefiting from the opium trade with heavy taxation and briberies from both the foreign merchants and the Qing officials (Su and Zhao 1998, 136–137; Wakeman 1978, 180–181).

Proponents of opium legalization argued that the enforcement of opium laws was impractical unless the emperor was willing to rule by terror, and that the continued enforcement of a drug ban would only further engender official corruption.[43] Concerned mainly with the shortage of silver due to the opium trade, legalization proponents proposed an alternative solution to the evolving drug problem and the "silver famine" crisis: (1) to allow foreigners to continue importing opium but only to trade opium with goods; (2) to permit domestic cultivation of opium in the hopes of eventually cutting off the opium trade with foreigners; (3) to allow those who do not have public duties (with an exception of public officials and soldiers) to continue to smoke opium because it would not interfere with regular governmental operations. These measures were intended to replace foreign opium with domestic cultivation to address the economic side of the opium trade and to control the spread of opium addiction from the top.[44]

Opponents of opium legalization objected to this proposal primarily on moral grounds. From their perspective, "the infraction of a law was no reason for its annulment" and legalization of opium would result in an epidemic of drug use and further erode the morality of the Chinese society.[45] Citing the Confucian doctrine of filial piety, it was asserted that if opium addiction continued, "Fathers would no longer be able to admonish their sons, husbands would no longer to able to admonish their wives; masters would no longer be able to train their pupils... it would mean the end of the life of the people and the destruction of the soul of

---

43   Opium smuggling brought governmental officials in contact with gangsters and secret societies, further precipitating the already rampant government corruption. For example, Qing's special patrol fleet, created to catch opium smugglers in 1826, ended up being turned into a protector of the very illegal trafficking activities for a monthly fee of 36,000 taels (Wakeman 1978, 179–181).

44   Several contemporary writers suggest that this view about the legalization of opium imports and use had some merit, especially given the complex political and social conditions of the late Qing dynasty. This opium control policy might have a better chance to achieve some success when compared with the hard-line approach (Su and Zhao 1998, 149–150).

45   The moralistic proponents refuted each and every one of the legalization arguments. First, the reason why opium prohibition law could not be carried out with success was because the public officials lacked the will to see it through. They argued that even though the opium trade involved foreigners, it must rely on the Chinese to complete the transactions. If the Chinese people were resolute about stopping this trade, it could be ultimately stopped. Second, if foreigners were to be allowed to trade opium with tea, what happens when the tea ran out? Would silver still be used to buy opium? In addition, if silver could be effectively prevented from flowing out of China, why could opium not be effectively prevented from coming into China? Third, to allow certain section of the population to smoke opium and prohibit others from smoking is inherently morally contradictory. And lastly, domestic cultivation of opium would not prevent opium imports but would result in the loss of productive lands (Su and Zhao 1998, 149–150; Wakeman 1978, 181).

the nation" (Wakeman 1978, 179). In addition, opium was viewed as an agent of "barbarian", Western aggression, a moral poison to deprave Chinese people.

While carefully weighing the arguments for and against legalizing the opium trade, it is important to note that Emperor Daoguang was also an opium addict himself, as his predecessors, and learned from personal experience about the lethal nature of opium and its potential impact on family and the nation.[46] By 1836, Emperor Daoguang concluded the opium debate and adopted the moralists' position.

What followed in subsequent years were a series of aggressive campaigns against native smugglers and dealers.[47] Even though these enforcement campaigns achieved some progress, millions of Chinese people remained addicted to opium. To eradicate this addiction problem, another official in 1838 proposed to Emperor Daoguang that a death sentence should be imposed on drug addicts, arguing that opium smuggling would continue as long as there was high demand for it.

This proposition on opium addiction stirred a second major debate on drug policy. Opposition to this approach of stern punishment of drug addicts argued that the only beneficiaries of this policy would be local policemen and clerks who could extort money from addicts and non-addicts. Instead, they contended that existing laws should be enforced more carefully and forcefully, rather than enacting new laws (Wakeman 1978, 181–182). In contrast, Lin Zexu, a *Hanlin* scholar, argued that even though it sounded harsh to punish opium addicts with death, it was morally acceptable to pressure addicts into giving up their habit with the threat of the death penalty. He also proposed that the state should intervene to help addicts quit their habit, implemented through a four-phase program to gradually increase the punishment if the addicts failed to quit their habit (Wakeman 1978, 184).

A more menacing drug problem for the Qing government, however, was the fact that these enforcement policies had little apparent impact on the large quantities of opium that were available through foreign importation and smuggling. To deal with this supply-side issue and to put forth a stronger anti-drug stance, the Qing government issued an *Act of 39 Regulations on the Banning of Opium* in 1839 (Su and Zhao 1998, 538–539). This act represented the most comprehensive anti-drug law to date in the Qing dynasty and had several characteristics:

- it specified various types of opium-related offenses including opium import, opium cultivation, opium manufacturing and processing, opium sale, opium use, operating opium dens, and manufacturing tools for opium smoking.
- it specified severe punishments for particular opium offenses such as strangulation for smuggling and transporting opium, decapitation for manufacturing, transporting, and stocking opium with foreign partners,

---

46   Emperor Daoguang said that "if opium were not banned, it could destroy family and the entire nation" (Su and Zhao 1998, 151).

47   It was recorded that 2,000 opium dealers were arrested and trafficking in drugs was almost at a standstill in 1837 (Wakeman 1978, 181).

suspended death penalty for cultivating opium,[48] and a death penalty for opium smokers who failed to quit their habit within one and a half years.

- it established a system of lighter sentences for voluntary confession.
- It established a system of collective responsibility that held parents responsible for their child's opium use.
- it subjected officials and civilians with equal punishment.
- it subjected foreigners who smuggle opium into China to decapitation.

To enhance the enforcement of the anti-drug laws, the Qing government appointed Lin Zexu as a special Imperial commissioner. Lin was authorized to enforce opium suppression laws, to manage and pacify dubious activities of the British and other foreigners, and to resort to force if necessary.[49]

Lin employed a two-pronged approach involving both domestic and foreign suppliers to bring the opium trade under control. Domestically, with the assistance of the Cantonese Opium Suppression Committee primarily composed of local gentries, Lin conducted sweeping investigations, detentions, arrests, and seizures of those who were suspected of being involved in opium trafficking.[50] These aggressive efforts achieved some results. For example, the authority investigated hundreds of cases involving opium smuggling, arrested 2,200 people involved in the trade, and confiscated 711,024 *liang* of opium, 75,726 opium pipes, and 726 opium woks. Even though these achievements were impressive for Lin, the confiscated goods represented less than 1% of the total 90,000 estimated chests of opium imported in this time period (Su and Zhao 1998, 152–153).

The major obstacle Lin encountered, however, involved the dealing with foreign opium smugglers. Lin made various efforts to try to cut off the import of opium. One effort was to hold hostage the Chinese partners of foreign smugglers. On March 18, 1839, Lin directed the Chinese merchants to persuade their foreign partners to turn over their opium stocks in three days and sign bonds promising

---

48   The death penalty was one of the sentencing options available in the Qing dynasty. The most common methods of execution were strangulation and decapitation, even though slicing was also used. Two types of death sentences could be rendered: death with immediate execution (*zan lijue*) and death with suspension (*zan jianhou*). Offenders who were given the suspended death sentence typically had their death sentence converted into a lighter sentence (e.g., life imprisonment). This system of suspended death sentence was set up in accordance with the Confucian view of differential punishment and cautious imposition of the death penalty (Zhang 2004, 1–10).

49   It was stated that Lin was given sweeping authority to eradicate the opium problem by severing the trunk from the roots, which meant to eradicate opium brokers, opium houses, warehouses, divans, and officials' corruption by strictly enforcing the laws (Wakeman 1978, 183–185).

50   Knowing that authorizing the local gentry class the power of arrest and detention could potentially jeopardize the balance of power in the locale between magistrates and the local gentries, Lin showed his willingness to risk everything to eradicate drug trafficking (Wakeman 1978, 185–187).

never to trade opium again. Otherwise, one or two of these Chinese merchants would be executed, and the others would lose their property. Under pressure, the foreign community agreed to surrender 1,056 chests of opium. However, it has been noted that Lin now believed that the key supplier was Dent, President of the British Chamber of Commerce (Wakeman 1978, 187). Four days later (March 22, 1839), Lin issued an order for Dent's arrest and took two Chinese merchants as hostages for Dent's self-surrender to the Chinese authorities (Wakeman 1978, 187). Lin's actions heightened the conflict between the Chinese and the British governments.

What quickly followed were the Chinese trade embargo, labor boycott, the blockade of the opium factories, and the holding of 350 foreigners as hostages. Out of desperation, Elliot, the British Captain at Macao, commanded the surrender of 20,283 chests of opium, valued at USD 9 million. Buoyant with initial success and foreign merchants' deference, Lin pressed forward with the signing of bonds – if a foreigner did sign and then smuggled afterwards, he would expect to be executed. This produced major contention between the Chinese and the British on the issue of extraterritoriality.[51] Meanwhile, another criminal incident, involving several drunken English seamen beating Chinese farmers with sticks and resulting in one death, stirred more conflicts over criminal jurisdiction between the two countries.[52] Failing to obtain satisfactory results from neither the bond signing nor the murder case, Lin was determined to push a little further by cutting off Macao (the sanctuary for the British merchants) from China's produce and supply list. Out of pressure, the Macao government gave in and forced the British out of Macao. The British then anchored their ships near Hong Kong. Lin's tough measures were taken as an affront and a provocation. As tension mounted, the two sides drifted into open hostilities that ultimately led to the Opium Wars.

Although the details of the Opium Wars are not important to this current research, what is clear from historical records is that the Qing government was ill-prepared for war.[53] On the military front, China's military equipment and

---

51   Based on the British rule, an Englishman could expect the protection of his own government from arbitrary foreign prosecution no matter where and under what circumstances. Because of the fear of blockade, Elliot asked Macao, under the Portuguese control then, for sanctuary and obtained permission to move to Macao (Wakeman 1978, 188–189).

52   This criminal incident not only touched upon the already sensitive issue of extraterritoriality but also symbolized the resistance and tension between the Chinese and the British government over trade disputes (Wakeman 1978, 189–191).

53   Historians have summarized the significance of the Opium War. In particular, it forced the Chinese government to realize that China was facing a new situation that it had never faced in thousands of years. Changes must be made on several fronts: diplomatic relations with foreign countries, recognition of the military superiority of the West, economic encroachment, and political imperialism (Hao and Wang 1980, 153–161). In addition, China's defeat in the Opium War marked the beginning of the disintegration of its traditional polity (Gentzler 1977, 17–18).

training was severely outdated, the armies were undermanned, about half of the soldiers were opium addicts,[54] and the local militia consisted of former bandits, salt smugglers or rural hoodlums who used their militia status to prey on local residents.[55] Perhaps more devastating was the severe underestimation of the British military strengths and their determination for free trade with China and making profits in China's unparalleled consumer market. This was evidenced by the involvement of the leading opium traders in the war efforts[56] and the 1842 Nanjing Treaty after China's defeat in the Opium War that involved, among other provisions, the opening of five ports for trade and the appointment of British consuls at each port.[57]

Even in defeat, however, the Qing government did not abandon the opium prohibition law after the first Opium War. In fact, it stressed the importance of the opium ban on several occasions. For example, the Qing government issued a regulation on the prohibition of opium in 1839, and Emperor Daoguang in 1843 issued another edict stating the importance of carrying out the law. In 1854, the successive emperor, Xianfeng (1850–1861), rejected a request for legalizing opium imports with taxation from England and stressed the resolution of banning opium. Nevertheless, because of its weak political and military power, the Qing government had little sanctioning power over the opium trade and this practice became de facto legal after 1843.[58]

After the second Opium War (1856–1860), the Beijing Treaty created by the British and French governments formally legalized the opium trade in 1858

---

54   Soldiers' addiction to opium and low morale were recurring themes in the Qing history (Liu and Smith 1980, 202–273).

55   A statecraft writer, Wei Yuan, in his influential work entitled the *Record of Imperial Military Achievements*, stated that the Qing's polity, particularly its military, may be responsible for the defeat in the Opium Wars. More specifically, he suggested the following major reforms: (1) to adopt new policies to improve the caliber of soldiers and officers; (2) to stabilize the monetary system and reduce the treasury deficits; and (3) to careful monitor military rosters to ensure against desertion and false registration (Jones and Kuhn 1978, 150–151). See also Wakeman 1978, 190–208.

56   It was reported that the leading opium traders were involved in helping the British statesman Lord Palmerston work out the aims and the strategies, supply intelligence and offer advice, lease opium vessels to the fleet, staff as pilots and translators, and, most importantly, use the opium profits to subsidize the army and navy expenditures (Fairbank 1978b, 213).

57   Other provisions of the Nanjing Treaty included the payment of USD 21 million, equal intercourse between officials of corresponding rank, abolition of the Cohong monopoly, moderate tariff on imports and exports, and cession of Hong Kong to the British territory (Wakeman 1978, 211–212). See also Gentzler 1977, 29–32.

58   For example, opium exports from India (only Bombay and Kolkata) increased from 42,699 chests in 1843 to 58,681 chests in 1860 and the destination was mainly China (Su and Zhao 1998, 161).

(Fairbank 1978, 251). By 1860, previous edicts banning the opium growth and trade were repealed (Candlin 1973).

In an effort to revitalize the Qing dynasty and under Western pressure to change, the Qing government engaged in a series of political and institutional reforms from 1901 to 1911.[59] Targets of these political reforms were the administration of justice, law, and the military system. For example, the *1907 New Criminal Law* stipulated in Article 21 the offenses of opium. The specific opium-related offenses included opium manufacturing, selling, stocking with the intention of sale, smuggling, manufacturing tools for opium smoking, selling opium tools, stocking opium tools with the intention of selling, smuggling opium tools, providing shelter for opium smoking, cultivating opium, and opium smoking. For the first time in Chinese history, fines were imposed as punishment for some opium-related offenses and the penalties for all types of opium offenses were much lighter than that in earlier eras (e.g., the maximum penalty in the new law was 10 years of imprisonment rather than death). Public officials were subjected to more severe punishment than civilians for these drug offenses (Su and Zhao 1998, 540–541). The *1909 Opium Smoking Prohibition Decree* also stipulated that those who cultivate, manufacture and deal opium, and those who operate opium dens were all subject to imprisonment (Su and Zhao 1998, 215)

In addition to the law and decrees, Emperor Guangxu issued an edict to prohibit opium in 1906 in an effort to eliminate a variety of "bad customs".[60] This edict contained the following orders:

- cultivation of poppy was to be gradually reduced and to be eradicated within 10 years;
- it was prohibited to take up opium smoking, to start opium dens, or to import opium; and
- officials who indulged must quit opium smoking within six months (with an exception of people over 60 years old) (Ichiko 1980, 410; Su and Zhao 1998, 213–214).

Two months later in November 1906, *A Ten-Article Decree on Opium Prohibition* was issued. This decree dealt with all fronts of the opium problems including banning poppy cultivation, banning new smokers, treatment of existing

---

59   Major political and institutional reforms included the reforms in education, military, financial section, and a constitution. For details of these political and institutional reforms, see Ichiko (1980, 375–415).

60   See Ichiko 1980, 410. Prior to the prohibition of opium, the Qing government also took a stance in opposing foot-binding practices in 1902. Cited in Reins (1991, 103–104), the royal edict demonized opium because "the opium smoker wastes time and neglects work, ruins his health, and impoverishes his family, and the poverty and weakness which for the past few decades have been daily increasing amongst us are undoubtedly attributable to this cause."

smokers, and closing opium dens. After Emperor Guangxu's death in 1908, the succeeding Emperor Xuantong issued another edict in 1909 stressing that officials, soldiers, teachers, and students must quit their smoking habits (Su and Zhao 1998, 215). The Qing government also negotiated with the British government on the reduction of opium exports from India to China. After rounds of discussions, the British finally agreed in 1911 to stop opium trade from India by 1917.[61]

The other major issue surrounding opium was domestic poppy cultivation. Eradication campaigns to stop domestic cultivation began in earnest at the end of the Qing dynasty. Historical accounts of production activities suggest that these eradication campaigns resulted in major reductions in poppy cultivation in various regions by early 1911 (Wright 1968, 292–293). In fact, the crusade against opium during the first decade of the twentieth century was characterized as the "largest and most vigorous effort in the world history to stamp out an established evil" (Wright 1968, 14). However, the collapse of the Qing dynasty and the subsequent takeover by the Nationalist Party in 1911 altered the nature of the political and legal responses to opium.

Facilitating and Constraining Factors in Opium-Related Activities

Over the entire history of Imperial China, a number of particular political, economic, and cultural factors have influenced patterns of change and stability in opium-related activities and its legal regulation. Major facilitating and constraining factors associated with the prevalence of opium-related activities in Imperial China are described below.

Political Forces

Despite numerous royal edicts banning opium-related activities, the political structure of Imperial China and the basic characteristics of this society placed serious constraints on the effectiveness of these legal decrees in regulating opium activities. The challenge of effective governance was magnified by the physical isolation of the emperor(s), the vastness of the Chinese territories, limited technology for mass transportation and communication, and the harsh reality of peasants' lives in this agrarian society.

Under the political structure of Imperial China, the primary agents of social control were the local magistrates and the neighborhood organization systems (*baojia, lija*). Most peasants were more responsive to the orders of these local leaders because they either represented the local interests better than the central government or they represented a much more imminent threat to the peasants'

---

61   The concession of the British government was due to the growing public opinion against opium exports in Great Britain and the Chinese students' protests (Ichiko 1980, 410–411).

daily well-being than that of the central government. From this perspective, it would not be surprising to find that many royal decrees and edicts banning opium were often ignored at the local levels because they were too remote from the local, daily activities of peasants' lives. Corruption and self-interests are other aspects of these local socio-political organizations that may have led to high rates of non-compliance to legal prohibitions on opium in the vast areas of rural China.

Economic Forces

A primary explanation for the persistence and growth in opium-related activities in Imperial China involves the economic aspects of its consumption, trade, and cultivation. In fact, opium was a lucrative "cash crop" for nearly all parties involved in the opium business over much of the Qing dynasty. Foreign governments (e.g., Great Britain, Holland, India, and Portugal) and their merchants reaped enormous economic profits from the opium trade. Chinese business partners of foreign merchants and local distributors of opium also received large financial gains from this trade. Similarly, both local and central governments of the Qing dynasty used taxes and surcharges from opium to subsidize their operations. Even the local poppy farmers benefited from the greater economic yield in opium cultivation than that of other crops.

While multiple explanations exist for the changes in opium-related activities across the history of Imperial China, particularly in the Qing dynasty, economic factors seemed especially relevant to some particular changes in opium's use, trade, and cultivation. These economic-related changes surrounding opium in Imperial China included the following:

- opium was initially a foreign luxury item that could only be afforded by the royal court and the wealthy/powerful (e.g., high-ranking officials and merchants). The domestic cultivation of a lower-quality opium and widespread use of opium resin for re-smoking reduced the economic costs of opium consumption and fostered its use by all social strata in Chinese society.
- the Qing government's ban of opium imports and domestic cultivation in 1833 was a direct response to the serious "silver famine" and growing budget deficit due to the opium trade.
- the switch of Qing's opium policy from reliance on foreign imports to domestic cultivation of opium was seen as economically advantageous because it would eventually cut off the opium trade with foreigners and solve the problems associated with this trade imbalance. Royal edicts and decrees in the nineteenth century often reinforced this position by focusing on opium activities that conflicted with the government's economic interests (e.g., smuggling, foreign importation).
- foreign interests in China's opium market diminished dramatically by the end of the nineteenth century as indicated by a substantial drop in

the volume of opium imports in this time period, which eventually led to foreign nations' agreement to stop the opium trade.

As both a benefit and cost, however, the economic factor underlying China's opium-related activities was a double-edged sword. After all, the Qing governments, both the central and the local governments, had relied on opium profits to support the governmental operational budget (i.e., the revenue generated from opium trade between 1887–1906 [at least 5 million taels[62] annually] accounted for 5–7% of the Qing government's national budget) (Reins 1991, 104). From this perspective, the opium eradication campaign was also a serious threat to taxes and other financial gains that derived from all forms of opium-related activities (i.e., consumption, trade, and cultivation).

Cultural Forces

The primary aspects of China's culture that are linked to opium-related activities in the Imperial era involved its dominant schools of philosophical thought (e.g., Confucianism and Daoism) and the nature of the consumption culture associated with them. Each of these cultural forces is described below.

Confucianism   Several core principles in Confucianism, relevant to discussions below, are filial piety, ritual propriety, and hierarchy (for a more detailed discussion of these Confucian ideas see Lu and Miethe 2007a, 29–31).

Filial piety stresses the importance of family as a unit in the society, and how family members should behave in accordance to their role/status in the family (e.g., wives must be obedient to the husbands, sons should obey their fathers). Ritual propriety is the manifestation of the hierarchical order within the family, the clan, and the society by emphasizing that no one should step out of the boundary of one's social obligations and roles.[63] Visible symbols of one's privileges were displayed in the routines and rituals of everyday consumption of products like tea, tobacco, and opium. Under the notion of ritual propriety, the prevalence of opium smoking in public places may have served an important symbolic function.

Another aspect of the Confucian philosophy that may be linked to the prevalence of opium use involved the concept of shame and its value as a mechanism of social control. From this perspective, the preference of opium smoking over alcohol consumption is that opium smoking may be harmful to the individual but it imposes little shame and disruption to the wider society (unlike what would happen in external outbursts from being drunk and disorderly). Indeed, the prevailing view of opium use for a long time in China and abroad was that with wealth and self-control, opium was not necessarily a more pressing social problem than gambling

---

62   1 tael = 40 grams.

63   For discussions on the relationship between individual and family, see Gentzler 1977, 117–121; Grasso, Corrin and Kort 2004, 69–70; and Hsu 2000, 69.

or prostitution, or more addictive than tobacco smoking (Forges 2000, 168). Under these conditions, the choice of opium for many Chinese consumers may be a deliberate act, weighing their familial and societal duties and personal desires. Although a Confucian moral system would not have actively encourage any type of frivolous and excessive behavior, the ritualistic smoking of opium was far more palatable with this belief system than the outward displays of disorderly conduct that are often associated with alcohol abuse.[64]

Daoism   Compared to Confucianism, Daoism has never achieved a status of becoming a dominant official or social philosophy in China. Instead, it was more of an individual philosophy. Nevertheless, Daoism had important political implications, particularly in the context of exploring the underlying causes for the widespread use of opium in the nineteenth and early twentieth centuries in China.

The most famous Daoist doctrine was *wu wei* (translated literally as "without action"). This is manifested in its view of a good government as one that takes the *laissez-faire* approach to governance because any attempt to solve all problems might create more problems. The slow, reactive Qing policy on opium may have been a reflection of this basic Daoist principle.

In the aspect of one's personal life, Daoism is well known for its ideal of a carefree lifestyle, the desire of maintaining status quo, and of conspicuous leisure (Zhu 2002, 53–63). Many Chinese individuals, including governmental officials, cherished this laid-back, carefree lifestyle, particularly during the late Qing period, when the court was largely saturated with corruption and personal "back stabbing". Under these conditions, opium use might have provided some individuals with a temporary escape from the harsh social and political reality of Imperial China.

The most basic cultural essence of Daoism is that it perpetuated a fatalistic attitude towards life and indulgence in earthly joys. Drawing on the theory of *yin-yang*, a holistic approach to body, mind, and spirit, and the theory of *qi* (energy) from the traditional Chinese medicine (Hoizey 1993; Wang, Chen and Xie 1999), Daoism also created a belief system that maintained that one could gain the "soft and invisible" power by achieving a state of perfect equilibrium between man and nature and by allowing the *qi* to flow freely (Gentzler 1977, 6). This belief system may have also influenced the national psyche of passiveness and retreat, resulting in China's capitulation to the use of opium (Su 1997, 6–8, 173–177).

Consumption Culture   Beyond its medical use, opium had gradually become a source of status and conspicuous consumption in the Chinese society. It turned

---

64   As suggested earlier, it is important to emphasize that Confucianism has also been used to oppose the legalization of opium. Given these diverse applications of Confucianism, it seems that this philosophy served as a double-edged sword with regard to opium use and eradication. On the one hand, it seemed to offer a platform for the widespread use of opium, and on the other hand, it served as a moral compass when the state launched its anti-opium campaigns.

into a recreational drug for the royal family and the wealthy class who started their leisure use of opium to enhance sexual performance and sexual pleasure during the Ming dynasty. Being a rare, imported, and expensive commodity, opium possession and smoking became a privilege of the wealthy and powerful class and remained a luxury item into the early nineteenth century. Opium was desirable because of its image as a foreign luxury item, its medical and narcotic benefits, and its symbolic value in signifying the social position of its user. In addition, since the mid-eighteenth century, smoking opium and offering opium to guests also became a way of displaying one's privilege.[65]

Box 2.9 Opium's Symbolic Value

Throughout much of China's history, opium has been a symbol of wealth and power because of its importation as a foreign commodity. For wealthy scholars and rich merchants in the early nineteenth century, opium smoking became an object of connoisseurship surrounded with exotic rituals (e.g., having a specialized opium "chef" for proper preparation for cooking and smoking). However, during the nineteenth century, there is little debate that opium use spread throughout all segments of Chinese society, including laborers, merchants, performers, officials, women, nuns, and monks.

See Dikotter, Laamann and Xun 2002, 57–62.

Like tea and other commodities, opium came in different grades that were catered and marketed to different consumer groups. During the nineteenth century in China, consumers were classified into hierarchical groups based on their political, economic, and social differences, ranging from the highest group such as the Machuria aristocracy, high-level officials, and wealthy merchants; to the intermediate group including middle and lower rank officials and professional groups such as lawyers, bankers, or clerks; to the lowest social group including laborers, performers, prostitutes, beggars, and criminals. Imported opium and the best domestic opium produced in Yunnan were catered to the upper rank of opium consumers, the less expensive opium produced in Sichuan was the main product for the middle-ranked consumers, and the remnants of the opium boiling process were sold to the lower classes of opium consumers (De 1936, 36–38).

---

65   Dikotter et al. (2002) stated that opium, as a luxury item, gradually acquired new meanings starting from the mid-eighteenth century. Opium smoking, very much like the tea ceremony, conferred social status to the ruling elites. Its preparation (e.g., the way it was prepared for lighting and smoking, the quality of the opium) and consumption (when, where, and how it was smoked) became a socially prestigious and ritually complex event.

Social stratification in opium consumption was not only manifested in the grade of opium, but also through the frequency and mode of consumption. It was recorded that while wealthy elites commonly consumed opium in their private gardens and mansions, the less privileged groups of people often smoked opium in public places such as theaters, teahouses, and opium dens. As the price for opium became more affordable in the late nineteenth century, opium smoking became frequent, widespread, and truly an epidemic, particularly in some regions of China (Dikotter, Laamann, and Xun 2002, 317–336).

Summary

Opium-related activities were a major aspect of social life in Imperial China. Initially used for medical purposes, the practice of smoking opium became widespread in the nineteenth century. A wide array of royal edicts and decrees were pronounced in the Imperial period for the apparent purpose to regulate and control opium use, trade, and cultivation. By the end of the Qing dynasty in 1911, both the foreign importation and domestic cultivation of opium had been reduced through various control efforts. However, opium remained a widely used drug among the Chinese population.

Our review of the major structural conditions suggests that the prevalence of opium use in the Qing dynasty was tied to the unique philosophical beliefs in Confucianism and Daoism. These beliefs involved ritual propriety, family and status orientation, desire for a carefree lifestyle, and a general absence of political activism. China's tradition of herbal medicine (i.e., the body-mind-spirit connection) and the social rituals and symbolic meanings of tea drinking and tobacco smoking were also major antecedents in the evolution of opium consumption culture.

The social and economic conditions in the late Qing period (i.e., poverty, heavy taxation, rapid population growth) perpetuated domestic poppy cultivation as a way to improve poor peasants' living standards, ease people's physical pain, and imitate the powerful and wealthy when opium finally became affordable and available to the average person. The growing crisis of opium consumption and cultivation in this period was also sparked by the increasingly aggressive efforts of foreign merchants to gain profits from smuggling opium into China, and the Qing government's inability to control the smuggling activities at the border. It is these social forces that led to various attempts at the legal regulation of opium-related activities in the later historical periods of Imperial China.

Chapter 3
Drug Laws and the Social Context in the Republic Era

This chapter surveys the historical development of drug laws during the Republic Era from 1911 to 1949. During this period of the twentieth century, China experienced major transformations from an imperial, dynastic rule to a semi-colonial, semi-feudal, and semi-capitalist system. We will first discuss the unique political, economic, and social conditions of the Republic Era that are linked to the nature of its drug-related activities. Available data on patterns of consumption, trade, and domestic cultivation of opium will be described, followed by a review of specific legal regulations and drug control efforts in this historical period.

Political, Economic, and Social Conditions

Despite its governance for a relatively brief historical period, the Republic Era (1911–1949) represented one of the most politically turbulent times in the entire history of China. The era was marked with civil wars, revolutions, and foreign invasions at the military-political level, and with basic change and substantial growth in economic, social, intellectual, and cultural realms of Chinese society. This period was characterized by both internal struggles (i.e., conflicts among the feudal, capitalist, and communist ideologies) and external concerns (i.e., Western imperialism, new ideas of individual rights, democracy and technology). Among the various internal and external factors facing China in this historical period, we focus on the major socio-political changes that have been linked to drug-related activities (i.e., consumption, cultivation, trade) and their legal regulations and control.

Weak Central Government and Strong Foreign Presence

When the Nationalist Party overturned the Qing government in 1911, it inherited a social system that derived from more than 2,000 years of a feudal tradition. These feudal institutions and practices were highly ineffective and inflexible to, and in many cases resistant to, new changes. The existing social institutions were guided by out-of-date officials trained in Confucian classics, the literati whose prerogatives let them monopolize higher education and elite culture, landlords who exploited tenants, courts that did not respond to social needs, and a general populace who lacked interests in public and national affairs (Fairbank 1978a, 4).

The Nationalist government also inherited a semi-feudal and semi-colonial state, under the oppression of both feudalism (from within) and imperialism (from Western Europe and Japan). Compared to other times in China's history, the degree of foreign influence in the Chinese life during the Republic Era was striking – ranging from the presence of foreign consulates, banks, schools, hospitals, and churches, foreign interventions during the Chinese civil war, the influence of foreign political system (e.g., constitution and parliament), and their impact on educational training (e.g., many young people went abroad to receive Western education). In fact, even the first Nationalist leader, Sun Yat-sen (Sun Zhongshan), was a Western-educated doctor.

The strong Western presence and influence during the Republic Era was a consequence of two legacies of the previous Qing government: (1) the closed-door foreign policy and (2) unequal treaties with foreign governments. Ironically, the Nationalist revolution was rooted in the Nationalist sentiment against Western imperialism but it also relied on Western ideas (e.g., democracy and science) and foreign assistance to achieve its revolutionary goals.[1]

The foreign presence within China was primarily felt along the delta river regions, particularly in the large, urban, coastal cities such as Shanghai. Foreign diplomats, merchants, and their families lived a lavish lifestyle along with their elite Chinese friends who were often officials and businessmen. They were frequent guests in high-end tea houses and night clubs, served with tobacco, cigars, and opium. Numerous lavishly decorated Shanghai opium houses were testament of their lifestyles in the early twentieth century (Feuerwerker 1983, 133–141).

Box 3.1 Weak Government and Strong Foreign Influence

- Political and military powers were shared among the Nationalists, Communists, and various warlords after the collapse of the Qing dynasty in 1911.
- Foreign presence was a direct result of unequal treaties that forced the opening of Chinese ports; and an indirect result of Chinese elites seeking Western ideas and assistance during this revolutionary era.

The short-lived Republic Era also marked acute military conflicts among the Nationalists, warlords, and, later, the Communists. Each of these groups was striving for the national power after the collapse of the Qing dynasty. This military strife produced a very weak and fragile central government led by the Nationalist Party. For example, following the death of Yuan Shikai in 1916, China entered

---

1   For example, the revolutionaries sought protection from foreign administrations in Hong Kong and Shanghai; the revolution was financed by Chinese merchant communities overseas; ideas of individual rights, freedom, democracy, and sciences were certainly from the West (Fairbank 1983, 2–6).

the period of warlordism from 1916–1927. The warlord period was marked by "constant warfare, the fragmentation of agriculture, and the dissolution of orderly government (Hoyt 1989, 51)."[2] The Nationalist Party was also under constant threat from both external forces (e.g., invasion by Japan) and internal concerns (e.g., the need to defend its control over the vast territories of China from local warlords, the Communists, and peasant riots).

In their efforts to strengthen the political and military control over the claimed territories in China, these various parties were in fierce competition for military supremacy. The race for the military supremacy soon turned into a race for money. Within this context, taxes collected from opium cultivation and sale (and sometimes licensing fees for smoking opium) became one of the most viable means for the warlords and the Nationalists to sustain their military operations. It was thus not a coincidence that opium cultivation peaked during the period of warlordism in the 1920s, and the Nationalist government utilized opium monopoly and licensing policies to further make profits from the very evil that it tried to completely eliminate in the first place.

Emerging Capitalism in Urban Area and Poverty-Stricken Rural Economy

During the early twentieth century, China's economic structure appeared to be undergoing a dramatic transformation from the feudal economy to a (pre-)capitalist economy. These changes were most evident in large urban coastal cities such as Shanghai, Qingdao, and Guangdong. The social forces of foreign trade, Western imperialism, domestic commercialization, urbanization, and modernization were all major precipitating factors in this economic evolution.[3]

Box 3.2 A Slow Yet Dramatic Transformative Economy

- The economy of post-Qing China was undergoing dramatic transformations due to the collapse of the feudal system and the influence of Western trade (i.e., urbanization, commercialization, and modernization).
- Yet the demand for a dramatic economic transformation was met with strong resistance from the old political, economic, and social relations.
- Internal political and military conflicts in China hindered the economic transformation during this period of time.

---

2   Given the strong presence and influence of Western countries during this time, the only positive aspect to warlordism was perhaps the fostering of nationalism that China belonged to the Chinese and that foreigners must be deprived of control. This sentiment was particularly strong in this time of widespread foreign control and presence both in foreign nations' physical presence in major coastal areas (e.g., Shanghai, Nanjing, Tianjin, and Guangdong) and their coercive stance on trade (Hoyt 1989, 51).

3   For instance, financial reform, technological improvement in communication, and industrial development had made significant inroads during the brief Republic Era (Hsu 2000, 565–577).

In reality, however, China's economy was only slowly evolving, hampered in a large part by its long steady feudal structure and social relations that reacted slowly to the political and economic changes (see Rankin, Fairbank and Feuerwerker 1986, 1–73). For example, China remained an agrarian nation in the first half of the twentieth century, with a large rural sector encompassing 75% of the population and agricultural products accounting for 65% of its national output by 1949 (Arbor 1983, 28–29). In addition, far different from the lavish lifestyles of the wealthy and powerful in Shanghai, peasants' daily lives were constantly interrupted by a series of political and military conflicts, including the Nationalist revolution in the 1910s, then the warlordism in the 1920s, the Japanese invasion in the 1930s and 1940s, and the civil war between the Nationalists and the Communists in the late 1940s. Within this context of anomie and civil unrests, cultivation and consumption of opium may have served as a coping mechanism for millions of Chinese farmers, particularly those who relied on opium for economic well-being and personal comfort.

Table 3.1 Edicts, Decrees, and Laws on Drug Activities in the Republic Era

1912	Sun Yat-sen issued a Decree on Banning Opium Smoking. In the same year, the Beiyang government issued the *Temporary Criminal Code of the Nationalist Government.* It essentially adopted the Qing's Criminal Code and retained in Article 21 the offenses of opium.
1928	The Nationalist government passed the *Temporary New Criminal Law* in which 15 different types of drug-related offenses were included. Fines were widely used as a mean of punishment, and the maximum of criminal sentence was five-year imprisonment for any drug related offenses. In the same year, the Nationalist government issued the *Prohibition Law on Opium Smoking and the Detailed Regulation on How to Carry out the Ban on Opium Smoking.*
1935	The Nationalist government passed the *Criminal Code* in which it modified several drug related offenses and imposed much harsher criminal penalty with a maximum possibility of life imprisonment. It also launched a six-year drug prohibition plan.
1937-1945	During the Sino-Japanese war, the Japanese military suspended the opium and narcotics regulations of the Nationalist government in their controlled territories. The Wang Jingwei government, a largely "puppet" government supported by the Japanese military (1940–1945), adopted a drug trade policy through legalization and licensing. Meanwhile, numerous decrees were issued by Border Area governments controlled by the Communist Party. The most noticeable ones included, for example, the *1939 Decree on Banning the Cultivation of Opium* issued by the Administrative Committee of the Jin-Cha-Ji Border Area; the *1941 Decree on the Temporary Sentencing Guidelines for Drug Offenders* issued by the Jin-Ji-Lu Border Area government; the *1942 Decree on the Temporary Searching and Confiscating Opium Regulations* issued by the Shan-Gan-Ning Border Area government.

Legal Regulations on Opium Activities

By the time that Sun's revolutionary army overturned the Qing government in 1911, it had to deal with the legacy of Qing's policies on opium-related activities. This legacy involved the most aggressive opium eradication campaigns in China's history with significant progress made on domestic cultivation, elimination of opium consumption, and an agreement with the British government to stop opium exportation from India by 1917 (Ichiko 1980, 410–411).

The Nationalist government seemed to have showed its resolution to eradicate opium. In 1912, President Sun issued a *Decree on Banning Opium Smoking*. In the same year, the Beiyang government (1912–1928), headed by Yuan Shikai, passed the *Temporary Criminal Code of the Nationalist Government*, which retained in Article 21 the offenses of opium smoking from the Qing law. In a well-documented and influential speech, Sun tied opium suppression together with good governance.

Nevertheless, Sun's opium eradication policy took a control approach through the establishment of a government monopoly on opium. Due to financial pressure, Sun set up this monopoly in 1924 that combined the enforcement of the prohibition law, managing the "controlled" supply of drugs to addicts, and collecting taxes from the "controlled" drug sales to achieve the dual purpose of the opium control and revenue increase for the military.[4] However, because of the conflict of interest, rampant corruption, and resistance by local Guangdong merchants, Sun's plan failed (Slack 2001, 72–77; Spence 1975, 173). This Guangdong opium monopoly system set up by the Nationalists was only a microcosm of the warlords' financing in its early years throughout China. Given the critical importance of the opium revenue for civil and military rule at the time, its complete eradication was only a symbolic ideal but not an attainable reality.

Upon the establishment of the Nationalist government in 1927, the Jiang Jieshi (Chiang Kai-shek) government announced a three-year prohibition plan to control opium and other narcotics. This plan required the following actions:

---

4 The policy of suppression through taxation represented Sun's ambiguous stance on opium. However, later he stated that after the Nationalists destroyed the warlordism and established a national government, a complete prohibition law would be implemented (Slack 2000, 248–269).

- with the exception of medical use of morphine and heroin, narcotics drugs are banned from importation;
- drug addicts who are younger than 25 years old must rid their habits; those who are older than 25 years old need to obtain a license and progressively get rid of their habits in three years;
- tax on drugs used to treat opium addiction were 70% in 1928, 100% in 1929, and 200% in 1930; and
- opium will be publicly auctioned so that the government can receive high tax (Su and Zhao 1998, 268–269).

Among these provisions, the idea of publicly auctioning opium was met with protests from virtually all levels of Chinese society because of its weak anti-drug stance and the blatant motive to profit from it.

As a result of the public pressure to take a strong stance in the anti-drug movements, the *Criminal Law of the New Republic* was passed in 1928. This law specified 15 different types of drug-related offenses, including manufacturing, selling, smuggling, cultivating, smoking, and injecting narcotic drugs. It dramatically expanded the use of fines as a punishment and significantly reduced the penalty of drug-related offenses. The maximum possible punishment was five years of imprisonment for those who manufacture, sell, or smuggle opium, morphine, or heroin or other synthetic narcotic drugs. Up to three years of incarceration was mandated for those who manufacture, sell, or possess opium pipes, harbor drug addicts, or plant opium poppies, whereas those who keep opium dens would receive imprisonment for between six months to five years (Su and Zhao 1998, 269, 544–545). During this same year (1928), the Nationalist government also issued the *Prohibition Law on Opium Smoking* and the *Detailed Regulation on How to Carry out the Ban on Opium Smoking.*

Based on various historical records and data sources, the new law and its enforcement policies did achieve some effects. According to a survey, a total of 585,553 *liang* (1 *liang* = 50 grams) of opium, 7,580 *liang* of morphine, and 2,297 *liang* of heroin were confiscated by the customs service in 1929. In 1932, a total of 66,490 opium pipes were confiscated, 25,471 drug dealers were arrested, and 146,121 *liang* of drugs were seized (Su and Zhao 1998, 270–271). By the end of 1933, there were 2,121 drug detoxification centers.

Despite these achievements, however, several commentators considered the Nationalist government's efforts to ban drugs in the Republic Era to be largely doomed for several basic reasons. First, it is not difficult to see that the monopoly of opium trade was the real intent of the government rather than a complete ban of the opium trade because of the potential lucrative tax revenue. Second, there was a need to use opium-generated taxes and revenue in civil war among the warlords. Third, corruption among all levels of governmental and military leaders made effective enforcement almost impossible. Fourth, there was a lack of complete sovereignty due to the presence of the extra-territorial jurisdiction that further dampened the enforcement of the new law (Su and Zhao 1998, 271–274).

During the first two decades of the twentieth century, historical accounts indicated that drug addiction increased markedly in China both for opium and morphine (due to the shortage of opium) and later for heroin and cocaine. The Japanese entered China and became the major narcotics trader in China during that time.[5] To ensure that their political and military aggression met little resistance from the Chinese populace and government, the Japanese government carried out a narcotics trading campaign that was designed to debauch the population, weaken the national will to resist, and to corrupt the government and military.[6]

As a result of the Japanese drug campaign, it was estimated that in the city of Tianjin, one of the major locations for narcotics trafficking in China by the Japanese, approximately 10% of the residents were addicted to drugs, and the number was rapidly increasing between 1932 and 1937.[7] Another development since the Japanese invasion of China was the rising price for opium due to its scarcity and the drop of price for other narcotic drugs first in the east coastal area, and then inland, resulting in many opium addicts switching from opium to other narcotic substances (Brook 2000, 328).

---

5   For example, it was reported that of the total 5,000 Japanese residents in Tianjin, 70% of them dealt in morphine or other illegal substances (Brook and Wakabayashi 2000, 1 30). In addition, the Tokyo War Crimes Trials (1946 1948) declared that Japan's wartime opium operations violated international anti-opium treaties (Kobayashi 2000b, 152–166).

6   Candlin (1973) pointed out that nations engage in psycho-chemical warfare to gain political and military advantages and the Japanese aggression toward the Chinese in the early decades of the twentieth century was a good example. Starting from the 1930s, Japan replaced Europe to become the major player involved in the narcotics trade in China. They made large quantities of purchases of Indian opium and shipped opium to Kobe and Qingdao. Candlin (1973) further stated that the psycho-chemical warfare engaged by the Japanese military and government during its invasion of China attempted to achieve several goals, including undermining the fabric of Chinese society and weakening the authority of the Nationalist government through exploiting Chinese people's susceptibility towards drugs, breaking down the Chinese resistance at all levels, using narcotics as a means of persuasion to recruit agents and collect military intelligence, a means of raising revenues, reducing the threat of the established Chinese organized secret societies, and establishing partnerships in narcotics trading.

7   It was recorded that most of the drug addicts were poor laborers and coolies, and despite the low price of these drugs, they could hardly afford the habit. During that time period, heroin began to make its way into the Chinese market, first reaching the more educated and wealthy individuals because of its dollar to dollar value compared to opium (Candlin 1973).

To further increase the Chinese people's addiction to and reliance on drugs, the Japanese military offered protection and transportation to drug rings and syndicates that ran opium dens and small establishments connected with drug trafficking. After the Japanese invasion of China in 1937, they immediately suspended the opium and narcotics regulations of the Nationalist government, released drug addicts and peddlers, commissioned opium traffickers, gangsters, prostitutes, and geishas to dispense opium and narcotics, and permitted retail shops selling opium.[8] The Japanese also issued notices to urge and reward farmers to grow narcotics plants.[9] All of these Japanese narco-chemical warfare efforts were further enhanced by the inability of China's Opium Prohibition Bureau to control drugs under the government led by Wang Jingwei, whose main function was not to suppress the narcotics trade but rather to legally license the trade (Boyle 1972).

Meanwhile, in 1935, the Nationalist government passed the *Criminal Code*. Compared with the 1928 *Temporary Law*, the new law increased the penalty from a maximum of five-year imprisonment to life imprisonment for manufacturing, selling, or smuggling opium, morphine, heroin, or other synthetic narcotic drugs. It also increased the fines from a maximum of 5,000 Yuan (CNY) to CNY 10,000 for these offenses (Su and Zhao 1998, 544–545). During this same year, the Nationalist government also launched the *New Life Movement* and unveiled a six-year drug prohibition plan. The *New Life Movement* was aimed at curtailing corruption, extravagant spending, and unsavory traditional social customs such as spitting or urinating in public. Opium smoking was also one of the bad customs to be unlearned. In addition, in one of the anti-opium propaganda meetings, the three evils including opium, gambling, and prostitution were once again linked to Western imperialism, in particular, the Japanese plot to destroy the Chinese race with opium, morphine, and heroin (Slack 2001, 106–107).

The six-year anti-opium plan had dual goals. One was to monopolize opium trade and its profits; the other was to reduce and eliminate opium consumption.[10] This control or suppression approach was not new. In fact, the Qing government had a system of opium suppression based on licensing that allowed the government to have some involvement in the trade-for-profit sharing as well as claiming moral purity.[11] Fully aware of the potential traps of this approach, the Jiang government came up with a new way of thinking about opium that would culminate in the elimination of opium in six years. The core idea was for the government to take

---

8   It was estimated that 2,150 kilograms of opium were sold monthly by mid-1939 after the Japanese invasion (Eykholt 2000, 360–379).

9   The reward included exempting from land tax to military service (Boyle 1972).

10   The six-year plan was also seen as a good example of the instrumental value of opium for the purpose of nation-building (Baumler 2000, 270–291).

11   In particular, the government in the late Qing period developed an opium suppression system that licensed opium growers and users to produce and consume gradually decreasing amounts of the drug so as to achieve the purpose of ultimate elimination (Baumler 2000, 271–272).

control of the opium trade before eliminating it – in Jiang's words, "killing two birds with one stone" (Baumler 2000, 271; Wakeman 1995, 274). This position of the Jiang government was hailed by both domestic and foreign critics for its public honesty and recognition of China's culpability in the opium problem rather than simply blaming foreigners for it.[12]

In its effort to eradicate domestic cultivation, Jiang's six-year plan adopted a divide-and-conquer approach by setting up "poppy-free zones" in areas with light poppy cultivation (mainly the east region) and "gradual reduction zones" in areas with medium and heavy cultivation (in the southeast and the northwest). In the gradual reduction zones, a licensing scheme was adopted to allow growers to gradually reduce their opium production (Baumler 2000, 286–289). These eradication plans were also accompanied by crop substitution to meet the financial needs of the farmers.[13] To strengthen the eradication enforcement, opium suppression committees were set up at provincial, municipal and county levels. Despite peasants' resistance to the enforcement of these laws, there was some evidence that these laws achieved some effects and domestic cultivation of opium decreased.[14]

Compared to its position on opium, Jiang's six-year plan was far more severe in punishing drug activities involving heroin and morphine. For example, the new policy imposed the death sentence for anyone convicted of manufacturing, transporting, or selling heroin or morphine and mandatory prison sentences and confiscations of property for their accomplices. In addition, addicts of morphine and heroin had eight months to voluntarily enter treatment facilities. Otherwise, they would be forced into detoxification if arrested. Starting in 1936, convicted

---

12   For example, Jiang publicly acknowledged that the drugs that the government sold in the market was opium, not anti-opium medicine; and Jiang, in a speech addressing the opium problems, departed from previous rhetoric of blaming Western imperialism but rather cautioned that the Chinese people look at the problems within their own country (Baumler 2000, 286–289).

13   For example, cotton, tea, corn, peas, sorghum, wheat, soybean, and tung trees were commonly used as substitutes for poppy in most regions (Slack 2001, 150–151).

14   According to the official data gathered by the Central Commission for Opium Suppression, raw opium production in the seven gradual reduction zones was reduced from 5,571 tons in 1934, to 3,673 tons in 1935, to 1,583 in 1936, and to 873 in 1937. These official data were challenged by an U.S. estimate of 12,000 to 18,000 metric tons in 1935, accounting for more than 90% of the total global production that year (Slack 2001, 151). Local resistance, particularly by peasants, was a common theme for every anti-opium enforcement policy during the nineteenth and the early twentieth centuries. Using Sichuan as an example, its opium production accounted for 74% of the total production in China in 1904, of which only 10% was exported, and 90% was consumed locally. With an estimated 7% of the 45 million-strong population addicted to opium in Sichuan, poppy cultivation was not only important for the economy but also for consumption reasons (Wyman 2000, 212–227).

addicts would receive five or more years of incarceration and after 1937 they could receive life imprisonment or the death penalty.[15]

To systematically and scientifically address narcotic addiction problems, Jiang's plan divided the country into drug-free zones where smoking was completely banned and gradual reduction zones where smoking was conditionally permitted.[16] For managing the addict population, smokers were required to purchase a permit to use drugs legally while allowing the state to monitor their progress (Slack 2001, 152–153). However, this registration of drug addicts was seriously flawed because elderly people were terrified by the process, wealthy addicts and governmental officials were afraid of losing face, and migratory laborers refused to purchase the permit as the smuggled drugs were readily available (Slack 2001, 153). Nevertheless, during the three years from 1935 to 1937 when addict registration regulation was carried out, a total of 1,665,209 people registered with local governments in 1935, 3,628,162 in 1936, and 4,160,285 in 1937 (Slack 2001, 152).

The plan was also designed to establish opium detoxification centers to treat young and less-dependent smokers, and allow more time for the elderly and chronic smokers to become less dependent on drugs with substituted medicine. Accordingly, the number of detoxification facilities that were reportedly established between 1934 and 1937 ranged from 597 to 1,499 and these facilities successfully treated a total of 1,076,612 opium addicts during these years.[17]

By the end of the sixth year in 1941, most historical accounts indicated that drug use remained an epidemic, particularly in the southwestern region of China. In response to its limited success, President Jiang announced another plan that would completely get rid of narcotic drugs in two years and even enlist the military court

---

15   Users of opium were also differentially treated than users of morphine and heroin in other aspects. For example, while heroin and morphine users were typically convicted as felons and executed by firing squads in public areas with press coverage, opium smokers were typically ordered to undergo mandatory detoxification in health clinics, even though they often were threatened with the death penalty after the grace period of one to two months to get rid of their drug habit (Slack 2001, 104–110). The particularly harsh treatment of heroin and morphine transportation and sale might be due to these harder drugs' direct link with the Japanese and indicative of these drug dealers' unpatriotic conduct (Slack 2001, 108–109).

16   The drug-free zones included provinces such as Zhejinag, Shandong, and Qinghai, and seven counties in Jiangxi, Zhongshan in Guangdong, and the municipalities of Nanjing, Qingdao, and Weihaiwei. Other provinces (Jiangsu, Hebei, Henan, Hubei, Hunan, Anhui, Jiangxi, Fujian, Guangdong, Guangxi, Sichuan, Guizhou, Yunnan, Gansu, Chahaer, Suiyuan, and Ningxia) allowed smokers to register to continue legally using drugs until they received treatments (Slack 2001, 152).

17   These numbers should be viewed with caution as the Jiang government, when reporting these data, did not differentiate types of drug addictions: opium, heroin, or morphine. In addition, it did not specify whether the number in treatment refers to treatment per person or per visit because as many as 20% of addicts undergoing treatment could be recidivists (Slack 2001, 153).

to enforce the ban (Su and Zhao 1998, 355). However, due to internal corruption, local resistance,[18] vacillating allegiance from the warlords, natural disasters, the Sino-Japanese war (1937–1945), and the civil war between the Nationalists and the Communists (1945–1949), none of these plans were able to seriously affect drug consumption.[19] After 22 years of combating narcotic drugs and before they left mainland China in 1949, the Nationalist government left a legacy of 20 million drug addicts, 600,000 drug dealers and smugglers, and 10 million farmers who planted opium poppies on 20 million *mu* of land (Su and Zhao 1998, 364).

During the eight years of the Sino-Japanese war, numerous decrees were issued by the Border Area governments led by the Communist Party. These decrees included the *1939 Decree on Banning the Cultivation of Opium* issued by the Administrative Committee of the Jin-Cha-Ji Border Area, the *1941 Decree on the Temporary Sentencing Guidelines for Drug Offenders* issued by the Jin-Ji-Lu Border Area government, and the *1942 Decree on the Temporary Searching and Confiscating Opium Regulations* issued by the Shan-Gan-Ning Border Area government.

Many of these decrees had similar tenets and can be summarized by the following observations. First, their detoxification measures generally specified that opium users must quit their habit in three months if they were under 25 years

---

18   Local resistance by poppy growers and users was a recurring theme throughout the late Qing period and the Republic Era. Bianco (2000, 296–300), citing numerous sources of local newspapers and scholarly writings at the time, compiled major civil resistance and revolts that occurred from 1907 to 1947 that included major provinces such as Sichun, Zhejiang, Fujian, Yunnan, Shaanxi, Jiangxi, Shanxi, Guizhou, Gansu, Henan, Guangxi, Heilongjiang, Liaoning, Fujian, Anhui, Guangdong, Rehe, Jiangsu, Xikang, and Hunan. What was interesting in Bianco's research was his analysis of the temporal and spatial distribution of the media's portrait of these movements. He noted that civil resistance movements were most readily reported by the news media when they occurred in coastal areas such as Zhejiang and Jiangsu, but less likely to be reported and reported favorably when they occurred in remote Western regions such as Sichuan and Yunnan. This might coincide with the official determination of opium suppression in the east coastal areas but less resolute practices in the more remote areas (Bianco 2000, 295, 300–301). In an interesting twist, the warlords' coercive measures to compel farmers to grow poppy during the warlordist time period also met some local resistance because of the fear of higher taxes, even though the majority of peasants voluntarily chose to plant poppy due to huge profits (Bianco 2000, 301–303). The tricks used by farmers to resist uprooting poppy plants ranged from planting poppy with alternate rows of other crops, uprooting poppy plants only along visible areas such as roads and main paths into the fields, bribing officials, and armed resistance (Bianco 2000, 303–304). Resistance to uprooting poppy plants was the strongest when farmers were compelled to plant poppies a few years ago and when the officials handled poppy control unfairly (Bianco 2000, 307–308).

19   In addition to the larger structural reasons, the failure of Jiang's anti-opium policy was also due to his inherently conflicting goals to both suppress drugs as well as monopolize the drug trade to raise revenue and achieve its political objectives of pacifying the warlords, fighting the Japanese, and eradicating the Communists (Slack 2001, 115–148).

of age, in six months if they were between 25 and 40 years of age, and in nine months if they were older than 40 years of age. Opium smokers unable to quit their habit within the time limit would be subject to one year of penal servitude and up to CNY 3,000 in fines. After three repeat offenses, opium smokers who could not quit their habit would be subject to the death penalty. Second, these decrees generally imposed severe penalty (e.g., the death penalty) for manufacturing and selling opium. However, economic penalties (i.e., fines, confiscating properties) were also utilized as punishments for other opium-related offenses (Su and Zhao 1998, 547–548).

Patterns of Narcotic Consumption, Trade and Cultivation

Following similar methodologies in data collection and analysis of the previous chapter, we are able to provide some detailed accounts of patterns of narcotic consumption, trade, and cultivation in the Republic Era. During this period, other narcotic drugs like morphine and heroin became more common in use and trade.

Box 3.3 Change of Consumption Patterns

• Newly emergent drugs in the Republic Era:
  − Opium in the past
  − Heroin and morphine now
• Methods of drug intake:
  − Smoking in the past
  − Injection now

Narcotic Consumption

While there is much debate about the absolute level of opium dependency and addiction in the late Qing period, there is no question that opium consumption was common in this era for medicinal, festive, and recreational purposes. After the Nationalist revolution that overturned the Qing government in 1911, both the nature and gravity of narcotic drug consumption changed in China. Many of the major changes in this time period were linked to the rise in anti-opium campaigns and the subsequent emergence of morphine injections as a relatively inexpensive and convenient alternative to opium smoking and as a dominant form of narcotic consumption.

A number of studies and reports were initiated during the Republic Era to investigate patterns of consumption of opium and other narcotics. For example, a 1929 study conducted by the National Anti-Opium Association (NAOA) estimated that there were more than 19 million opium addicts at the time, constituting about 4% of the estimated 500 million people in China (Slack 2001, 42).[20] A 1934 Nanjing Ministry of the Interior report suggested that the number of opium, heroin and morphine addicts could total 30 million people (Slack 2001, 42–43). Another source suggested that there were probably 50 million opium smokers in the 1930s and an estimated 10 million of them were addicts (Slack 2001, 153). Another regional report suggested that by mid-1939, the monthly sales of opium was about 2,150 kilograms in Nanjing (the unofficial estimate puts the number close to 2,550 kilograms). This was enough opium for daily use by 60,000 people out of 500,000 residents in Nanjing (Eykholt 2000, 362).[21]

In contrast, data collected from local governments under the mandate of the Nationalist government's six-year drug prohibition plan, by the end of 1935, indicated a total of 1.67 million registered opium smokers (This number represented a severe underreporting problem because many provinces such as Guangdong, Ninxia, Guangxi, Qinghai, Zhejiang, Shangdong, Hebei, and Chahaer did not even report their numbers). By 1936, the number of registered opium smokers increased to 3.63 million (again, several key provinces including Guangdong, Guangxi, Zhejiang, Shandong, and Chahaer did not report their data). By 1937, the recorded number reached the highest at 4.16 million. Even though the number of registered opium smokers dropped to 2.02 million and 2.81 million in the subsequent years of 1938 and 1939 respectively, the overall number remained very high (Jiang, Qiuming, and Qingbao Zhu 1997, 368–369, 408; see also Qi, Lei and Hu, Jinye 2004, 210–211).

Meanwhile, the Nationalist government also reported data on smokers who quit their habit. For example, between 1935 and 1939, the total number of drug addicts who quit their habit was 1.6 million.[22] After the Japanese invasion and its pro-narcotics policy, the number of opium smokers jumped to 32 million people (Qi, Lei and Hu, Jinye 2004, 97).

Even if these national figures were accurate estimates of opium use and addiction, they were far from an adequate portrait of opium use within geographical areas of heavy poppy cultivation such as Sichuan, Yunnan, and Gansu. In these regions,

---

20   According to Wakeman (1988, 12), there were an estimated 5 million addicts in the Yangzi valley area alone during the 1920s and approximately USD 1 billion worth of opium was consumed annually by them during this time period in the Republic of China. Between USD 40 to USD 100 million worth of narcotic drugs passed through Shanghai annually.

21   It was argued that the percentage of opium users among residents in Nanjing should be far greater than 10% because these official and unofficial estimates did not account for: (1) the large illegal distribution of opium, (2) opium ash reused several times more by poorer users, (3) different drug use habits (i.e., some were not frequent daily users), (4) children and women probably being less involved in narcotics, and (5) other narcotic drugs such as heroin not being included in the numbers (Eykholt 2000, 362).

22   The annual number of smokers who quit their habit was 339,198, 339,046, 319,024, 181,518, and 386,591 respectively from 1935 to 1939. See Qi, Lei and Hu, Jinye 2004, 212; Jiang and Zhu 1996, 408.

more than half of the population was suspected of being addicted to opium, based on the reports of the National Anti-Opium Association (Slack 2001, 43).

Similar to the profile of opium use in the late Qing period, opium smoking was considered ubiquitous in the Republic Era, particularly evident in urban centers and densely-populated river deltas (Wakeman 1978, 178). As a leisure activity, opium smoking continued to serve as a commodity for conspicuous consumption for all social groups (Dikotter, Laamann and Xun 2002, 58–62; Zheng 2005, 59). The prevalence of opium use was evidenced by thousands of opium dens in cities and towns, including Shanghai where there were more stores selling opium than selling rice, and more opium halls and dens than restaurants in the early twentieth century (Forges 2000, 170).

The emergence of hypodermic injection as a method of narcotic consumption in the early twentieth century has been attributed to the confluence of various cultural, political, technological, and economic factors. In particular, the idea of injecting drugs with needles easily resonated with China's population because of the long cultural tradition of using acupuncture as a medical technique for various types of pain relief. Technological developments (e.g., the mass industrial production of syringes, increased pharmaceutical knowledge, production of tablets and ampoules with accurately measured dosages) provided the raw materials for hypodermic-based consumption. Politically, government policies and anti-drug organizations in the early twentieth century focused primarily upon the abolition of opium trade and use but morphine injections were viewed more positively as an essential part of the prevailing medical culture (e.g., as a cure against opium addiction or remedy for sleeplessness) (Dikotter, Laamann and Xun 2002, 179). The primary economic benefit for the drug consumer was that morphine injection was far cheaper than smoking opium, often reducing the costs for habitual users by more than 80%.[23] It is the joint distribution of these factors that helped explain the use of morphine injections as a quick, potent, economical, odorless, and legal alternative to opium smoking in this time period.

Evidence of the prevalence of narcotic injections during the Republic Era can be derived though various observations and inferences. For example, claims about a rising needle culture for injecting narcotics and other substances in this period were supported by the following observations:

- China experienced explosive growth in pharmaceutical products in the early decades of the twentieth century. The use of syringes to administer numerous types of drugs was widely accepted and the packaging of many patent medicines in glass ampoules greatly simplified and shortened the injection process. Starting in the early 1920s, local factories began manufacturing

---

23   Similar to the tax revenues generated by opium, the regulation of the importation of morphine and syringes was also a source of government revenue, with taxes levied on both morphine and syringes through the passage of legislation in 1909 (Dikotter, Laamann and Xun 2002, 177–179.

injectable products. For example, nearly 60 pharmaceutical companies were found in Shanghai alone by 1937, producing 120 medical substances designed for hypodermic application and turning out over 300,000 ampoules each month (Dikotter, Laamann and Xun 2002, 179–180).

- From the 1920s onward, the hypodermic syringe was widely used in China to administer vaccines and serums for numerous health concerns (e.g., typhus, cholera, meningitis, gonorrhea, tuberculosis, smallpox, diphtheria, bubonic plague). Many of these injections were often mandatory in times of epidemics (Dikotter, Laamann and Xun 2002, 181–182).
- Medical handbooks on injection methods and other "how to ..." manuals were widely published and circulated within China in the mid-1920s and 1930s.[24] These materials showed both doctors and public consumers the proper methods and best points for injecting these substances.
- Most morphine injectors shifted to injection because they could no longer afford opium smoking. This was especially true of narcotic users in China's working class. For example, many poor customers in Shanghai switched to morphine injections because it cost about a third as much as an average pipe of opium (Dikotter, Laamann and Xun 2002, 188).
- Customs reports indicated that the number of syringes illegally imported into China increased from 940 in 1924 to 3,892 in 1927. A total of 13,402 morphine needles that were being smuggled into China were seized between 1924 and 1928 (Dikotter, Laamann, and Xun 2002, 186).

Narcotic Drug Trade

Even though the agreement between the Chinese and the British on banning opium importation took effect in 1917, smuggling of opium and other narcotic drugs never stopped. From 1917 to 1937, Persia (modern day Iran), Turkey, and India were the three major countries that exported narcotic drugs (e.g., opium, heroin, morphine). China received these exported narcotics either directly from these countries or indirectly via other locations such as Hong Kong, Macao, Taiwan, Japan, France, and the United States (Su and Zhao 1998, 321–322). Domestically, local bandits and secret societies were continuously involved in drug trafficking to support their existence. For example, according to Wakeman (1988, 12–15), the underworld consisted of an estimated 100,000 hoodlums who were involved in opium, morphine and heroin trade in Shanghai alone.

According to various reports, the total annual opium exports between 1925 and 1931 from these three countries (Persia, Turkey, and India) were 3,135,523 pounds. China imported annually an estimated 113,318 pounds of narcotic drugs from the port of Dalian in the Northeast region of China. The remaining amount of narcotics was smuggled into China. Between 1932 and 1933, with the tightening of the drug

---

24   For a listing of some of these medical handbooks and manuals, see Dikotter, Laamann and Xun 2002, 181–182 and the references therein.

prohibition enforcement, the total combined annual opium export from these three countries dropped considerably to 1,603,973 pounds, with legally imported opium at 137,789 pounds coming through the Dalian port (Zheng 1935).

Before the Sino-Japanese War broke out in 1937, the Japanese had already started exporting narcotic drugs to China. The "psycho-chemical warfare" that aimed at weakening the Chinese government, its resources, and Chinese people's will to resist the military aggression and occupation had intensified since the start of the war in 1937. While no detailed records exist on the amount of narcotic drugs smuggled into China by the Japanese, the suspension of drug prohibition laws, the establishment of the monopolized drug sale committee controlled by the Japanese military, and the promotion of various drug related activities (cultivation, sale, and use) suggested widespread drug smuggling occurred in the Japanese-controlled territories (e.g., Manchuria) (Su and Zhao 1998, 323–326).

Various reports suggested that the opium trade during the Republic Era remained a lucrative business and attracted people from all walks of life (Slack 2001, 16–19). For example, a survey conducted by National Anti-Opium Association (NAOA) in 1929 indicated that merchants, officials of high and low rankings, soldiers, and individuals involved in organized crimes contributed to about 70% of the opium trade (Slack 2001).

The NAOA survey in 1929 identified several categories of individuals and groups involved in the opium trade. These participants in the opium trade included: (1) opium merchants who were involved in various levels of production, transportation, and sale of opium; (2) wholesale merchants who had considerable capital and were engaged in a large-scale buying and selling of raw opium; (3) retail merchants who purchased opium from the wholesale merchants and sold it to the boiled opium merchants for further processing; (4) boiled-opium merchants who processed raw opium into a smokable form and sold it to customers; and (5) opium den keepers who provided smokers a place to enjoy the product on the basis of status or social class (Slack 2001, 16–19).

Because of the need for revenue to launch campaigns against the communists or recalcitrant militarists, the Nationalist government took advantage of its connection with the Shanghai Green Gang, a secret society, to have a stake in the illegal opium trade (Bailey 2001; Martin 1996). It was also reported that in the Shaan-Gan-Ning Border Region both before and after 1949 the Communists relied on opium revenue to survive due to the economic blockade imposed by the Nationalist government (Bailey 2001, 142; Chen 1995).

Domestic Cultivation

Due to the cultivation eradication campaigns in the late Qing period and the early Republic Era, opium cultivation had mostly been eliminated and growth was only restricted to remote provinces, according to an observer of the British Minister in Beijing (Feuerwerker 1980, 8). Based on this report, opium crop acreage dropped substantially during the years between 1914 and 1919, even though opium continued to be smuggled into China each year.[25] During this time period, there was a significant price increase for opium due to market speculation about the shortage of opium.

The first leader of the Republic Era, Sun, made an important statement on opium policy on behalf of the Nationalist Party in 1924. He linked the success of opium eradication to a democratic government and said that "the problem of opium suppression in China is synonymous with the problem of good government. For the traffic in opium cannot coexist with a National[ist] government deriving its power and authority from the people. Until political workers in China are in a position to implement civil authority in the administration of government, it will be nearly impossible to prohibit opium completely" (Slack 2001, 71).

However, a decade of warlordism starting from the death of Yuan Shikai in 1916 brought back poppy cultivation to support the warlords' private armies.[26] Warlords imposed heavy taxation on every source of revenue possible, including opium. They encouraged poppy cultivation and even levied a "laziness tax" on those who did not plant it. In addition, the warlords extracted protection money from opium and gambling houses (Sheridan 1975, 86–87). Sun's death in 1924 further weakened the Nationalist Party's influence in national politics. Warlordism became rampant. Poppy cultivation surged to the level of the 1900–1906 period, producing an estimated 9,000 to 35,000 tons per year in the mid-1920s.[27] Based on a report of the International Anti-Opium Association of Beijing presented at the Geneva opium conferences in 1924–1925, China was growing at least 15,000 tons of opium annually, accounting for approximately 88% of the total world production (Slack 2001, 6). From 1929 to 1933, poppy cultivation took up 80 million *mu* of land, approximately 6% of productive land; yielded 60 million kilograms (120 *dan*) of opium annually. Four provinces including Shanxi, Gansu, Yunnan, and Sichuan were major areas of production (Qi and Hu 2004, 194). According to data released from the 1934 International Conference on Opium Prohibition, the annual Chinese production of opium was 12,000 tons in 1930, whereas there were only 1,990 tons produced in other countries. In other words, the annual production of

---

25   For example, from 1904 to 1909, it was estimated that 14% of the total reported crop area was planted with opium. That number was reduced to 3% during the 1914–1919 period but climbed back to 11% in 1924–1929 and reached 20% by the 1930–1933 period (Feuerwerker 1980, 8).

26   Warlordism referred to the brief period of military and political chaos after the collapse of the Qing dynasty and the birth of the Republic of China in 1911, particularly during the period between Yuan's death in 1916 and the establishment of the Nationalist government in 1927. Bianco (2000, 293) called the warlords' competition to monopolize opium trade to strengthen their army "intense", and the start of the "new opium wars" (Sheridan 1983).

27   Under warlordism, large areas of land were given over to raising the profitable poppies. The amount of cultivated land used for opium increased from 3% in 1914–1919 to 20% in 1929–1933. This rise in opium cultivation was partly responsible for the widespread famine in 1929 (Sheridan 1975,102–103; Young 1971, 306).

opium in China was six times as high as that of other all nations combined (Qi and Hu 2004, 194).

During the Republic Era, farmers in many provinces were cultivating opium poppies. Sichuan, Yunnan, and Guizhou provinces were the heavy cultivating areas, whereas moderate levels of cultivation were found in provinces such as Shaanxi, Gansu, Rehe, Fujian, Anhui, Henan, Heilongjiang, and Jilin. Low cultivation areas included Hubei, Hunan, Suiyuan, Chahaer, Jiangsu, Xikang, Guangdong, Shandong, Jiangxi, Ningxia, Xinjiang, Hebei, Liaoning, Zhejiang, and Guangxi. Other provinces such as Xizang (Tibet), Qinghai, and Mongolia had no record of poppy cultivation, probably due to the lack of favorable weather conditions and production technologies.[28]

Poppy cultivation was extremely labor-intensive, requiring an average of 109 working days per *mu* for opium when compared with only 26 days for wheat, 82 days for rice, and 88 working days per *mu* for tobacco.[29] Farmers cultivated poppy for two main reasons: (1) economic benefits and (2) pressure from bandits, landlords, merchants, and military and civil officials.[30]

Policies on opium cultivation changed over time and space during the early twentieth century. This was mainly because the Nationalist Party in the post warlordism period struggled to articulate a national policy on opium. Conflicted between the moral obligation for eliminating the most blatant symbol of Chinese humiliation and helplessness in the past century or so and the need for the lucrative revenue generated by a thriving narco-economy, the successive leaders of the Nationalist Party such as Sun and Jiang came up with a paradoxical policy of control through taxation (Baumler 2000; Slack 2000, 248).[31] In addition, the weak

---

28   Poppies required rich land and heavy fertilization and drought and hailstorms may ruin a crop, which might explain why in some regions poppy cultivation was not recorded (Slack 2001, 7).

29   Tea was the most labor-intensive product, requiring an average of 129 working days per acre (Slack 2001, 8).

30   Opium, called "black rice", simply earned farmers more than any other crops, even with higher taxes and a fine due to its planting being illegal at the time. In addition, during the warlord period, farmers were coerced into planting poppy and were labeled as patriotic by the warlords. In places where farmers refused to plant poppy, they were subject to penalties three times higher than the regular "fine" for illegally planting the poppy, leaving farmers with no choice but to plant poppies (Slack 2001, 10–12).

31   According to Slack (2000, 248–266), other visible anti-opium forces during the Republic Era involved the Christian missionaries and their Chinese converts, and non-Christian urban elites. Two non-governmental organizations were formed respectively by each of these prominent groups: the National Christian Council of China (NCC) and the National Anti-Opium Association (NAOA). The views expressed by these organizations on opium were very different from that of the governmental officials. Contrary to the governmental official policy of "suppression through taxation", these social groups advocated a policy of complete prohibition of opium production, trade and consumption. They allied themselves with the international organizations on opium prohibitions such

Republic central government and the strong local and regional control under various warlords also contributed to the weak enforcement of the drug control policy. Cultivating opium poppies was at one time compulsory and at other times illegal. Peasants were threatened with death if they did not plant poppy at one time and later if they did plant poppy. Taxes were also used as a means to either stimulate production or eradicate the crops and at times, regardless of whether opium poppy was planted or not, the land was heavily taxed. The general high taxes on opium cultivation, combined with the changing policies and their economic impact on peasants, resulted in a series of peasant riots between 1910 and 1935.[32]

Based on a variety of sources, the annual opium production averaged between 12,000 and 15,000 tons from 1924 to 1937. The high level of opium production was strongly tied to its price value when compared with other important crops. For example, the average yield per *mu* (1 *mu* = 0.16 acres) of important crops in China between 1931 and 1937 showed that rice yielded 365 pounds per *mu*, corn yielded 207 pounds, 168 pounds resulted from tobacco cultivation, and wheat yielded 145 pounds per *mu*. In contrast, opium yielded only 4.2 pounds per *mu* (Slack 2001, 164). Although the yield per *mu* for poppy cultivation was extremely low, the adjusted farm price for poppy was incomparably high. For example, data in 1929 indicated that rice received CNY .036 per *mu* compared to CNY 14.5 per *mu* for opium (Slack 2001, 166).

After the establishment of the Nationalist Government in 1927, Jiang launched several plans to address poppy cultivation, opium trafficking and smoking. As a

---

as the International Anti-Opium Association and were actively involved in international meetings such as the Geneva Opium conferences. By doing so, they urged the Nationalist government to adopt a policy of zero tolerance on opium and other narcotics drugs (Slack 2000, 248–266). The NAOA's main mission was to enforce the laws prohibiting opium consumption, cultivation, and trade, to limit the importation of foreign narcotic drugs to the amount required for medicinal needs, and to promote treatment of drug addicts and anti-narcotics education (Slack 2000, 252). During its 14 years of operation (1924–1937), the NAOA experienced a rise in power with its increased influence on the Nationalist government to transform the policy from suppression to prohibition during 1924–1930 and gradually lost its power while Jiang Jieshi was gaining political and military control over China and reinforcing the opium monopoly system. The association was finally dissolved in 1937 (for detailed review of the mission, function, and activities of the NAOA, see Slack 2000, 248–266).

32   In many regions, peasants were levied with heavy taxes as a means to phase out poppy cultivation. However, the reality was that regardless of whether peasants grew opium poppy or not, they were levied with heavy taxes, leaving them no choice but to cultivate poppy as no other crop could bring in enough to make such high taxes viable. Peasants were also personally threatened with the punishment of death if they did not uproot their plants within two weeks in a Gansu official inspection in 1932. The prohibition of opium also had a devastating effect on peasants' economic prospects as it made the value of land drop overnight. All of these factors precipitated peasant riots in areas where poppy growth was common such as Sichuan, Gansu, and Fujian (Bianco 1986, 285–288).

result, poppy cultivation was drastically reduced. Data on raw opium production suggested annual reductions from 5,571 tons in 1934 to 873 tons in 1937 (Slack 2001, 151). Even though significant disparities existed between the above data provided by Jiang's central government and data collected by the U.S. consulates (the latter put the number around 12,000 to 18,000 metric tons in 1935), there was little dispute that opium production had indeed been reduced significantly.[33] Nevertheless, with the outbreak of the Sino-Japanese War in 1937 and the subsequent civil war between 1945 and 1949, drug eradication campaigns by the Nationalists were disrupted. The Japanese government's narco-chemical warfare policy toward China led to increased cultivation activities (e.g., the production of opium reached 20,000 tons in Japanese occupied territories) (Qi and Hu 2004, 97).

Before the Communist Party took over China in 1949, it was estimated that at least 10 million people were involved in planting and cultivating opium poppy, more than 20 million *mu* of land were used for planting opium poppies, and approximately 20 million people were drug addicts (more than 4% of the national population) (Su and Zhao 1998, 364). In heavy opium-producing regions of southwestern China drug problems were even more staggering. For example, in Yunnan province, about 21% of its residents were estimated to be drug addicts and 33% of its productive land was used for the cultivation of opium poppy (Xu 2007, 29–32). The City of Kunming alone (in Yunnan Province) had 1,187 opium houses. According to an observer, "every household had an opium pipe and every household held gambling gatherings" (Su and Zhao 1998, 363). In Jinyuan County of Sichuan Province, the cultivation of opium poppy only started from the early Republic Era. However, by 1930, it quickly grew to cover 20% of the productive land, and between 1940 and 1950, the coverage further expanded to 40% of the total productive land (Su and Zhao 1998, 363).

Summary

This chapter explored the nature of drug control laws, drug-related activities, and their social context within the Republic Era. During this historical period, China was experiencing dramatic transformations in its political, economic and social systems. The conflicts and contradictions that are associated with these socio-economic conditions of the Republic Era and their impact on drug-related practices will be further analyzed in Chapter 5.

---

33   For example, the U.S. Consuls estimated a 50% reduction in cultivation since 1934 in the provinces of Sichuan, Yunnan, and Guizhou that historically had heavy poppy cultivation (Slack 2001, 151–152).

Chapter 4
Narcotics Control in the People's Republic of China

1949 was a watershed year in the long history of China's struggle with narcotics. After defeating the Nationalist army led by Jiang Jieshi (Chiang Kai-shek), the Chinese Communist Party (CCP) declared its victory and founded the People's Republic of China (PRC). As part of its effort in building a new China, the Communist government targeted opium use, cultivation, and trafficking in the 1950s and successfully eradicated narcotics problems through nationwide, intense public campaigns and stiff political, administrative, and legal sanctions. In the next two decades, China remained a "drug-free nation".

Drug problems, however, re-emerged after China's commencement of its economic reforms in 1978, first in the southwest region of the country and then they quickly spread to other areas. Despite its increasing effort to regain control over narcotics use and crime, China struggled along with other nations in the resurgence of this "old" problem. The "people's war" tactics, which was so effective in the 1950s drug suppression campaign, seemed to be losing its ground and effect in the new era.

This chapter describes these patterns of narcotic consumption, cultivation, trafficking and the PRC's responses to it. We focus on two distinct historical periods: (1) the initial years of the PRC in the 1950s and (2) the economic reform era since 1978. Important economic, political, and social conditions in each period are identified and discussed in terms of their impact on the nature of drug-related activities and governmental control in both historical periods.

People's Republic of China (1949–1978): The Building of a New Socialist Nation

The defeat of the Nationalist government and the victory of the CCP in 1949 embarked a beginning of a new political and economic system in China – the People's Republic of China (PRC). The political, economic, and cultural conditions associated with the initial development of a new socialist country under Mao are examined below.

Political Structure under the People's Democratic Dictatorship

The political system established by the CCP was fundamentally different from China's feudal political system and the Western-style capitalist political structure. Instead, this political system was primarily based on Mao's theory of New Democracy that adapted Marxism-Leninism to China in its critical transition from semi-colonialism and semi-feudalism to socialism.

The political structure was characterized as a People's Democratic Dictatorship that was led by the CCP as a vanguard of the working class, and was supported by a four-class alliance (i.e., the workers, the peasants [nearly 90% of the population had an origin of peasant then], the petite bourgeoisie, and the national-capitalists). The CCP had a membership of 4.5 million in 1949 (Hsu 2000, 646–651).

Based on the *1949 Organic Law* and the 1954 Constitution, the highest organ of the state was the National People's Congress (NPC). The NPC was in charge of making major policy decisions and electing top government officials. Other important political offices at the central governmental level included the Chairman of the Republic (Mao was the first appointed to that position), the State Council, the National Defense Council, Supreme People's Court (SPC), and Supreme People's Procuratorate. The leading party was the CCP (Hsu 2000, 449).

Box 4.1 Political Structure of the PRC: People's Democratic Dictatorship

> - Led by the Chinese Communist Party as a vanguard of the working class
> - Supported by a four class alliance
>   - Workers
>   - Peasants
>   - Petite bourgeoisie
>   - National-capitalists

A critical feature of the original structure of PRC was its merging of the leadership between the CCP and the government. As a result, most of the governmental administrative positions were filled by the Communist Party members, making it clear that it was the CCP that set the agenda for the state. For example, Mao served as the Chairman for several key positions including the CCP Central Committee, the Central Secretariat, the People's Republic, and the NPC (Hsu 2000, 650).

At the provincial and local (districts or county) levels, the political structure was organized in a similar fashion of dual roles: the Party and the local government. Similar to the state's political structure, higher ranking party officials almost uniformly held important positions in the provincial governments.

This setup of political institutions certainly had its advantage: it ensured the Party's leadership in managing important state and local governmental affairs so that the Party's directives could be effectively carried out at all levels of the governments. Nevertheless, the drawbacks of this particular arrangement involved its inability to insert necessary and appropriate checks and balances between the Party and the government. It also had a limited ability to detect or curb various types of governmental abuse and corruption.

The potential problems with this model of government was soon manifested in a series of political and economic movements such as the Great Leap Forward (1958–1960), the Three-Anti Campaign (1951) and Five-Anti Campaign (1952), the Anti-Rightists Movement (1957–1959), and the Cultural Revolution (1966–1976). In these particular movements, Mao's personal view turned into the Party's view, and the Party's view turned into the government's position. This strong interdependency of views was pivotal in starting China on a dangerous slippery slope of personal worship and dictatorship of Mao throughout the 1960s and the 1970s. It was during these turmoil years that the initial success of political reforms were eroded by personal and ideological conflicts among the Party leaders, resulting in the isolation, exclusion, and even extra-judicial convictions and executions of many political dissidents that characterized the lawless era of class struggle and the Cultural Revolution (For a detailed account of this period of the PRC history, see Hsu 2000, 645–706).

Mass-Line and Popular Justice

After the establishment of the PRC, all laws from the Nationalist government were abolished. Initiatives were made to enact new laws that reflected the socialist political and economic interests and objectives. Indeed, the 1950s was the golden age for lawmaking in China, when many of the first laws of the PRC were enacted including the 1954 Constitution.

Box 4.2 Mao's View of Law

- Law is a tool used by the ruling class to maintain state domination
- Law is elitist, too static and slow to reflect social change
- Living law is preferred over formal law
  - popular justice
  - mass-line policy
  - class struggle
  - extrajudicial organizations, procedures, and measures replaced judicial ones

One of the fundamental differences between Western capitalist democracy and Chinese Communist government was the view on law and its value in national political economy. Contrary to Western conception of law's supremacy and independence, the Chinese Communist leaders led by Mao believed that law was a tool for the maintenance of state domination. For Mao, law was not independent entity but rather an instrument for the preferential treatment of the ruling class (Chen 1973, ix). In addition, Mao viewed law as static, elitist, and slow to reflect social change.

To facilitate rapid political, economic, and social transformation, Mao essentially saw law as a burden and roadblock to effective social changes. Instead, mass mobilization and popular justice of the grassroots movements were regarded more favorably. The preference for these methods of social change was understandable when one considers that the Communist Party's successful fight against the Nationalist government and Japanese invasion in the 1930s and 1940s was a direct result of its close relationship with and reliance upon the peasants and its use of rural areas as revolutionary bases.

Mass-line policy and class struggle achieved great success in the rural areas first before it spread to the urban areas, primarily because self-reliance and self-sufficiency were not new concepts for the peasants and local residents in China. In fact, these ideas can be traced back to feudal China. What was new in the PRC, however, was the intensity and the scale of the mass mobilization.

Such a policy of mass mobilization had major consequences on various aspects of social life in China. In its heyday, it tragically paralyzed the legal system. For example, during the Culture Revolution period (1966–1976), courts, procuratorates, and police organizations were almost completely abolished. It also replaced the law and the legal system with the living law (i.e., justice was contextualized depending on one's class membership), and employed extra-judicial organizations, procedures, and measures to impose sanctions and settle disputes. As a result of these activities, political dissidents (e.g., those who were labeled as "leftists" or "rightists") and/or unpopular social elements (e.g., petty capitalists, landlords) were disenfranchised and excluded. "Educational" sessions involving self-criticism were mandated for some dissents, whereas others were sent to "thought reform" labor camps, imprisoned, and/or executed.

The intense social control under the ideology of socialist popular justice was further assured through the establishment of neighborhood committees in urban cities and the household registration system. The establishment of these two basic systems of social control in urban areas effectively tied individuals to their residential neighborhood and workplace.

State-Planned Economy

The PRC also built a completely different economic structure to achieve socialist objectives. The socialist economic system was envisioned to consist of three sectors: (1) the state economy, (2) the agricultural economy, and (3) the private economy. The state economy was comprised of major industries, mines, enterprises, and public utilities, all controlled by the government. The state economy represented a large share of the total production and led other sectors in the economy to achieve the socialist economy. The agricultural economy was collectively owned by the rural communes where farmers participated in the collective agricultural production. The private economy was only operated by the middle and small capitalists and comprised a very small percentage of the socialist economy (Hsu 2000, 646).

Box 4.3 PRC's Socialist Economic System

- State economy
    - Major industries, mines, enterprises, public utilities all controlled by the government
    - representing a large share of the total production
    - leading other sectors to achieve socialist economy
- Agricultural economy
- Private economy

If there were any resemblance of the PRC economy to the Qing's feudal economy, it was its closed-door policy and its emphasis on self-reliance and self-sufficiency. Unlike Qing's self-chosen closed-door trade and diplomatic policy, however, the PRC's closed-door policy in its early decades was due primarily to Western economic embargos and the "Cold War" ideology.

Box 4.4 PRC's Agrarian Reforms

- First agrarian reform in1950
    - Redistributing the land.
    - 700 million *mu* of land distributed to 300 million peasants by 1952.
- Second agrarian reform in 1952
    - Collectivization of the rural economy.
    - Establishment of the People's Communes across the rural sectors by 1958.

To achieve this goal of reconfiguring economic sectors and ownerships, the PRC launched two agrarian reforms in the 1950s. The first agrarian reform in 1950 achieved the goal of redistributing the land from the landlords to the peasants. By the end of 1952, approximately 700 million *mu* of land had been redistributed to 300 million peasants. The second reform launched in the December of 1952 was aimed at collectivization of the rural economy. By 1958, People's Communes were spread across rural sectors in all areas of the country.[1]

Meanwhile, recognizing that the backbone of the socialist economy was a strong industry, the PRC launched its first *Five-Year Plan* in 1955, which aimed at doubling the industrial output through the construction of 694 projects, and incorporating private industry and commerce into the state system by the end of the plan. The plan achieved great success and surpassed expectations in many areas such as steel, iron, electric, and coal production (Hsu 2000, 654). The initial, unprecedented success prompted a more ambitious plan in the next five years, which called for an overall increase of 75% in both industrial and agricultural production by 1962 and a 50% increase in national income. To meet these demands of rapid economic growth, the government revamped higher education by eliminating the general education and the liberal arts education within universities and focusing on technical institutes and specialized fields in science and technology (Hsu 2000, 655).

What followed was a series of movements designed to continue accelerating economic productivity. For instance, the Great Leap Forward (1958–1960) was designed to rely on China's vast population to rapidly transform the agrarian economy into an industrialized economy. It rejected the centralized planning policy adopted in the beginning of the PRC and encouraged self-reliance in building small-scale manufacturing facilities in rural areas.

The development of People's Communes accompanied these changes. These Communes were designed as the nation's basic social and organizational units for agricultural and industrial production. They were the ultimate grassroots self-reliant local organizations, which assumed many functions of the government such as collecting tax and providing policing, education, and health services. They were also primary economic production units, responsible for providing the living necessities for people in the Commune. In addition, these Communes were also a means of mass mobilization, critical for the class struggle, popular justice and the mass-line policies (Grass, Corrin and Kort 2004, 179–207). These pushes for rapid modernization and social transformation added tremendous strain to an already overheated economy. This strain was reflected by periods of Party's opposition in the 1950s and the 1960s, the slowdown of the economy in 1960s and the 1970s, and some disastrous consequences of mismanagement of the economy (e.g., depression and famine in the 1960s).

Externally, the Communist success of 1949 ended foreign concessions and settlements. At the same time, China also became ostracized from the world order by the Western capitalist democratic alliance of the Post-World War II era. This larger international context forced Communist China to develop an isolated political and diplomatic policy, a self-sufficient economy, and a closed society literally free from the influence of Western ideologies and values. Ironically, this

---

1 Several phases were involved in achieving the collectivization including mutual aid, semi-socialist agricultural producers' cooperatives, the fully-socialized cooperative, and finally the People's Communes (Hsu 2000, 653).

period of isolation made it easier for the PRC to control the supply-side of the drug problems that emanated from international trafficking.

Consumption, Cultivation, and Trafficking of Narcotics Drugs

By the time that the CCP took power in 1949, the new government was confronted with a staggering problem of drug trafficking and drug use. Reportedly, there were an estimated 20 million drug addicts, 300,000 drug traffickers and manufacturers, and the poppy cultivation reached over 1 million hectares nationwide (Zhao and Yu 1998, 27; He and Fang 1998; Dupont 1999; "China Always Says 'No' to Narcotics, 2004). To address this problem, the new government employed many of the same techniques that were used to develop the emergent political and economic structures of the PRC. These drug-control strategies focused on a mass-line policy that incorporated grassroots support, mass mobilization movement, political campaign, "educational" programs, and other formal mechanisms of social control (e.g., incarceration, execution).

Consumption Patterns in the Early Years of the People's Republic

No official statistics are available on narcotic drug consumption, cultivation, and trade, both during and after the drug prohibition and eradication campaigns launched after 1949. With regard to consumption, after five years of strict enforcement of drug prohibition laws and public campaigns, an estimated 20 million drug addicts quit their drug addiction through either mandatory detoxification or voluntary treatment programs (Su and Zhao 1998, 371). In 1953, the Chinese government proclaimed to the world that the "sick man of Asia" was gone and China became a "drug-free nation" (Su and Zhao 1998, 374). This was partly confirmed by the dramatic reduction in the number of temporary measures and governmental decrees issued about drug-related activities in the 1950s compared to those pronouncements during the 1960s and the 1970s.

Box 4.5 Consumption Patterns in Early PRC

- An estimated 20 million drug addicts were successfully treated with their addiction between 1949 and 1953.
- Chinese government declared "a drug-free nation" to the world in 1953.

Poppy Cultivation in the Early Years of the People's Republic

In light of the absence of systematic data on the national level, studies on a particular province may provide a useful snapshot on the scale of poppy cultivation and the effect of eradication campaigns. For example, Gansu province was one of the primary areas of drug use and cultivation in the northwestern region of China.

During the first ten years after the establishment of the PRC, there were more than 10 eradication campaigns in Gansu province alone that eliminated more than 600,000 *mu* of poppy plants (Su and Zhao 1998, 386). For example, Gannan was one of the areas most heavily infiltrated with drugs in Gansu Province. Gannan was historically inhabited by Tibetans and it had severe problems with opium cultivation and use. Drug eradication campaigns significantly reduced the drug problems in this area as well (Su and Zhao 1998, 386).

Box 4.6 Poppy Cultivation in Early PRC

• No available national statistics
• Eradication campaigns used comprehensive measures
   – Persuasion
   – Education
   – Coercion
   – Punishment
• Virtually complete eradication between 1958 and 1978

Through a combination of measures (e.g., persuasion, education, coercion, and punishment), a total of 385,000 *mu* of poppy plants were eradicated in Gansu province and 12 million grams of opium were confiscated by 1956 (Su and Zhao 1998, 386–388). By the late 1950s, opium cultivation was almost completely eliminated in this province. Similar outcomes were replicated in other parts of the country. As a result, most authoritative accounts suggest that China enjoyed a period of 20 years (1958–1978) without major problems with domestic cultivation of poppy (Su and Zhao 1998, 388).

Narcotics Drug Trade in the Early Years of the People's Republic

After the establishment of the PRC, the narcotic drug trade was declared strictly illegal. However, due to China's physical proximity to the "Golden Triangle" region (i.e., Laos, Thailand, and Burma) and the huge drug addict population estimated at 20 million people, drug smuggling was quite common during the early 1950s. Given the long history of drug trade and cultivation in China, drug smuggling and sale networks were massive and extremely well-financed and well-organized.

By the end of 1949, it was estimated that at least 600,000 people were involved in manufacturing and trafficking narcotics (Su and Zhao 1998, 364). In the early 1950s, more than 500,000 people were estimated to be involved in drug dealing and smuggling, and slightly more than 10% of the drug dealers were government officials, who utilized their official positions as cover to facilitate and protect the illicit trade (Su and Zhao 1998, 370–371).

Box 4.7 Narcotic Drug Trade in Early PRC

- Rampant drug trade problems in 1949
  - China's unique physical proximity to the "Golden Triangle" region.
  - Strong domestic demand for narcotics.
  - Drug smuggling and sale networks given historical reasons.
  - An estimated 600,000 people involved in manufacturing and trafficking.
  - People of all walks of lives involved in trafficking, including an estimated 10% public officials.
- Five year campaigns (1949–1953)
  - 220,000 drug cases were tried.
  - 80,000 offenders were convicted for manufacturing, smuggling, and selling drugs.
  - More than 800 were sentenced with the death penalty.

Source: Su and Zhao 1998: 370–371.

To illustrate the magnitude of the drug trade in the early 1950s, consider China's official statistics on the criminal cases involving drugs. Between 1949 and 1953, a total of 220,000 cases involving narcotic drugs were tried in the People's Courts at all levels. Among these cases, 80,000 involved convictions for manufacturing, smuggling, and selling of drugs. More than 800 of these offenders were sentenced to death (Su and Zhao 1998, 370–371; Mao and Wang 2002, 492; Zhou 2000b, 388).

After five years of strict prohibition and major anti-drug campaigns, it is widely assumed that China became a virtually drug free nation between 1955 and 1978. Limited information is available about the nature of drug activities during this period. Only sporadic episodes of isolated drug smuggling are noted in the available information and these incidents mostly occurred in the remote Western region of China (Su and Zhao 1998, 371).

Legal Regulations on Narcotic Drugs

The CCP had longstanding anti-drug policies since its establishment in the 1920s. During the late 1920s and early 1930s, opium poppy cultivation was declared illegal in the Communist controlled regions.[2] In the 1940s, several temporary measures and decrees were issued by regional Communist governments to combat cultivation, sale, and use of opium and other narcotics drugs such as morphine and heroin. However, because of the civil unrest and military conflicts at the time, none of the measures achieved visible results.

As mentioned earlier, by the time the CCP took over the political power from the Nationalist government in 1949, there were an estimated 20 million drug addicts, 600,000 drug dealers and smugglers, and 10 million farmers who planted opium poppies on 20 million *mu* of land (Su and Zhao 1998, 364). The PRC government immediately confronted these drug problems with a series of national and regional laws and initiatives. Achieving unparalleled success, these anti-drug initiatives dramatically transformed China's image from the "sick man of Asia" to a virtually "drug free" nation. For analytic purposes, this "people's war on drugs" waged by the CCP before and after the establishment of the PRC can be divided into three phases: (1) 1920–1949, (2) 1950–1954, and (3) 1955–1979 (Su and Zhao 1998, 549).

Drug Suppression Decrees (1920–1949)   Laws used in combating opium and other narcotics drugs in Communist revolutionary bases during this period were primarily in the form of decrees and temporary measures issued by various regional governments controlled by the Communist Party. These decrees and temporary measures are summarized in Table 4.1.

Based on these measures and decrees, it appeared that the Communist revolutionary governments utilized criminal punishment of various sorts including fines, fixed-term sentences, life imprisonment, and the death penalty as means to deal with drug trafficking, poppy cultivation, and addiction. In addition, the punishment meted out for drug offenders appeared quite stern as well as discriminatory, much harsher toward those activities involving hard drugs such as morphine and heroin. For example, the *1941 Temporary Decree on the Prohibition of Opium in Northwest Jin*[3] specified that:

---

2   There was evidence that the Communists did cultivate and sell opium outside their controlled regions in exchange for needed currency and materials, though the discussion of this issue was forbidden due to its sensitive nature within China (Zhou 2000b, 381; 1999, 94).

3   Those who transport, sell, and possess opium with valid governmental license were exempt from this decree (Su and Zhao 1998, 1536–1537).

Table 4.1 Decrees and Laws on Drug Activities (1930–1977)

Communist Revolutionary Based Governments before 1949

1939	Decree issued by the Jin-Cha-Ji Border Administrative Committee Regarding Prohibition of Poppy Cultivation.
1941	Temporary Decree on the Prohibition of Narcotics Drugs in the Jin-Ji-Lu-Yu Border Region.

- Subjected those who manufacture narcotics drugs such as morphine, heroin and other synthetic drugs to the death penalty and confiscation of property.
- Subjected those who traffic, harbor traffickers, or sell narcotics drugs to life imprisonment or the death penalty, with an exception with reduced sentences for the first time offender, those involving extremely small quantities, or those deceived or forced into the activities.
- Subjected drug addicts to quit their habit in three months (25 years old or younger); in six months (25–40 years old); in nine months (older than age 40); those who do not quit beyond the time limit are subject up to one-year forced labor and a fine up to 3,000 yuan; second offense will subject to more than one year of imprisonment and a fine up to 3,000 yuan; third offense will result in the death penalty.

1942	Temporary Measures for Searching and Seizing Narcotics Drugs in the Shan-Gan-Ning Border Region.
1943	Temporary Measures for Prohibiting and Punishing Narcotics Offenders in Shandong Province.
1946	Temporary Measures for Searching and Seizing Narcotics Drugs in the Liao-Ji Region.
1946	Decree on Prohibiting Opium Smoking and Narcotics Drugs in the Liao Ji Region.
1949 (July16)	Temporary Measures for Prohibiting Opium Smoking and Narcotics Drugs in the Northern Region.
1949 (August 20)	Temporary Measures for Narcotics Drugs Detoxification in Suiyuan Province.

The People's Republic (1949–1978)

1949–1952	During the early years of the People's Republic of China, numerous decrees were issued by local governments. For example, the 1949 Temporary Measures on Prohibiting Opium and Other Narcotic Drugs in the Huabei Region; the 1949 Temporary Measures on Prohibiting Opium Smoking in Suiyuan Province; the 1950 Measures on Completely Eradicating Opium issued by the Southwestern Military Government Committee; the 1951 Measures of Eradicating Opium Smoking in the Inner Mongolia Autonomous Region; the 1952 Directive on Prohibiting Opium and Other Narcotic Drugs issued by the Northeastern People's Government .
1950	The Executive Administrative Ministry issued a Decree on Banning Opium.
1963	The Chinese Communist Party and the Central Government issued a Notice on Banning Opium and Morphine.
1973	The State Council issued the Notice on the Banning of Cultivating, Selling and Smoking Opium and Other Narcotics Drugs.

Source: Su and Zhao 1998: 1534–1547.

- those who transport, sell, and posses opium for the purpose of selling were subject to more than two years and less than 10 years of imprisonment with a fine up to CNY 5,000;
- when the amount exceeded 200 grams, the offender would be subject to the death penalty;
- den keepers were subject to 3–10 years of imprisonment and a fine up to CNY 5,000; and
- opium smokers were allowed up to a year to quit their habit; smokers older than age 25 may have up to three years to quit their habit; those who did not quit after the specified time limit would be subject to a three-year incarceration.

Another decree on eradicating narcotic drugs and opium in the Liao-Ji Region issued in 1946 tackled both opium and other more lethal, narcotics drugs such as heroin and morphine. This decree showed differential treatment for opium and other narcotic drugs. In particular, the use, transport, sale and possession of "hard" narcotic drugs like morphine and heroin were treated much more harshly than similar activities involving opium (Su and Zhao 1998, 1543–1544). For example, the decree specified that:

- Those who transport opium were subject to 3–5 years of imprisonment for less than 100 grams, 5–10 years of imprisonment for less than 500 grams, and life imprisonment or the death penalty for more than 500 grams.
- Those who transport and sell hard narcotic drugs (like morphine and heroin) were subject to life imprisonment or the death penalty regardless the amount involved.
- Opium smokers must register with the government. Those who are younger than 20 years of age must quit within one month no matter the degree of addiction; those under 30 years of age, three months; those under 45 years of age, six months; those under 60 years of age, 10 months. Those who cannot quit their habit within the time frame will be detained and undergo forced detoxification with a fine more than CNY 5,000 yuan; if reuse after detoxification, the smoker will be sentenced to life imprisonment or the death penalty.
- Narcotic drug addicts must quit their habit of using morphine or heroin within three months; those who cannot quit the habit within this time limit may use opium as a substitute under the same conditions as opium users. If drug addicts do not quit their use of hard drugs within three months, they will be subject to life imprisonment or the death penalty.

However, due to political turmoil and military conflicts among various warlords and the Nationalists as discussed in the previous chapter, the effect of anti-drug efforts by the Communists was very limited during the 1930s and the 1940s.

Drug Suppression Laws (1950–1954) During the initial phase of drug prohibition under the PRC, several major national and regional laws and decrees were issued. These included the *1949 Temporary Measures on Prohibiting Opium and Other Narcotic Drugs* in the Huabei Region, the *1949 Temporary Measures on Prohibiting Opium Smoking in Suiyuan Province*, the *1950 Decree on Banning Opium* issued by the Executive Administrative Ministry, the *1950 Measures on Completely Eradicating Opium* issued by the Southwestern Military Government Committee, the *1951 Measures of Eradicating Opium Smoking* in the Inner Mongolia Autonomous Region, and the *1952 Directive on Prohibiting Opium and Other Narcotic Drugs* issued by the Northeastern People's Government. These anti-drug laws were similar to previous legal regulations in their definitions of particular types of narcotic offenses. However, these new drug laws also had several distinct characteristics that contributed to their effectiveness.

First, these laws established a reward system for offenders who voluntarily turned themselves in, confessed to their crimes, showed remorse, and/or provided important leads for criminal investigations. These offenders were given favorable treatment with lighter sanctions or no punishment in an effort to effectively target more "hard core" criminals who refused to cooperate with the authorities.

Second, these laws and decrees imposed severe sanctions on criminals who committed serious drug-related crimes such as transporting narcotics with arms, cultivating, manufacturing, and transporting drugs, and operating opium dens. Many of these crimes were subject to the death penalty.

Third, multiple types of economic sanctions (e.g., fines, confiscation of properties) and corporal punishments (e.g., imprisonment, death sentences) were utilized in combination to control particular offenses. For example, a decree by the Northeastern government specified that offenders who transport or manufacture drugs must have their drugs, money, and property confiscated along with other appropriate criminal punishment.

Fourth, the content of laws and decrees were rather vague and brief, leaving huge discretionary power for the local authorities to mete out punishment (Su and Zhao 1998, 551–552).

Drug Suppression Laws (1955–1979) After the first five years of the anti-drug campaigns, the epidemic narcotic drug problem in China was to a large extent effectively controlled and eliminated. Nevertheless, from the late 1950s to the early 1970s, drug problems persisted in some parts of China, particularly in the remote southwestern, mountainous areas such as Yunnan and Sichuan.

In 1963, the CCP and the central government issued a *Notice on Banning Opium and Morphine*. It specified that those who sold, stocked, and used narcotic drugs, cultivated poppy, or operated drug dens must be severely punished. It further stated that drug addicts must undergo forced detoxification. The forced detoxification process was to be managed and supervised by designated governmental agencies and under the surveillance of the local people. Those who refused detoxification would receive severe punishment.

During the 1970s, the growing global drug problem and abuse also spilled over to certain areas of China. To address this concern, in 1973 the State Council issued the *Notice on the Banning of Cultivating, Selling, and Smoking Opium and Other Narcotics Drugs* (Zhao 1993, 55). The Notice called for mobilizing the masses to combat the selling, cultivating, and the using of opium and other narcotic drugs. It particularly stressed severe punishment for those who smuggle and transport narcotic drugs. In addition, it required a more stringent detoxification plan to force drug addicts to quit their habits.

Eradication Campaigns against Narcotics Drugs in the Early PRC Period

Anti-Drug Campaigns   The initial success achieved by the Communist government on opium and other narcotic drugs control in the early years was accomplished through a series of comprehensive anti-drug campaigns. The Chinese government launched its first nationwide anti-opium campaigns immediately after the founding of the PRC in 1949. These comprehensive campaigns aimed at both the supply and demand of the drug problems and adopted various measures including extensive propaganda campaigns, poppy cultivation eradication campaigns, strict prohibition of cultivation, trafficking and selling, demanding the public to turn in their supplies of opium, and drug addicts registration and rehabilitation (Zhou 2000b, 282). As a result, more than 165,000 drug offenders were uncovered during these campaigns (Zhou 2000b, 386).

Despite such efforts, the first round of campaigns was not viewed as complete and effective for several reasons. First, there lacked comprehensive plans and execution strategies in implementing the central government's directives of waging the war on drugs, particularly in light of the monumental tasks of its nation-building (e.g., reviving economy, regaining social order, fighting the Americans in Korea), and drug suppression was not made the priority. Second, the new government lacked resources to carry out its ambitious drug eradication plan nationwide, particularly at the local level. Third, the punishments rendered during this round of campaign were viewed as too lenient to be effective (Zhou 2000b).

Box 4.8 Anti-Drug Campaigns in the 1950s

- Mass mobilization
  - Establishment of neighborhood committees.
  - Extensive use of propaganda meetings (760,000 meetings).
- Widespread effects
  - 75 million people were educated.
  - 400,000 drug offenders were identified.
  - 82,000 arrests were made.
  - 52,000 offenders were convicted.
  - 34,000 were given criminal sentences.
  - 880 offenders were executed.

Source: Mao and Wang 2002; Zhou 2000b.

A second wave of anti-drug campaigns was launched in 1952 to consolidate and strengthen the first campaigns. This round of campaigns mobilized the general public to identify drug users and conduct mass education about the harmful effects of narcotics drugs on the individual and society. Meanwhile, neighborhood committees that were established to provide surveillance and education significantly improved the effectiveness of the anti-drug campaigns. According to official statistics, the second round of campaigns held a total of 764,423 propaganda meetings nationwide, through which 74,595,181 people were educated (Zhou 2000b, 392; 1999, 103; Reins 1991; Slack 2001; Wong 2000). These massive public campaigns uncovered more than 370,000 drug offenders and resulted in 82,100 arrests (22%). Among 51,600 convicted offenders, 880 were executed (5%)[4] and over 33,800 were given criminal sentences (Mao and Wang 2002, 492; Zhou 2000b, 388).

During these campaigns, drug manufacturers and traffickers were heavily targeted, while drug addicts were forced to quit. There was very little record with regard to the total number of drug addicts mandatorily rehabilitated by the government. Available regional data suggested that in Guizhou, for example, 49,646 *mu* (3,310 hectares) of poppies were wiped out, 3,000 opium dens were closed in 1951, 11,700 opium addicts were rehabilitated, and 6,333 drug offenders were arrested (Zhou 2000b, 383). In Nanjing, two rehabilitation centers were set up to treat 1,120 drug addicts (711 male and 409 females) in 1952. Most of those addicts reportedly undertook rehabilitation at home with the help of family members and "under surveillance of the masses", and only 50 addicts were put on compulsory

---

4 The number of execution, though not small, was relatively insignificant when compared with executions in the campaign against counterrevolutionaries, estimates of which range from 500,000 to 800,000 (Zhou 2000b, 393; 1999, 105).

rehabilitation under the supervision of the public security authority. By the end of the year, all 50 addicts were officially cured (Zhou 2000b, 388).

By the end of the second round of campaigns, China became a virtually drug-free society, though the anti-drug campaign continued in some ethnic minority regions in the late 1950s (Zhou 1999; 2004).

A State-Building Process   As commonly acknowledged, in hundreds of years of China's drug control history, the Communist government's success in the 1950s was virtually complete and unprecedented (Wong 2000; Zhou 2000a, 2000b). This unique success was not accomplished through a formal modern lawmaking process. Rather, it was achieved in a process of state-building when dramatic changes happened in many aspects, including the changes in economic, political, and social conditions previously mentioned. In this state-building process, a number of key factors are worth special attention.

First, due to China's unique history, opium use was blamed as the evil of the feudal Qing society and foreign nations' imperialism. To build a new communist society meant to get rid of the image of the "sick man of Asia". Unlike other political campaigns during the same period, the rationale of the anti-drug campaign was not based on class struggle, but on building a new national identity. The Communist government was eager to show several contrasts: the Old China versus the New China; the Nationalists versus the Communists, the Imperialists versus the Chinese people (Zhou 2000b). The new government took the anti-drug campaign as an opportunity to show the world that only a Communist society was able to eradicate drug problems that deeply plagued China over the past hundreds of years. This powerful ideological rhetoric mobilized the public to participate in anti-drug campaigns, and prompted the government to extend the campaigns in the second half of the 1950s to ethnic minority regions and "saved" ethnic minorities from their "backward" lifestyles and helped them build their new socialist society (Zhou 2004).

Second, the Communist government effectively tied its anti-drug campaigns to the notion of nationalism and patriotism. In the first half of the twentieth century, nationalism was directly tied to anti-imperialism in China. Both the Nationalists and the Communists deliberately incorporated anti-drug campaigns into their efforts of state building, and tried to strengthen their authority and tighten their social control. The anti-drug campaigns in the 1950s were no exception, and contributing to the success of the campaigns was regarded as being patriotic. For example, the new government mobilized anti-American sentiment in China because of the ongoing Korean War and successfully kept its anti-drug campaign invisible to the outside world – this explained why there was little public record of the anti-drug campaign during this period.[5]

---

5   Zhou (2000b) pointed out that during this time, there were accusations by the Americans that China was exporting drugs to Japan. To safeguard its "new China" image, the Chinese government decided to keep a low profile of the 1952 anti-drug campaign. This

Third, the success of the anti-drug campaign was made possible by the Communists through the building of an unprecedented social control system in the Chinese society. A series of social control mechanisms such as neighborhood committees, public security committees, the household registration system, and mandatory drug addict registration were established nationwide and restrained free movement of the populace in general and drug addicts and traffickers in particular. Mass rallies and public trials were utilized frequently to mobilize public participation and facilitate anti-drug campaigns. In some instances, fervent "patriots" were even reported to have disclosed their family members and relatives for their drug use (Zhou 2000b). When the campaign was extended into remote ethnic minority regions in the late 1950s, the Communists took a deliberately different, gradual approach towards ethnic minorities, partly due to its incomplete social control over these groups and regions, until they gained increasing full control by the end of the campaign (Zhou 1999, 2004).

Fourth, and lastly, the success in the 1950s was further buttressed by economic and political policies implemented by the Communist government internally and China's foreign policies externally. The centralized national economy and collectivized private sectors both in urban and rural areas had significant impact on opium cultivation and manufacturing. For example, land reform conducted in the rural areas in the early 1950s facilitated the reduction of poppy-cultivation, as the redistribution of lands generally weakened the ability of big landowners to engage in mass cultivation of opium poppies. In the spring of 1952 alone, more than 147,000 *mu* of opium poppies were pulled up in the course of rent reduction and land reform (Zhou 2000b, 384). Politically, a series of movements during the early years of the new nation such as the Three-Anti Campaign in the 1951 and the Five-Anti Campaign in the 1952 greatly facilitated the anti-drug campaigns and many drug traffickers indeed were rounded up and executed as counterrevolutionaries (partially due to lack of anti-drug laws and regulations) (Zhou 2000b). Externally, as discussed above, Communist China became largely isolated after 1949 in the international arena. Its economic self-sufficiency policy and its isolation ironically cut off potential routes for opium trade and international trafficking, and allowed China to remain "drug free" for the next two decades.

In sum, the new Communist government's unique economic, political, foreign, and social conditions in the 1950s greatly facilitated its state-building strategy. Tight social control and relative isolation from the outside world cut off possibilities of drug trade, trafficking, cultivation, and consumption. Though not based on modern formal laws, the CCP's zeal of building a new China along with its nationalism propaganda made possible a complete eradication of drug problems. As a result, China proudly enjoyed a drug-free reputation until its economic reforms and its "open-door" policy by the end of the 1970s.

---

image of China becoming a major drug dealer in the international arena and poisoning its enemies has been lingered and emerged from time to time. See, e.g., Chen (1974).

The Reform Era (1978–Present):
Resurgence of "Old" Drug Problems

Mao's death in 1976 marked the end of the Cultural Revolution, and Deng's rise to power in 1978 sent China on a completely different path. Deng championed two philosophical shifts of the CCP's policies: *gaige* and *kaifang* (literally translated into reform and openness). These new policies led to dramatic economic reforms that embarked in 1978, and resulted in major legal, political, and social changes.

Economic Reform: China's Market Economy and Socialism

As a victim himself, Deng well realized the disastrous impact of Mao's class struggle policies and mass public campaigns. The first task was to abandon class struggles and to save the national economy. At the third plenary session of the 11th Central Committee in 1978, the CCP officially acknowledged that "the principle contradiction in China today is no longer class struggle but between the growing material and cultural needs of the people and the backwardness of social production" (Leng 1985, 36).

In order to increase economic productivity, major changes of socialist economic structure have been made in both rural and urban areas. In the rural areas, the "contract responsibility system" was adopted, replacing collective commune production, and greatly promoted farmers' incentives and enhanced agricultural production. From 1978 to 2005, for example, the gross output value of farming increased more than 16-fold, from CNY 111.76 billion to CNY 1.96 trillion (China Statistics Yearbook 2002–2006). In the rural areas, non-state-owned modes of organizations, such as township and village enterprises, (foreign) joint ventures, wholly foreign, and private enterprises, were gradually reintroduced into industrial sectors. Those non-public productive activities were deemed as the "tail of capitalism", and to be collectivized and eliminated under the 1975 and 1978 PRC Constitution (Lin, Cai, and Li 1996). After 1978, however, it was those non-public modes of production that greatly contributed to China's economic development.

Box 4.9 China's Market Economy and Socialism

- Rural sector
  - Contract responsibility system replaced collective commune production.
  - Promotion of farmers' incentives to enhance agricultural output.
  - Formation of township and village enterprises, and joint ventures.
- State-Owned Enterprises (SOEs)
  - Gradually replaced by private enterprises.
  - Produced less than 50% of the total national GDP by 2005.

Source: Lin, Cai, and Li 1996; *China Statistics Yearbook* (1980–2002); the *People's Daily*, November 13 and December 1, 2006; February 28, 2005.

Official data showed that by the mid-1980s, the number of non-state- and non-collective-owned industries already far exceeded the total number of state- and collective-owned industries. Around the turn of the new millennium, the gross output value of non-state and non-collective industries also caught up to that of state and collective industries (Li, Cai and Li 1996; China Statistics Yearbook 1980-2002). Due to their accelerating development, non-public-owned sectors started absorbing more and more laborers. In 1994, the number of workers employed by non-public sectors surpassed that of urban collective-owned units, and in 2002, it further passed the shrinking state-owned enterprises (SOE). Official data in 2005 and 2006 showed that non-public owned economies already contributed more than 50% of China's total GDP annually (the *People's Daily*, November 13 and December 1, 2006; February 28, 2005).

In carrying out its economic reforms, the Chinese government realized that major adjustments had to be made to the old planned economy. In the early 1980s, plans were proposed to supplement the planned economy with market regulations, and this was the first step in making adjustments (World Bank 1997). Next, the term "commodity economy" was proposed to meet the needs of the new market under the planned economy (Chen 1995, 82). Though the difference between a commodity economy and a market economy was vague, the government showed a strong reluctance to use the term "market economy" because of its association with capitalism. In 1987, the CCP acknowledged that China's socialism was still at a preliminary stage. Rather than "carried out on the basis of a highly-developed capitalism" as orthodox Marxism suggested, China's socialism was "constructed in backward industrial conditions, with backward productive forces and an underdeveloped commodity economy" (Lo 1995, 29). This acknowledgment paved the way for further structural changes.[6] For example, income derived from bonds and shares was viewed as unearned under orthodox Marxism. At the preliminary stage of socialism, however, it became acceptable to receive some income that did not come from one's own labor (Epstein 1991, 97).

In 1988, Zhao Ziyang, General Secretary of the CCP, rejected the orthodox Marxist dichotomy that characterized socialism and capitalism in terms of a planned and a market economy (Lo 1995, 30–31). Under the new interpretation, a market economy no longer belonged to capitalism and could be used by socialist countries as a means to regulate the economy as a supplement to the planned economy. From 1989 to the early 1990s, the official position was that China's economy was an economy with "organic integration with both planned and market regulations" (World Bank 1997). The triumph of the market economy over the planned economy, however, looked unstoppable. In 1993, the market economy officially replaced the planned economy in the revised national Constitution as

---

6 It is further added and underscored in the revised 1999 Constitution that "China is going to be at the 'preliminary stage' for a long time." the *People's Daily*, March 17, 1999.

the main economic mode at the socialist preliminary stage. Since then, the official term has been the "socialist market economy with Chinese characteristics."

The impact of the economic reforms and the market economy was enormous and reached every corner of the society. For once, getting rich was no longer shameful but glorious, and people were willing to take any means to be rich, including committing crimes (Rojek 2001). Drug trafficking turned out to be exactly such a means, and gaining profit was the number one reported reason for drug traffickers. Market economy and economic reforms intensified social economic competition and opened up opportunities for drug offenses.

The "Open Door" Policy and International Cooperation

Along with domestic reforms in 1978, the Chinese government established an "open door" policy as its first step toward rejoining the outside world. The first trial of this policy was the establishment of special economic zones (SEZs) for international trade and foreign investment. In 1979, Shenzhen, Shantou, and Zhuhai in Guangdong province became the first three SEZs, and Xiamen in Fujiang province became the fourth SEZ in 1980. In those SEZs, measures of market operation were introduced, and enterprises were given special preferences (such as tax breaks and exemptions, land use privileges, and duty exemptions) to attract foreign capital and technologies.

Box 4.10 "Open Door" Policy in Reform Era

- Establishment of SEZs in 1979 and 1980
  - Shenzhen
  - Shantou
  - Zhuhai
  - Xiamen
- Utilization of market incentives and special preferential treatments
  - Tax incentives
  - Land use privileges
  - Duty exemptions
- Expansion of the SEZs to coastal zones in the 1980s and the 1990s
  - Hainan (1984)
  - Shanghai (1990)

The trial project turned out to be very successful. In 1980, the foreign currency holdings of Guangdong and Fujian rose to six times their 1979 levels (Gross 1988). Seeing the fruitful outcome, the central government quickly granted similar preferences to Hainan Island[7] and 14 coastal cities[8] in 1984, to the entire coastal zone in 1988, to Shanghai in 1990, and to 21 additional (non-coastal) cities along the Yangtze River and in the northeast in 1992 (Shirk 1994, 39; Wang 1996, 253; Yan 1992).

Since the establishment of those SEZs, both foreign trade and investment have tremendously increased. From 1978 to 2006, China's trade (both imports and exports) increased from USD 20.6 billion to USD 1.76 trillion, with an average annual rate over 15%; China's national ranking in the world trade (merchandise) jumped from the 32nd place in 1978 to the 3rd place in 2004 (after just the U.S. and Germany) (Collection of Statistics of Foreign Economic Relations and Trade of China 2001; China Statistical Abstract 2002; WTO, International Trade Statistics 2005). Total foreign capital investment also increased steadily throughout the 1980s until 1989 when the Tiananmen Square protest broke out and scared off many investors.

Foreign investment quickly bounced back in the 1990s and only showed a decrease in the second half of the 1990s due to the influence of the financial crisis in Asia before it picked up a new momentum in the new century. The total realized foreign capital value, based on official data, increased from USD 1.26 billion in 1979 to USD 6.4 billion by 2004 (Collection of Statistics of Foreign Economic Relations and Trade of China 2001; China Statistical Abstract 2002; Chinese Statistical Yearbook 2005; 2006). The total accumulated foreign direct investment (FDI), an important indicator of the total foreign investment, reached USD 622.4 billion in 26 years from 1979 to 2005. China has been the largest FDI recipient in all developing countries since 1991 and was the third-largest FDI recipient in 2005 (only after the U.S. and the Great Britain) (Qiu Xiaohua, Commissioner of the National Bureau of Statistics of China (NBSC), posted at www.legalinfo.gov.cn, October 2, 2006).

With the massive entry of foreign capital, China became a new hot market for the direct operation of foreign enterprises. By the end of 2005, approximately 470 of the top 500 transnational enterprises had come to China to invest in direct operations (Qiu Xiaohua, Commissioner of the National Bureau of Statistics of China (NBSC), posted at www.legalinfo.gov.cn, October 2, 2006). Over time, foreign invested enterprises (FIEs) have shown rigorous growth and become more and more involved in China's economy. At the beginning of the reforms, the involvement of FIEs in both exports and imports was very minimal, less than 1% of the total exports and imports values. However, the involvement of FIEs increased very quickly over the years, especially in the 1990s. At the turn of the new century, the share of FIEs in both exports and imports reached and then surpassed 50% (Data from Collection of Statistics of Foreign Economic Relations and Trade of China 2001. "Invest in China" (www.fdi.gov.cn), Ministry of Commerce of the

---

7   In 1988, Hainan Island was separated from the Guangdong province and became a new province in China.

8   Those cities are: Dalian, Qinghuangdao, Tianjin, Yantai, Qingtao, Lianyuangang, Nantong, Shanghai, Ningbo, Wenzhou, Fuzhou, Guangzhou, Zhanjiang, and Beihai.

PRC). FIEs are becoming more and more critical to China's foreign trade, and the success of foreign investment and international trade has become an important impetus for China's economic development.

Despite its huge success, the "open door" policy made China's relative isolation in the 1960s and 1970s impossible in the new reform era. One consequence of this change was the increased international drug trafficking, noticeably from the Golden Triangle and the Golden Crescent, two notorious drug centers in Asia (Zhou 2000a). The Chinese government realized that it cannot go back to its pre-reform days, and must move forward to join the global world and fight against the drugs. Indeed, the Chinese government had already ratified such international treaties as the *1961 United Nations (UN) Single Convention on Narcotics Drugs*, *1971 UN Convention on Psychotropic Substances*, and the *1988 UN Convention against Illicit Traffic in Narcotics Drugs and Psychotropic Substances* (Su and Zhao 1998). In more recent years, the Chinese government has gradually and steadily increased its effort seeking international cooperation and support on its domestic war against drugs.

Social and Ideological Transformations

China's economic reforms and the "open door" policy not only transformed China's economic structure but also facilitated China's social and ideological transformations in the new era. This is evident in several aspects.

First, China's urbanization finally took off in the reform era. From 1960 to 1981, China's total population increased from 662 million to 1 billion but the percentage of rural residents stabilized around 80% because of tight control of people's migration. After the reform, the percentage of rural residents decreased to 70% by 1997, and reached its lowest level of 56.1% by 2006 (China Statistics Yearbook 2001; 2005; 2006; Almanac of China's Population 2001; China Statistical Abstract 2002; 2006 data from the *People's Daily* March 1, 2007).

Box 4.11   Social Transformations since 1978

• Structural change in urbanization
− Rural to urban population ratio at 80:20 in the early 1980s.
− Rural to urban population ratio was lowered to 56:46 by 2006.
• Population movement from rural to urban areas
− 147 million migrants by 2005.
− Household registration system faced challenge.
• Deepened social stratification and widening inequality
− Gini-Coefficient increased from .21 in 1981 to .41 in 2000
• Ideological control no longer effective.

Source: *China Statistics Yearbook*, 2001, 2005, 2006; *Almanac of China's Population*, 2001; China Statistical Abstract, 2002; 2006.

Second, when extra labor became free after the reform, China witnessed waves of population migration from rural areas to the inner cities. Solinger's study showed that the average percentage of floaters (i.e., migrants) in the permanent residents of major cities (such as Beijing, Shanghai, Tianjin, and Guangzhou) increased from 12.6% in 1984 to 22.5% in 1987, and to 25.4% in 1994 (Solinger 1999, 17). From 1993 to 1995, the estimated number of migrants nationwide ranged from 20 million to 110 million based on different reports and measurements (Solinger 1999, 19–21). Data from National Bureau of Statistics of China (NBSC) showed that the floating population reached 144 million in 2000 and further increased to 147 million by 2005 (the *People's Daily*, August 30, 2006).

Third, as urbanization and migration quickly developed, the arbitrary separation between the rural and the urban based on the household registration (*hukou*) system began to collapse. The *hukou* system worked very well before the reform, consistent with the planned economy. However, it is losing its effect in the reform era, especially on migrants. To control the new migrants in major cities, the Ministry of Public Security issued *Provisional Regulations on the Management of Population Living Temporarily in the Cities* in 1985. On the one hand, it recognized the migrants' status by granting them a semi-legal status in the cities; on the other hand, it continued the *hukou* system with a goal of regaining the lost control (Mathaus 1989; Solinger 1999). In the same year, the Standing Committee of the sixth NPC in its 12th meeting passed *Regulations of Residents' Identification Cards* to strengthen the *hukou* system, and after 1989 resident cards became mandatory for everyone over the age of 16. From 1985 to October 2002, a total of 1.14 billion resident cards were issued (Data from online news posted at Xinhuanet, October 25, 2002). Although the central government tried to keep the *hukou* system alive, both its effect and existence have become increasingly questionable.

Fourth, with deepened social stratification the problem of social inequality emerged in China. The Gini coefficient, a standard measurement of income inequality, increased from .21 in 1981 to .41 in 2000, a strong warning of income inequality in China (Whyte and Parish 1984; Selden 1985, 211; World Bank 1992; the *People's Daily* July 9, 2002; Khan, Griffin, Riskin and Zhao 1992). In addition, social inequality has become substantially diversified and shows discrepancies between rural and urban residents, among geographical locations, and within different occupations, besides other increasing gaps.[9] Further, the increasing unemployment rate in China aggravated the problem of social inequality. Official data showed that the unemployment rate increased from less than 2% in the mid-1980s to over 4% in the new century (see China Statistics Yearbook 1980–2006).

Fifth, when China implemented dramatic changes economically and socially, the old ideology control under Mao's era started waning, and the younger generations quickly took up new ideas, values, and lifestyles. When the society

---

9   For example, Maurer-Fazio, Rawski and Zhang (1999) showed how gender wage gaps actually increased from 1980s to 1990s in China.

became more diversified, mobile, and economically driven, individuals, their relationships, and their basic unions (families) also became more versatile, unstable, and economically (rather than politically) binding. The government clearly felt the pressure from losing ideological control and took measures to fight the comeback of old vices (such as drugs and prostitution) and defend the invasion of the Western "spiritual pollution". The Tiananmen Square event in 1989 to some extent signified the apex of such ideological crisis and challenge.[10] Despite these governmental measures, China has been experiencing dramatic changes in the new era, and its old social control mechanisms and ideological beliefs are waning to a significant degree. Under such a transitional period, new phenomena arise, including drug use and trafficking.

The Rule of Law in the Post-Reform Era

To protect the political and economic reforms and to maintain domestic stability and attract foreign investment, the PRC started its legal reform in 1978 (see Liang 2008, for a comprehensive study of the changing Chinese legal system in the reform era). Since then, China's legalization has been carried out through several means.

Box 4.12 China's Legal Reform

> * Increasing lawmaking activities:
>   - Passage of 301 laws.
>   - 7 law interpretations.
>   - 122 decisions regarding laws.
>   - Building a preliminary legal system by 2002.
> * Rebuilding an effective legal system:
>   - Judicial system.
>   - Procuratorate system.
>   - Lawyers and lawyering.
>   - Judicial power and independence.

First, the Chinese legislature (i.e., NPC and its Standing Committee) and other governmental branches have been extremely active in creating new laws, decrees, and regulations. From 1978 to August 2002, for instance, the NPC and its Standing Committee passed 301 laws, seven law interpretations, and 122 decisions regarding laws, among which included the Criminal Law, Criminal Procedure Law, Lawyer's

---

10 For the impact of losing ideology on the Tiananmen Square event, see Zhao, 1997.

Law, and Judge's Law (Data from Law Yearbook of China 1986–2005). It was officially announced in 2002 that China had accomplished its task of building a preliminary legal system.[11]

Second, along with the accelerated lawmaking process, China's legalization efforts have had a strong emphasis on rebuilding its legal system, including the judicial system, the procuratorate system and lawyers. Take the growth of professional lawyers as an example. In 1979, there were only 2,200 lawyers and 685 law firms in the whole nation; by the year 2005, China has had 12,988 law firms with a total of 153,846 lawyers (*China Judicial Administration Yearbook 1995–2000*; *Law Yearbook of China 1978-2005*; *Chinese Statistics Yearbook 2005; 2006*).

Third, in the legalization process, a new term, legal professionalism, was proposed to designate the legal profession as a unique profession with its own rules and practices; to recognize different players working within the legal profession; and to elevate the legal system to a higher level and grant it a relatively autonomous status (see a series of discussions on legal professionalism in the *People's Daily*, July 24, 2002).

In sum, in about 30 years, the PRC has made a rapid improvement from a lawless nation in the 1960s and the 1970s to a nation (at least thriving to become) ruled by law, despite a number of problems (Liang 2008). The immediate effect of China's legalization process on its drug control and regulations is shown in its increasing efforts of law-making, including the first ever comprehensive anti-drug law adopted by the end of 2007 (discussed below).

Effects of Social Changes on Drug-Related Activities in Post-Reform China

As described, China's economic, political, and social conditions in the new era are dramatically different from that of the 1950s. Within the new context of privatization, market economy, integration into the global system, social and ideological transformation, and the establishment of the rule of law system, there are several specific factors that may either facilitate or constrain efforts to control drug-related activities and other social problems in post-reform China.

First, the new conditions in the post-reform era have fostered an environment of greater tolerance of diversity and deviance. Old problems (e.g., drug use,

---

11   The *People's Daily*, September 26, 2002. It was later clarified that the goal of the ninth NPC and its Standing Committee was to set up a preliminary legal system (*chubu xingcheng*) as accomplished by 2002. The preliminary system covered seven major legal areas (including Constitution law, civil and commercial law, administrative law, economic law, social law, criminal law, and major procedural law) and three tiers of laws, rules and regulations (including laws, administrative regulations, and local regulations). The goal of the 10th NPC and its Standing Committee is to further strengthen the basic legal system (*jiben xingcheng*), and the final goal by the Chinese legislature is to set up a mature system by 2010. The *Outlook Weekly*, March 12, 2007.

prostitution, gambling) are no longer viewed as "problems" by some people, despite of the government's propaganda. Many drug users view their actions as personal leisure and do not accept the patriotism lesson any more as seen in the 1940s and 1950s.

Second, as realized by the government, drug control is no longer China's problem alone, and must be dealt with within the global system. Within this context, any national control efforts may have limited effect if they are circumvented by the activities of global drug markets.

Third, as part of China's legalization process, the tactic of fighting drugs has been adjusted. For example, China has defined social vices as crimes and passes laws that clearly define them as such. Appropriate legal procedures have also been spelled out and followed in order to hold people accountable for their actions. These requirements, to a large extent, have changed the nature of the people's war on drugs in the new era.

The zeal of building a socialist nation and mobilizing grassroots support as in the 1950s is no longer present in contemporary China. Instead, the government has to turn to formal modern laws and the legal system. Given that anti-drug war is now fought within this new context, it will probably be less effective and less complete in eradicating drug addicts, cultivators, and traffickers.

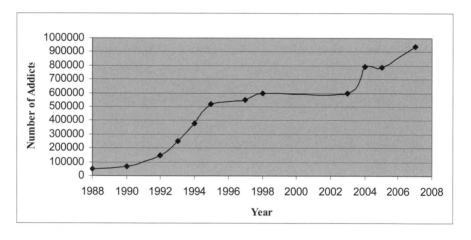

Figure 4.1 Number of Registered Drug Addicts, 1988–2007

Drug-Related Activities in the Reform Era

After being 'drug-free' for nearly two decades, drug problems re-emerged in China in the 1980s. Based on a variety of sources, the number of registered drug addicts has increased dramatically in the last two decades from an estimated 50,000 in

1988 to 937,000 in 2007 (see Figure 4.1).[12] Unofficial estimates of the number of drug addicts are even higher, reaching as high as 6–12 million drug addicts in recent years (DEA 2004; Kurlantzick 2002; McCoy 2004).

In the past two decades, heroin has replaced opium as the primary choice of China's narcotic users. This conclusion is based on the dramatic rise in the amount of seized heroin annually. For example, the Chinese government seized only 23 grams of heroin in 1983 and this amount of illegal drugs reached 5,000 grams by 1985. In 1990 alone, the seizures of heroin reached 1,600 kilograms (1.6 million grams), and the number further increased to 6,900 kilograms by the end of 2005 (Zhao and Yu 1998, 32; *People's Daily,* June 23, 2006). The number of heroin users reportedly reached 743,000 by 2007, 79% of all registered drug addicts in China (the *People's Daily,* December 21, 2007). Drug seizure data also indicate that opium, cocaine, methamphetamine, and marijuana are also commonly used in modern China (DEA 2004, 1996; Li, Zhou, and Stanton 2002; He and Fang 1998; IOSC 2000). In 2002, for instance, approximately 1.3 metric tons of marijuana were seized by the China authorities (DEA 2004).

Geographic patterns regarding drug trafficking and drug use indicated that narcotics drugs initially re-emerged in the southwest region of China, such as in Yunnan and Guangdong provinces, because of the historical tradition of tobacco and opium smoking in these provinces and their physical vicinity to drug-producing nations such as Burma, Thailand, and Laos. In the 1990s, narcotics drugs spread quickly into inner provinces such as Shanxi and Sichuan provinces (Dutton 1997).

Box 4.13 Demographic Profile of Drug Users

- Young
- Male
- Poorly educated
- Unemployed or self-employed
- Smokers
- Alcohol drinkers
- Sexually active
- Prior criminal record
- Disproportionate ethnic minorities

---

12 The Chinese Ministry of the Public Security keeps records of the number of registered drug addicts with its operations of compulsory drug treatment centers, "rehabilitation-through-labor" centers, and rehabilitation medical centers (The *Legal Daily,* December 21, 2007). The sources for the data in Figure 4.1 include: Zhou, 2000a; 1999; 1997; Li, 1994; DEA, 2004, 1996; He & Fang, 1998; 2003 data from online news report: http://news.sina.com.cn/c/2003-10-16/2004931476s.shtml; 2004 data from the *People's Daily,* May 27, 2005; 2005 data from the *People's Daily,* June 23, 2006; 2007 data from the *Legal Daily,* December 21, 2007.

In terms of the socio-demographic profile of drug users, previous research suggests that the majority of drug users are young males (DEA 2004, 1996; Dupont 1999; Kurlantzick 2002; McCoy et al. 1997; Wu et al. 1996; Zhao and Zhang 2004), poorly educated (DEA 2004, 1996; McCoy et al. 1997; Li, Zhou and Stanton 2002), either unemployed or self-employed such as entrepreneur and peasants (DEA 2004, 1996; McCoy et al. 1997; Zhao and Yu 1998). These studies also reveal that drug users tend to be smokers, alcohol drinkers, sexually active, and have a prior criminal record (Wu et al. 1996; Li, Zhou, and Stanton 2002; Zhao and Yu 1998; DEA 1996). It has also been noted that disproportionately more ethnic minorities were involved in drug related offenses than any other traditional offenses (DEA 2004 1996; Bonner 1994).

Along with the increasing trend of drug use in general, female drug use also increased in the post-reform era of China. There were very few female drug users before the mid-1980s, but the number escalated quickly in the 1990s (Yao 2001). By 1999, the number of registered female drug users reached 118,000, which further increased to 138,000 in 2000, and female drug users represented about 16% of all drug users nationwide in both 2002 and 2003 (Gui 2005; "China Always Says 'No' to Narcotics," 2004).[13] Some regional studies showed that female drug dependents made up 20%, sometimes even higher, of all drug abusers in cities such as Guangzhou in Guangdong province and Wuhan in Hunan province (Gui 2005; Yao 2001). For example, in Zhejiang province, there were 2,510 registered female drug users in 2001, who comprised 6.6% of all drug users in Zhejiang. This number increased to 6,365 (16.7% of the total) in 2002, 7,790 (18.8%) in 2003, and 9,374 (19.6%) in 2004 (Wang and Shi 2005; Wang and Zhou 2005). A study of juvenile female drug addicts showed a similar increasing trend over the years, though no specific statistics were reported (Hao 1998).

Box 4.14 Female Drug Use and Users

> •   Increasing involvement in drug use and offenses
> •   Reasons for drug use
>   –   Introduced by family members and intimate friends
>   –   Coaxed into drug use, engaged in prostitution and/or drug trafficking to support drug use
>   –   Pleasure seeking
>   –   Coping mechanisms, escaping from harsh reality

---

13   Zhao and Zhang's study (2004, 166) reported an even higher percentage (25%) of use among women.

A number of reasons were cited in previous research for the increase in female drug use. First, women started using drugs after they were introduced into using by family members (e.g., husband) or intimate friends (e.g., boyfriend) who were drug addicts. Second, some women became addicts after they were initially coaxed into drug use, and then had to take on illegitimate careers such as prostitution and drug selling to support their drug use. Third, an increasing number of young women, especially in urban cities, began and continued their drug use simply to pursue the sensation that resulted from drug use until they became addicts. Finally, a group of female drug users took on drugs as a means of seeking positive things after they encountered negative experiences and difficulties in their social reality (Gui 2005; Huang 2000; Li and Yang 2004; Xie 1995).

A few available studies on female drug dependents consistently showed similar demographic features as male drug users. For example, female drug dependents tended to be young (usually under 25 years old and many with a very young first-use age), unemployed, living in urban areas (medium or small cities), unmarried,[14] and having received little education (Gui 2005; Ji 1998; Ji, Wang and Pang 1997; Li and Yang 2004; Ruan 2007; Wang and Shi 2005; Wang and Zhou 2005; Yao 2001). Compared with male drug users, it seemed to take less time and a lesser quantity for women to become addicts (Yao 2001). Most female drug offenders committed crimes such as prostitution to support their drug use, and they tended to experience an extremely high risk of reuse even after intensive treatment, with over 90% of them reportedly resorting back to drug use (Huang 2000; Wang and Shi 2005; Wang and Zhou 2005; Yao 2001).

Narcotics Cultivation and Manufacture   Since the economic reforms in 1978, cultivation and processing of drugs started to emerge beyond the traditional growth of opium poppy and extended to include cannabis, ephedra, and synthetic drugs. Legal cultivation of cannabis still exists in China, and China produces approximately 14 metric tons of opium per year for domestic pharmaceutical uses under the control of the Ministry of Agriculture and the National Drug Administration Bureau of the State Council (DEA 2004). Illicit poppy cultivation is rare but in several parts of China, such as Xinjiang, Ningxia, Inner Mongolia, and Yunnan provinces, illicit cultivation of cannabis has re-emerged. For example, approximately 1.3 metric

---

14   Two surveys done in Gansu province and Yunnan province in the 1990s showed that slightly over half of the interviewed drug addicts and offenders were married, contrary to other research (Xie 1995; Ji 1998; Ji, Wang and Pang 1997). These findings might have something to do with both the timing of the research (in the early 1990s) and the geographical locations of both provinces (as being poor, remote border provinces in China). Due to their devastating economic and family background, many married women in these regions turned to drug selling and trafficking as a means of making a living.

tons of marijuana was seized in 2002 (DEA 2004). According to official reports, domestically cultivated cannabis was primarily for local consumption.

It was reported that the Chinese government frequently used advanced technologies such as aerial surveys and satellite remote sensing to detect drug fields in high-production regions. For example, 7,345 opium plants were eradicated in Sichuan province in 2004, and 1,170,000 opium plants were eradicated in 2005 in Heilongjiang province (Chen and Huang 2007, 105).

It appears that the manufacture of methamphetamine and synthetic drugs such as MDMA (Ecstasy) has been on the rise in the past 20 years in China. For example, 1.3 metric tons of methamphetamine was seized in 1995 and 4.5 metric tons was seized in 2003 (Drug Enforcement Agency Beijing 2002 and International Narcotics Control Strategy Report January 2003–June 2003). This rise in manufacture of these drugs has been attributed to the availability of precursor chemicals from making these drugs (e.g., pseudoephedrine and ephedrine) and the growing popularity of these substances among the young people in cities across China.[15]

Narcotics Trafficking   Drug smuggling in China began to seriously re-emerge in the early 1980s and gradually escalated in the 1990s. Due to the influence of international narcotic trafficking, particularly in the Golden Triangle region of the Southeast Asia, China was inevitably brought into this global trade network.

While no systematic data exists on the amount of narcotic drugs smuggled into China since the kickoff of the economic reform, data on drug-related arrests and drug seizures provides some circumstantial evidence of the increasing problem of drug trafficking in contemporary China. In particular, both the number of arrests and convictions increased steadily over the past decade (Chinese Government Information 1991–2002, the International Narcotics Control Strategy Report (INCSR), U.S. Department of State 2002, and INCSR January 2003–June 2003). Data on drug seizures (i.e., seizures of heroin, opium, precursor chemicals, marijuana, and crystal methamphetamine) indicate clear signs of escalation between 1983 and 2005 (see Table 4.2) (Chinese Government Information 1991–2002, and the International Narcotics Control Strategy Report (INCSR), U.S. Department of State 2002, and INCSR January 2003–June 2003).

---

15   For example, a total of 86 metric tons of precursor chemicals were seized in 1995 and in 2002, 300 metric tons were seized (International Narcotics Control Strategy Report (INCSR), U.S. Department of State, 2002, and INCSR January 2003–June 2003). In addition, it was reported that approximately 78% of drug addicts are between ages 17 and 35.

Table 4.2 Drug Seizures in China (in kilograms) (1983–2005)

Year	Opium	Heroin	Precursor chemicals	Marijuana	Methamphetamine	Amphetamines
1983	5.25	5				
1984	1.9					
1984	24	7				
1986	78	24				
1987	137	39				
1988	239	166				
1989	269	488				
1990	782	1,632				
1991	1,961	1,919	49,800		351	
1992	2,680	4,489	58,800		655	
1993	3,354	4,459	90,000		5	
1994	1,737	3,881	38,000		460	
1995	1,110	2,376	86,000	466	1,304	
1996	1,745	4,365	219,000	4,876	1,599	
1997	1,880	5,477	383,000	2,408	1,334	
1998	1,215	7,358	344,500	5,079	1,608	
1999	1,193	5,364	272,000	106	16,000	
2000	2,428	6,300	215,000	4,493	20,900	200,000
2001	2,820	13,200	208,200	751	4,820	2,070,000
2002	1,219	9,291	300,000	1,300	3,191	3,010,000
2003		9,530	72,800		5,830	409,000
2004		10,836	160,000		2,746	3,200,000
2005	2,300	6,900	157,900		5,500	2,340,000

Source: DEA 2004; Chen and Huang 2007.

Regional reports on the crackdown of organized criminal groups and drug seizures may also provide insight into the current problems of drug trafficking. For example, a 1997 report from Sichuan Province revealed that it solved one of the largest drug trafficking cases in recent years. This case involved three organized criminal groups with 55 members, working in several foreign nations of the Golden Triangle region, and five provinces and 27 different counties in China. A total of 2,924 grams of cocaine, CNY 165,000 in cash, more than 10 handguns and 400 rounds of ammunitions were confiscated (Su and Zhao 1998, 980–986). Another report from the city of Chongqing suggested that in three months of 1997, the law enforcement agencies had cracked 126 drug trafficking cases, confiscated 7,503 grams of heroin and arrested 106 drug dealers and 444 drug users (Su and Zhao 1998, 986–987).

Due to its geographical location in the southwest region of China, Yunnan province has a long historical tie with narcotics-related activities. Facing the re-emergence of the drug problems, the Yunnan government played a significant role fighting drug trafficking. For example, from 1982 to 2000, Yunnan province cracked a total of 83,743 drug cases, confiscated 88.1 tons of heroin, opium, "ice", and other refined drugs, and arrested more than 100,000 drug dealers. The heroin confiscated in Yunnan accounted for around 80% of the total confiscated in China, and opium accounted for between 60% and 70% of the total in China ("China Always Says 'No' to Narcotics" 2004, 52).

Studies have also indicated that China is increasingly becoming the world largest precursor chemical producer. Those legally produced chemicals can be easily used to manufacture illicit narcotics (Navarro 2007; Li 1994; DEA 2004; Zhou 2000a).

HIV and AIDS Problems   In addition to serious narcotics trafficking and drug use, drug problems have been related to an escalating HIV and AIDS problem in China (Bonner 1994; Kurlantzick 2002; McCoy et al. 1997). Since the discovery of its first HIV case in 1985, the official number of HIV cases in China reached 22,517 in 2000, 40,560 in 2002, and 840,000 in 2003 (with over 80,000 AIDS patients), and decreased a little to 700,000 (with 85,000 AIDS patients) by the end of 2007 (the *People's Daily*, April 12, 2001; Amnesty International 2004; http://news.sina.com.cn/h/2007-11-29/105814413675.shtml). Intravenous drug use reportedly accounted for 60% to 70% of these cases (the *People's Daily* August 24, 2001; Zhou 1999; China Always Says 'No" to Narcotics 2004). AIDS in 2005 became the third-largest life-taker (after tuberculosis and rabies) among all contagious diseases in China (the *People's Daily*, February 14, 2006).

Yunnan province reportedly had the highest prevalence rate of HIV infection due to its serious drug problems. By September 1990, Yunnan had nearly 98% of the total Chinese HIV positive cases (Zhou 2000a). The Chinese Ministry of Health reported that 80.4% (1,426 of a total of 1,774) of all HIV infections in China in 2000 were in Yunnan, and 60% of all confirmed AIDS cases were also found in Yunnan (Cherry 2002, 39). Most recently, a study by the Chinese Center for Disease Control and Prevention reported that the outbreak of AIDS in China could be dated back to 146 drug addicts in Yunnan province in 1989, further reinforcing the image of drug addicts as the major culprit of social diseases (both drug abuse and AIDS) (The *Beijing Daily*, November 29, 2007).

Governmental Responses to Drug-Related Problems in the Post-Reform Era

As noted above, the success of the CCP's anti-drug campaigns in the 1950s was closely related to its economic and political, state-building process. The success was not achieved through a formal, systematic law-oriented approach. Rather, it was achieved through the mass-line people's war on drugs. In comparison, the Chinese government's approach towards narcotics problems in the new era has been increasingly formalized through legislation, along with its effort in building a complete and systemic legal system. During the reform era, China had experienced two distinct periods of drug suppression laws: (1) 1979–1990 and (2) 1990–the present. These laws are summarized in Table 4.3.

Table 4.3 Decrees and Laws on Drug Activities (after 1978)

1979	The Criminal Law of the People's Republic of China went into effect in 1979. It stipulated the offense of manufacturing, selling and transporting narcotics drugs in Article 171.
1981	The State Council issued a Notice on Prohibiting Opium.
1982	The State Council issued an *Emergency Notice on Banning Opium*. In the same year, the Standing Committee of the National People's Congress issued a *Decision on Severely Punishing Those who Disturb the Economy*, in which it made drug crimes (i.e., manufacturing, selling, and transporting drugs) punishable by the death penalty.
1986	The Standing Committee of the National People's Congress passed the *Punishment Regulation of the Public Security Management* by subjecting drug addicts to up to 15 days of custody and/or up to 200 yuan in fines, or warning; and those cultivating drugs with up to 15 days of custody and/or up to 3,000 yuan in fines.
1987	The Supreme People's Court issued a *Response on Sentencing Standards for Imposing the Death Penalty on Narcotics Traffickers*.
1988	The *Supplemental Regulations regarding the Punishment of Smuggling* made drug smuggling a capital offense.
1990	The Standing Committee of the National People's Congress passed the *Resolution on Prohibiting Narcotics Drugs*.
1995	The State Council issued a *Measure on How to Carry out the Forced Detoxification*.
1997	The Criminal Law of the People's Republic of China was revised in 1997. It expanded the definition of narcotic offenses (i.e., illegal trading, transporting, carrying, and possessing opium, poppy plants, or other narcotic plants) and required more severe punishment of drug offenders (i.e., offenders who were involved in smuggling, selling, transporting, and manufacturing narcotic drugs would be held criminally liable regardless the amount of drugs involved).
2002	The Criminal Law of the People's Republic of China was revised in 2002. The definition and punishment for narcotic offenses stipulated in the 1997 Criminal Law remained intact.
2005	The State Council issued *Regulations on Administration of Precursor Chemicals* (Decree of the State Council of the People's Republic of China, No. 445), and *Regulations on Administration of Narcotic Drugs and Psychotropic Substances* (Decree of the State Council of the People's Republic of China, No.442).
2007	The National People's Congress passed the PRC's first comprehensive Anti-Drug Law to curb drug use and trafficking. The new law, which took effect on June 1, 2008, expanded the police power in cracking down on drug trafficking and specified the qualifications and conditions of drug treatment programs.

Drug Suppression Laws (1979–1990)   During this period, drug laws were made in various forms by different government branches, reflecting a concerted effort. In 1979, the government passed its first *Criminal Law of the People's Republic of China*. The new law criminalized the offense of manufacturing, selling, and transporting narcotics drugs. Drug offenders were subject to up to five years of incarceration or custody, and fines (Chapter 1, Article 171). Habitual offenders or offenses that involved a large amount of narcotic drugs were subject to more than five years of prison sentence and confiscation of property.

In 1981, the State Council issued a *Notice on Prohibiting Opium*. It stressed that incidents of cultivating, manufacturing, selling, and smoking opium had increased steadily in recent years, particularly with opium smuggling from foreign countries. In 1982, the State Council further issued an *Emergency Notice on Banning Opium*, stating that opium smuggling and cultivation in bordering provinces such as Yunnan had escalated. In the same year, the Standing Committee of the National People's Congress issued a *Decision on Severely Punishing Those Who Disturb the Economy*. This decision increased the penalty for offenders involved in manufacturing, selling and transporting narcotic drugs from 15-year incarceration to life imprisonment or the death penalty combined with confiscation of property.

In 1986, the Standing Committee further passed the *Punishment Regulation of the Public Security Management*. This law stipulated that those who smoke opium and inject morphine or other narcotic drugs damage the public security system and are subject to up to 15 days of custody, up to CNY 200 in fines, or warning. It also stipulated that those who violated governmental regulations by cultivating poppy or other narcotic plants are subject to up to 15 days of custody, and/or up to CNY 3,000 in fines with the eradication of the plants.

In 1987, the SPC issued a *Response on Sentencing Standards for Imposing the Death Penalty on Narcotics Traffickers*. This order specified that individuals who manufacture, sell, and transport more than 500 grams of heroin shall be given the death penalty and their property may be confiscated; for those who carry more than 300 but less than 500 grams of heroin, if the crime involves aggravating circumstances (e.g., the offender was a ringleader, repeat offender, armed trafficker, resisting arrests or inspection with violence, trafficking and providing shelter for others to use drugs, participating in international trafficking, re-offending after escaping from a labor camp), the individual may be given the death penalty along with confiscation of property.

In the next year, the Standing Committee of the NPC issued *Supplemental Regulations regarding the Punishment of Smuggling* to increase the maximum sentence for drug smuggling from 10 years to the death penalty (Su and Zhao 1998, 553–556).

Drug Suppression Laws (1990–2007)   Due to the acceleration of China's "open door" policy, its economic development, and the globalization of drug issues, narcotic drugs have become an increasingly serious problem in China since 1990.

The National People's Congress passed the *Resolution on Prohibiting Narcotics Drugs* in 1990. This law represented a landmark achievement on narcotic drugs for a number of reasons.

First, it clearly defined and differentiated illicit drugs from other drugs. It specified that illicit drugs include opium, heroin, morphine, marijuana, cocaine, and other narcotics drugs and psychotropic substances. This definition was consistent with the United Nations' definition of narcotic drugs.

Second, it expanded the scope of narcotic offenses to include harboring offenders who were involved in smuggling, selling, transporting, and manufacturing narcotic drugs, illegally providing drugs to others, illegally possessing drugs, and illegally selling narcotic drugs and psychotropic substances to others.

Third, it established a more systematic structure of criminal punishment by coupling the severity of the crime with the severity of punishment. In addition, it expanded the use of supplemental punishment such as fines and confiscation of property.

Fourth, it subjected not only the individual, but also institutions to punishment for violation of these drug offenses. It also stressed a heavier penalty for governmental officials who were involved in these offenses.

Fifth, it specified that habitual drug addicts are subject to forced detoxification. Addicts who revert back to drug use after detoxification are subjected to more labor-intense education and required to go through detoxification again while in the program (Su and Zhao 1998, 556–558).

Sixth, it specified that China has the jurisdictional authority over all drug-related offenses. Foreigners who committed crimes such as manufacturing, smuggling, transporting, and selling narcotic drugs outside China but entered into China's territory will be subject to China's laws in the absence of the multi-lateral and/or bi-lateral extradition agreements with other nations.

To better coordinate drug control efforts in the whole nation and enforce the new law, the Chinese government also set up the National Narcotics Control Commission (NNCC) in the same year. Composed of 25 key departments including the Ministry of Public Security, Ministry of Health, and General Administration of Customs, the NNCC leads the nation's drug control work and is also responsible for international drug control cooperation.

In 1995, the State Council issued a *Measure on How to Carry out the Forced Detoxification* based on the *1990 Drug Prohibition Law*. This new provision detailed the responsibilities and authorities of agencies that supervise, execute, and manage the process of forced detoxification (Su and Zhao 1998, 558–559).

In 1997, the *Criminal Law of the People's Republic of China* was revised. It retained all drug offenses stipulated in the 1990 law and added several new drug-related offenses (e.g., illegal trading, transporting, carrying, and possessing opium poppy or other narcotic plants).[16] In addition, it reaffirmed the death penalty as the potential

---

16 A total of nine offenses were stipulated in the 1997 Criminal Law, including (1) narcotics trafficking (Article 347), (2) unlawful possession of narcotics (Article 348), (3)

maximum penalty, and required that severe drug offenders involved in smuggling, selling, transporting, and manufacturing would be held criminally liable no matter of the amount of narcotic drugs involved, signaling a much more punitive policy towards drugs. The most recent revision of the *Criminal Law of the People's Republic of China* in 2002 retained all provisions on narcotic drugs in the 1997 version.

In 2005, the State Council issued both *Regulations on Administration of Narcotic Drugs and Psychotropic Substances* (Decree of the State Council of the People's Republic of China, No. 442) and *Regulations on Administration of Precursor Chemicals* (Decree of the State Council of the People's Republic of China, No. 445). Both regulations aimed at facilitating the government's war on drugs through tightened controls over psychotropic substances and precursor chemicals in numerous avenues such as manufacture, experimentation, use, purchase, management, transportation, imports, and exports. In addition, these regulations specified responsibilities of respective entities and procedures for supervision and inspection of psychotropic substances and precursor chemicals and their legal liabilities if not in conformity with the regulations.

Most recently on December 29, 2007, the Standing Committee of the National People's Congress adopted the PRC's first comprehensive *Drug Control Law*. The new law, which took effect on June 1, 2008, included seven chapters on general provisions, anti-drugs education, narcotics control and regulation, treatment and rehabilitation, international cooperation in drug control, legal liabilities, and supplementary provisions, respectively.[17] Opium, heroin, marijuana, methamphetamine hydrochloride (commonly known as "ice"), morphine, and cocaine were listed as banned drugs in the new law, and it sets strict rules on the clinical use of pharmaceuticals and other chemicals and medicines that could be used to make illegal narcotics, such as methadone and ephedrine. The new law allows drug addicts to recover in their communities for a limited period of three years and further specifies the conditions under which drug addicts could be confined to rehabilitation centers. The comprehensive nature of the law makes it clear that it is imperative for the Chinese government to crack down on drug-related crimes in order to protect public health, and maintain social order in the new century. At the same time, it calls for all-around anti-drug education and international cooperation.

---

providing shelter for traffickers (Article 349), (4) unlawfully transporting or carrying raw materials (Article 350), (5) unlawfully planting opium poppy, marijuana, or other plants (Article 351), (6) unlawfully buying, selling, transporting, carrying, or possessing live sheets of opium poppy or other plants (Article 352), (7) inducing, instigating, or deceiving others into inhaling or injecting narcotics (Article 353), (8) providing shelter for others to inhale or inject narcotics (Article 354), and (9) illegally providing state-controlled addictive narcotics to others (Article 355).

17   A full version of the new *Drug Control Law* (in Chinese) is available at the NPC's official website (http://www.npc.gov.cn/npc/xinwen/lfgz/zxfl/2007-12/29/content_1387811.htm).

To combat surging drug trafficking crimes in southern border regions, the SPC authorized the High Courts (i.e., the supreme courts) of Yunnan and Guangdong provinces to provide final review and approval of all death sentences for drug trafficking cases in the early 1990s (Chen 2002, 554–556). Technically, such a review and approval by lower courts lacked legal basis since both the 1997 Criminal Law (e.g., Article 48) and the 1996 Criminal Procedure Law (e.g., Article 199) clearly stipulated that "death sentences and executions shall be reviewed and approved by the SPC." However, a compromise was reached in the people's war on drugs until 2007 when the SPC decided to take the review rights back to its own hands (Liang 2008, 139).

Additional efforts to regulate and control narcotics drugs were made at the provincial level as well. For example, narcotic drugs were banned in Yunnan province through its own narcotics control administrative regulations in 1989 and *Narcotics Control Ordinance in 1991*, which covered not only cultivation, production, use, and shipment of narcotics, but also harboring of traffickers and abusers. Gansu province followed Yunnan's lead with similar regulations.[18] In addition to penalties provided by the *1979 Criminal Law*, these provincial regulations and decrees called for prison sentences of up to 15 days, fines, or detention at labor camps for minor offenders (Bonner 1994).

Official Crackdown and Campaigns against Drug Crimes   Along with increasing legislation, the Chinese government targeted drug offenses in its official crackdowns and campaigns, and punished offenders, especially traffickers severely. For instance, the number of drug cases uncovered by the police was 10,946 in 1991; it quickly increased to 88,579 by 1996 and decreased a little bit after the government initiated its second "severe-strike campaign" (For a study of China's "severe-strike campaigns", see Liang 2005), but regained its increasing momentum near the end of the 1990s and reached 112,947 by 2002, and then dropped significantly after 2004.[19] Unlike the fluctuating drug cases, drug arrests made by the police grew rapidly and continuously from 185 arrests in 1988 to 58,000 arrests in 2005 (See Figure 2) (Guo 1993, 196; He and Fang 1998, 137; Baum 1992; DEA 2004; 1995; IOSC 2000; Chen and Huang 2007; the *People's Daily* June 23, 2006; 2007 data from: http://www.legalinfo.gov.cn/misc/2007-12/26/content_769638.htm). Given that the Chinese population was at an official estimate of 1.3 billion in 2005, the arrest rate for drug-related crimes was 4.44 per 100,000 persons.[20]

---

18   A copy of the 1991 Ordinance is available at the Web site of the Narcotics Control in Yunnan at http://www.ynjd.gov.cn.

19   Notice that the third round of the government's "Severe Strike Campaign", kicked off in 2001, began to come to an end by 2004, and this could be one reason why the number dropped (Liang 2005).

20   This rate appears extremely low when compared with the arrest rate of 545 per 100,000 persons in its U.S. counterpart during the same year (Bureau of Justice Statistics, 2006).

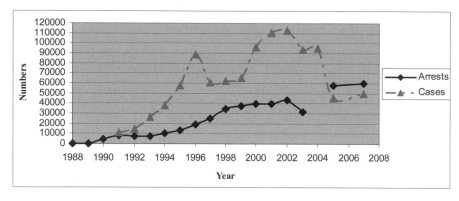

Figure 4.2 Recorded Drug Cases and Number of Arrests, 1988–2007

Consistent with the punitive legal climate on drug offenses, drug offenders had increasingly received harsh punishments, and mass executions, death and life sentences were utilized in anti-drug campaigns. In the late 1990s, for example, over 20% of all those involved in drug trafficking cases were sentenced to death or life imprisonment, and 68% were given a fixed prison sentence of more than five years. The latter far exceeded the average 30% of long-term sentences in all cases annually in China (He and Fang 1998, 141; Yao and Xue 2004, 297). More recently, in the first five months of 2005, courts at all levels sentenced 53,205 drug offenders, and 22,371 of them (42%) received harsh, long-term incarceration (over five years), exceeding the average 24.3% in all other cases (see online news at the following link, http://ww.cpd.com.cn/gb/newscenter/2006-06/26/content_621243. htm [last retrieved on July 13, 2006]). Similarly, a total of 55,671 drug offenders were sentenced nationwide from January 2006 to May 2007, and 21,223 (38%) received long-term incarceration (Statistics reported by the Supreme People's Court, posted online at www.chinacourt.org, June 25, 2007; see also reports in the *Legal Daily*, June 26, 2007, the *Beijing Evening News*, June 25, 2007; the *People's Daily*, June 26, 2007); in the first four months of 2008, courts at all levels tried 10,883 drug cases and sentenced 13,435 offenders, and 4,625 of these offenders received over five years of incarceration, life-time imprisonment or death sentences (34.3%) (Http://legalinfo.gov.cn/misc/2008-06/26/content_887345.htm).

In addition, drug offenses are among a few other crimes (e.g., murder, robbery) that have received swift dispositions in the "severe-strike" campaigns. For example, a nationwide mass campaign initiated in 1989 targeted the "Six Evils", of which drug use was one (Li, Liu and Cao 1992; Zhou 2000a, 1999). As a result, efforts from the public security organs stepped up: in 1987, public security organs nationwide cleared 56 drug-related cases, seized 137 kilograms of opium and 43 kilograms of heroin; the numbers increased to 268 cases, 239 kilograms of opium, 166 kilograms of heroin in 1988, and to 547 cases, 269 kilograms of opium, 488 kilograms of heroin in 1989 (Li et al. 1992). The number of drug trafficking cases further skyrocketed from 547 in 1989 to 3,670 in 1990, directly due to the pressure of the campaign (Baum 1992).

During this time period, sentencing rallies and mass executions of drug offenders were also quite common, particularly on special occasions, such as China's National Anti-Drugs Day (June 16) and the United Nations' International Day against Drug Abuse and Illicit Drug Trafficking (June 26). In 1996, for example, at least 260 drug offenders were executed to commemorate the Anti-Drugs Day on June 16 (Slack 2001, 155).

Information on China's death penalty practice (e.g., numbers of death sentences and executions) is still viewed as a state secret and therefore not officially available. As a result, there is a lack of systematic data on the numbers of death sentences and executions for drug offenses. However, Table 4.4 summarizes this information as it has been reported by different sources and suggests wide variability in these practices over time and regions. In recent years, the Chinese government tightened its control over death penalty practices (e.g., the retrieval of the final review and approval right by the SPC from the lower-level high courts in 2007) and seemed to have made diligent effort at reducing the number of death sentences and executions (see Liang 2008, 139). Nevertheless, the SPC has been consistently announcing its "get-tough" policy against drug offenses and emphasized its willingness to impose the most extreme penalty whenever appropriate.[21]

Table 4.4 Drug-Related Execution, Death and Life Sentences

Jurisdiction	Year	Number	Punishment	Sources
Yunnan	1989–1990	136	Execution	Baum, 1992: 10
Nationwide	1989–1991	4,093	Execution	Li, 1994: 31
Yunnan	1991	401	Death sentence	Zhou, 2000a: 13–14
Nationwide	1991	866	Death and life sentences	Zhao and Yu, 1998: 130
Yunnan	1992	464	Death sentence	Zhou, 2000a: 13–14
Yunnan	1994	> 400	Execution	Slack, 2001:155
Nationwide	1991–1995	7,000	Death and life sentences	Zhou, 2000a: 13–14; He and Fang, 1998: 137
Beijing	1996	> 260	Execution	Slack, 2001: 155

---

21   See, for example, such report in the *People's Daily*, June 26, 2007; http://www. chinacourt.org/html/article/200806/27/309476.shtml; the *Legal Daily*, September 24, 2008. From a comparative perspective, China's death penalty criteria noticeably are not among the harshest in Asian countries. Instead, they are rather average (Zhou, 1999: 13).

Female Drug Cases and Offenders   Although there is a general absence of systematic and comprehensive national crime data in China, available reports nonetheless revealed an upward trend in female drug offenses both at the national and the regional levels. For example, in 1986, female drug offenses made up 7% of all drug offenses nationwide but that number increased to 13% by 1992 (Gui 2005). Regionally, the people's courts at all levels in Beijing tried 239 drug cases involving 284 offenders in the first five months of 2002, of which 19% were female offenders, compared to 9% of female offenders in all other offenses (Gui 2005). Statistics reported by the Beijing First Intermediate People's Court and the nine district people's courts within its jurisdiction showed that cases involving female drug offenders grew 115% from 2003 to 2006. In 2003, 48 cases involved female drug offenders, and the number increased to 52 in 2004, 69 in 2005, and 88 in 2006. In addition, the percentage of female drug cases when compared to the total number of drug cases increased from 15% in 2003 to 16% in 2004, 20% in 2005, and 25% in 2006 (Guo and Wang 2007).

The people's court in An'yuan District in Jiangxi province experienced a similar pattern of rising numbers of female drug cases. There were very few female drug cases (usually two to three per year) before 2003, which was less than 5% of all drug cases handled by the court annually. The number, however, jumped to over 10 per year after 2003, representing about 20% of all drug cases. From 2003 to 2006, the court tried 57 female drug cases and sentenced 67 female offenders. Among them, 13 women received sentences less than three years, 10 women received sentences less than five years, and 44 women (65%) received long-term incarceration over five years (Wen and Zhong 2007).

In a review of female drug cases by the courts in Beijing, An (2003) categorized female drug offenders into four types: (1) a group of female offenders were manipulated by other major drug dealers as tools (mules) for drug trafficking (with their roles being limited in these cases) and they committed drug offenses for lucrative profit; (2) a number of drug offenders took on prostitution to support their drug use; (3) some female drug offenders participated in drug trafficking to support drug use; and (4) a small, but steadily increasing, number of female drug offenders became actively involved in drug trafficking and major drug dealers (*duxiao* in Chinese).

Other studies of women drug offenders showed that they tended to commit drug offenses with accomplices, very often with family members; their drug offenses often accompanied other property crimes such as robbery, larceny and fraud; seeking high-risk profit was cited as the major reason for their offenses; and a high percentage of those female offenders did not accept culpability for their behavior (Huang 2000; Ji 1998; Ji et al. 1997; Ruan 2007; Wen and Zhong 2007). In recent years, researchers have reported that female drug offenders have become more proactive and aggressive in their offenses, seeking profit in drug trafficking. For example, from 2003 to 2006, the Beijing First Intermediate People's Court and its nine subordinate people's courts sentenced 287 female drug offenders in 252 cases. One hundred eighty-one of these offenders (63%) actively participated in their offenses (Guo and Wang 2007).

Available data on drug sentencing usually does not provide gender-specific patterns. A rare exception to this pattern is a study of sentencing disparity in which gender significantly affected sentencing outcomes among drug traffickers. However, this gender disparity disappeared when judges considered and rendered the most important decision, death sentence and execution (Lu and Liang 2008; Liang, Lu, and Taylor 2009). This finding seemed to support another study's finding that a quarter of all executed offenders in Yunnan in the 1990s were females (He and Fang 1998, 152).

Drug Education and Rehabilitation   The Chinese government did not pay enough attention to the prevention of drug abuse in the early 1990s, and mistakenly believed that a mere repetition of the people's war as in the 1950s would stop and take care of the re-emerging drug problems in China (Zhou 2000a). However, the government realized its mistake in the second half of 1990s and initiated nationwide drug education to raise the public consciousness on the danger of drug use. From May to July, 1998, for instance, the Chinese government held a two-month national exhibition on drug control, with a theme as "Yes to Life, No to Drug". A total of 1.66 million people visited the exhibition (Narcotics Control in China 2000). In addition, the government attaches special importance to drug prevention education for youngsters, and asked governments at all levels to take the education of primary and middle school students as a basic part of narcotics control work.

Box 4.15 Anti-Drug Campaigns

- National exhibition on drug control.
- National Anti-Drugs Day.
- Utilization of mass propaganda.
- Sentencing rallies and mass executions of drug offenders.
- Creation of drug-free communities.
- Compulsory rehabilitation.

As noted above, during anti-drug crackdowns and campaigns, the government utilized all sorts of media sources to deliver public education. Sentencing rallies and mass executions of drug offenders were quite common, particularly on special occasions, such as China's National Anti-Drugs Day and the United Nations' International Day against Drug Abuse and Illicit Drug Trafficking. Given the claimed connection between drug use and AIDS, the Chinese government also began celebrating the World AIDS Day (December 1) every year, as public health departments organized all sorts of publicity activities, emphasizing themes such as "Refuse Drugs, and Prevent AIDS" (Narcotics Control in China 2000). In 2000, the Chinese government published a white paper "Narcotics Control in China". In this document, the government identified the rampant resurgence of drug problems in contemporary China, described its effort in drug legislation, enforcement, treatment and rehabilitation, and emphasized the importance of international cooperation and domestic drug education.[22]

Along with massive drug education, another important measure initiated by the government by the end of the 1990s was to create "drug-free communities." These communities would be so labeled when no drug use, trafficking, cultivation, or manufacturing is detected within the neighborhood. As such an example, "No Drugs Allowed into My Home" activities were kicked off in Nanning, Guangxi in 2000. By the end of 2002, 3,170 drug-free schools, residential areas, courtyards, and towns had been certified, representing a 90% success rate; 48,524 drug-free communities and 29 drug-free counties had been certified by the end of 2004 (Chen and Huang 2007, 106).

As in the 1950s, the Chinese government has been adamant about helping drug addicts quit their use. In 1995, the State Council issued *Measures on How to Impose Compulsory Rehabilitation*, which formalized drug addicts' compulsory rehabilitation procedures. In addition to voluntary rehabilitation, compulsory rehabilitation allows the imposition on addicts smoking or injecting drugs of pharmaceutical treatment, psychological treatment, legal education, and moral education over a given period of time to rehabilitate them through administrative measures. Supervised by the public security organs, compulsory rehabilitation usually lasts from three to six months, with possibilities of further extension. Addicts mainly receive treatment at compulsory rehabilitation centers, treatment and re-education-through-labor centers (labor-reeducation centers) or special schools for educating. In 2000, China reportedly had 746 compulsory rehabilitation centers and 168 labor reeducation centers (China Always Says 'No' to Narcotics 2004).

Although the numbers of drug addicts subject to compulsory rehabilitation and labor reeducation varied over the years, available reports at both the national and local levels suggested an upward increasing trend by the end of the 1990s and in the new century when the numbers reached six digits (see Table 4.5). By June 2006, drug addicts at the labor reeducation centers constituted over 50% of inmates (the *People's Daily*, June 27, 2006). Among those who were forced to participate at compulsory rehabilitation centers and labor reeducation centers, women were not uncommon. For instance, in regions and provinces that are plagued most severely by drugs (e.g.,Guangdong, Hainan, Shanxi, Guangxi, and Guizhou provinces), it was reported that more than 50% of female residents were drug users (Gui 2005; Yao 2001). By April of 2002, female drug addicts made up 35% of all addicts in the compulsory rehabilitation centers in Beijing as well (Gui 2005).

---

22   A full (English) version of this white paper is available at http://www.china.org. cn/e-white/1/index.htm.

Despite all these efforts, drug rehabilitation did not turn out to be very effective and promising. As showed in Table 4.5, with one exception, studies and reports recorded very high reuse rates among addicts after their official release from the rehabilitation centers. For example, in 1990 the recidivism rate of 598 rehabilitated addicts in Baoshan Yunnan province was 85%, and the recidivism rate of 132 female addicts was an amazing 100% (Zhou 2000a, 24). In Gansu province, the reuse percentage was reported as high as 70 to 80 percent (Mao and Wang 2002, 495). The Drug Enforcement Administration (DEA) reported drug addicts' recidivism rate as high as 90 to 95% (DEA 1996). A study on Kunming Drug Rehabilitation Center, which was established in December 1989 by the Kunming City government to provide treatment for drug addicts, revealed that the effect was not satisfactory despite its rigid regimen. From 1992 to 1996, the treatment center managed to follow up on 10% of all drug addicts who had been treated and found the relapse rate was 80% within 2 years (McCoy et al. 1997; Mao 1999, 151). In the new century, the reuse rate stays high, if not higher: it is not uncommon to find that over 90% reuse rates were reported (*The China Youth Daily*, July 27 2004).

Summary

This chapter has reviewed the PRC drug laws and decrees in two distinctive time periods: 1949-1978 and 1978-the present. To effectively explain the relevance and importance of these laws in dealing with the pressing concerns of narcotic drugs, we first discussed the important political, economic and social transformations during these two historical periods of time, followed by a detailed elaboration on the transformative patterns and characteristics of the consumption, cultivation/ manufacture, and trafficking of narcotics drugs. While our discussions of these critical structural and behavioral patterns involving narcotics drugs in socialist China may have explicitly or implicitly established a causal relationship between these factors and the related drug laws, we did not attempt to fully address how the content and the impact of laws were shaped by these structural and historical events. Nor did we try to explain whether and how these drug prohibition laws have achieved its intended results in contemporary China. We will address these research questions in the next chapter.

Table 4.5 Rehabilitation and Reuse

Jurisdiction	Year	# of rehabilitation centers	# rehabilitated people	Reuse percent	Sources
Yunnan	1990		598 (including 132 women)	85% (100% for women)	Zhou, 2000a: 24
Nationwide	1991		41,227 at compulsory centers		Qi and Hu 2004: 334–335
Shanghai	1992		12		Zhou, 2000a: 19
Nationwide	1992		46,000 at compulsory centers		Qi and Hu 2004: 334–335
Shanghai	1993		94		Zhou 2000a: 19
Nationwide	1993		50,000 at compulsory centers, 15,000 at labor-reeducation centers		Qi and Hu 2004: 334–335
Shanghai	First half of 1994		164		Zhou 2000a: 19
Nationwide	1994	251 compulsory rehab centers, 75 labor-reeducation centers	50,000 at compulsory rehab centers, 30,000 at labor reeducation centers	90–95%	DEA 1996; Qi and Hu 2004: 334–335
Yunnan	Early 1990s			80%	McCoy et al., 1997
Nationwide	1995	500 compulsory rehab centers, 65 labor-reeducation centers	78,000		Qi and Hu 2004: 299
Nationwide	(by June) 1997	187 new	30,000		Zhou 2000a: 15
Nationwide	1997	695 compulsory rehab centers, 86 labor-reeducation centers	180,000 at compulsory centers, 90,000 at reeducation centers		Qi and Hu 2004: 334–335
Nationwide	1998	632 compulsory centers, 61 reeducation centers	140,000 at compulsory centers, 120,000 at reeducation centers		Qi and Hu 2004: 334–335
Nationwide?	2000 onward			90–100%	He and Fang 1998: 177, *The China Youth Daily*, July 27 2004

Table 4.5 continued

Jurisdiction	Year	# of rehabilitation centers	# rehabilitated people	Reuse percent	Sources
Baotou, Inner Mongolia	1999			0.84%	Cited in Chen and Huang, 2007: 106
Nationwide	1999	746 compulsory centers, 41 reeducation centers	224,000 at compulsory rehab center, 120,000 at labor reeducation centers		Narcotics Control in China, 2000; Qi and Hu 2004: 334–335
Nationwide	2000	746 compulsory rehab centers, 168 labor reeducation centers			Narcotics Control in China, 2000
Nationwide	2001		216,000 at compulsory centers. 70,000 at reeducation centers		Qi and Hu 2004: 334–335
Nationwide	2002		252,579 at compulsory rehabilitation, 76,043 at labor education		China always says "no" to Narcotics, 2004: 39
Guizhou	2002		28,682 at compulsory rehabilitation, 7,020 at labor education		China always says "no" to Narcotics, 2004: 59
Guangxi	2002		15,500 at compulsory rehabilitation, 3,400 at labor education		China always says "no" to Narcotics, 2004: 61
Hunan	2002		16,000 at compulsory rehabilitation, 5,000 at labor education		China always says "no" to Narcotics, 2004: 67
Gansu	2002		35,288 at compulsory rehabilitation, 9,353 at labor reeducation		China always says "no" to Narcotics, 2004: 68
Nationwide	2005		298,000 at compulsory rehabilitation, 70,000 at labor reeducation; 135,000 voluntary rehabilitation		*Beijing Youth Daily*, June 23, 2006
Nationwide	2006		269,000 at compulsory rehabilitation, 71,000 at labor reeducation		http://news.sina.com.cn/c/2007-02-14/20291231 9427.shtml

Chapter 5

Theoretical Issues and Explanations of China's Drug Laws

Both functionalist and conflict theories of law and society have been widely used to explain the nature and effectiveness of legal development in a variety of socio-political contexts. As mentioned in Chapter 1, these theories provide fundamentally different images of the structure of society (e.g., whether society is characterized by consensus or conflict), the nature of law and social order, the functions of law, and how law responds to changing social conditions over time.

The current chapter explores the basic tenets underlying various theories of legal development and their utility in understanding historical trends in China's drug laws. These basic principles involve assumptions about: (1) legal evolution and societal complexity, (2) the instrumental and symbolic functions of law, (3) the causes and consequences of legal change, and (4) evaluating the effectiveness of law. The congruency of the historical pattern of China's drug laws with each of these prevailing assumptions about the nature of law and society is described below.

Legal Evolution and Societal Complexity

Most theories of law and society assume that the content of law changes as societies become more complex. For example, the transition from repressive to restitutive sanctions in modern society is a fundamental assumption of theories of legal change developed by several authors (e.g., Durkheim 1964; Nonet and Selznick 1978). Similarly, Black's (1976) theory of the behavior of law assumes that fundamental characteristics of social life in modern societies (e.g., complexity, diversity, stratification) influence both the quantity and quality of law. Under this formulation, societies with greater complexity and diversity are presumed to have more laws for purposes of social control, whereas the style of law (e.g., penal, compensatory, or conciliatory) is determined by elements of stratification (e.g., law is penal when applied to lower-ranking individuals but conciliatory when the offender is a high-ranking individual within the stratification system).

Box 5.1 Theories of Law and Society

- Transition of law from repressive to restitutive in modern society (Durkheim 1964; Nonet and Selznick 1978).
- Quantity and quality of law vary by complexity and diversity of society (Black 1976).
- These traditional theories of law and society are challenged by China's drug laws as both the nature and content of these laws are far more dynamic, non-linear, and context-specific than what was conveyed in these Western theories.

Our historical analysis of China's drug laws suggests that the assumption of a monotonic or linear transformation from repressive to restitutive laws over time does not adequately represent the nature of the legal evolution in this context. In fact, the nature and content of China's drug laws is far more dynamic, non-linear, and context-specific than is conveyed by this conventional image of law and society. This conclusion is based on the following observations about how the legality and severity of punishment for narcotic drug activities varied dramatically both within and across the major eras of China's history:

- After its introduction in the late fifteenth century, opium smoking was a legal leisure activity over much of the remaining years of Imperial China.[1] However, there were particular times in this historical period (e.g., 1813, 1839, 1906, and 1909) in which royal edicts and decrees banned opium smoking. During the Republic era (1911–1949), legal prohibitions on the consumption of opium and other narcotics (e.g., morphine, heroin) also varied widely over time and jurisdiction. The use of these narcotics was legally banned at the beginning of this era, followed by a series of policies directed at government control of drug addicts, and then a period of repeal of the bans on narcotic use in the Japanese occupied territories. In contrast, throughout the history of the PRC, the legal prohibition on the consumption of narcotics has been a consistent theme and these legal proscriptions have been applied to other drug offenses (e.g., cocaine, marijuana).
- The legality of opium importation and trade has vacillated greatly over China's history. Opium importation became illegal in the first half of the nineteenth century (1796–1843), de facto legal until 1858 when the ban on imports was formally repealed by "unequal" treaties with foreign nations, and remained legal until banned again by the royal edict in 1906. Opium importation was illegal throughout much of the Republic era, except in

---

1   Similar to social rituals that surrounded the consumption of tea and tobacco, opium smoking in this era was shrouded in symbolism and cultural status (e.g., as a foreign luxury item for conspicuous consumption).

the Japanese-controlled territories where prohibition laws were suspended from 1937 to 1945. The PRC has prohibited the importation of opium and other narcotics throughout its history.

- After its inception in the mid-1800s, opium cultivation has also experienced major shifts in its legality and criminality over time. Domestic cultivation of opium poppy was legal and actively encouraged to reduce various problems associated with foreign importation in the late nineteenth century. Drug cultivation was also de facto legal in the early twentieth century, when warlords used opium cultivation to subsidize their military operations. Similar to other drug activities, domestic narcotics cultivation was banned throughout the history of the PRC (except limited legal cultivation for domestic pharmaceutical uses under the control of the Ministry of Agriculture and the National Drug Administration Bureau of the State Council).

- Legal punishments for drug-related activities have shifted dramatically over historical eras, and they have not followed a progression from repressive to restitutive sanctions. Over China's long history of narcotics control, both repressive and restitutive measures were found. For example, death sentences for various opium-related activities (e.g., trade, cultivation, consumption) were mandated under an 1839 act of the Qing government, and these types of repressive sanctions are found in the current criminal code of the PRC. Mao's intense campaign for a "drug-free" nation that began in the early 1950s represented a very repressive period against narcotic use in China's history. "Strike hard" campaigns on drug activity and other crimes have continued in the twenty-first century. While various types of alternative sanctions have been available in the PRC (e.g., fines, confiscation of property, and more restitutive sanctions like drug treatment), repressive punishments like imprisonment and death sentences remain an essential mechanism of social control in modern China. Restitutive measures were also present in drug laws adopted by the late Qing government (e.g., detoxification program in the 1906 Decree), the Nationalist government (e.g., use of fines and treatment in the 1928 Temporary Criminal Law), and the PRC government. This use of restitutive sanctions over time also does not follow the theorized historical progression.

Given these trends in legal development and punishment, our analysis of China's history of narcotic drug activities provides little support for the common presumption that a linear progression from repressive to restitutive sanctions occurs as societies become more diverse and complex. Periods of legal tolerance and repression are found at various times within both the Imperial and the Republic eras. The "strike hard" campaigns throughout the history of the PRC provided additional evidence of the predominance of repressive sanctions for drug activity in contemporary China.

Black's theory about the quantity of law and its style is also incongruent with many of our observations about drug laws in China. For example, in the Qing dynasty (1792–1911), over 130 narcotics laws, regulations, and rules were enacted and promulgated, whereas over 250 national and local narcotic drug laws were enacted in the Republic era (1912–1949). In contrast, the PRC has adopted over 70 laws and 20 local regulations on narcotic-related offenses (Qi and Hu 2004, 422–423). Given that the measurable aspects of social life (e.g., greater stratification, diversity, centralization, less informal social control) are more dominant features of modern China, the lower number of drug-related laws in the PRC than is true in other historical eras (especially the Republic era) is in direct contradiction to the basic tenet of Black's theory.

Another proposition underlying Black's theory that is not supported by our analysis involves the style of law. In particular, Black (1976) contends that law will have a more penal style or form when applied to lower-ranking individuals and a compensatory style when applied to higher-ranking members. However, there are clear instances across China's history in which this assumed relationship between stratification and the style of law is not evident. For example, a decree of the Qing government in 1813 subjected palace personnel (e.g., the palace guards and eunuchs) to far more serious punishment for opium use than civilians. Customs' officials who did not effectively deal with opium smuggling were also singled out for more severe punishment in 1818. The more penal treatment of higher-ranking individuals is also observed in the more severe punishment given to narcotic drug traffickers than users across China's history. These drug traders in the Imperial era were often members of China's merchant class, whereas both party officials and well-connected "capitalistic" entrepreneurs are typical high-ranking individuals who have sufficient power or economic resources to organize complex drug trafficking networks in the PRC. Thus, while higher-ranking individuals may be more successful in avoiding detection or gaining immunity against prosecution, the greater punitiveness of some drug laws that either directly or indirectly target higher status groups is clearly contrary to this basic hypothesis in Black's theory.

The Instrumental and Symbolic Functions of Law

It is well known that laws serve various functions or purposes in a society. They preserve and protect social order by reinforcing public standards of morality. Criminal laws often serve this function because they criminalize particular conduct that threatens social order and provide the legal authority to incapacitate and punish violators. Other laws are designed specifically to regulate and coordinate social relations, especially the municipal ordinances, administrative rules, and regulatory codes that typify modern societies.

From a conflict perspective of social order, law serves as an instrument of power that is used to preserve, reinforce, or enhance special interests. It is not a neutral party that represents collective or public interests. For example, criminal law under a conflict perspective provides a means of controlling the conduct of some groups and legitimizing similar activities of those with power (see Chambliss and Seidman 1982; Quinney 1977). While the explicit or manifest function of these laws often suggests that they represent public interests, it is their implicit or latent functions that illustrate how special interests are served by particular criminal laws.

Under both conflict and functional perspectives, law serves an important function as a tool for the control and elimination of various types of social problems. This "social engineering" function of law emphasizes its role as an instrument for threat resolution and social change.

A major difficulty in studying the functions of particular laws in a comparative historical context involves the inability to identify their true purposes. This problem is especially germane in most historical research because there is often no accompanying written text of purpose or intent that serves as a preamble for a particular law. Under these conditions, the ultimate purposes of particular laws can only be implied from descriptive accounts of the social context in which these laws were implemented.

Our historical analysis of China's drug laws suggests that these laws were used for various functions over time. Depending upon the particular historical period and type of drug-related activity, these laws served both instrumental and symbolic purposes. These context-specific functions of China's drug laws and their abolitions are summarized below.

The Functions of Narcotic Drug Laws in Imperial China

Legal regulations on the consumption and distribution of opium served a wide array of instrumental and symbolic purposes over Imperial China. The regulation of opium-related activities was directly related to the prevailing economic, political, and cultural factors within this historical context.

Economic interests have played a prominent role in China's opium trade history. As a foreign commodity, taxes and duties on opium importation were a lucrative source of revenue for the government. Foreign trade companies and their domestic partners also reaped major financial benefits from the opium business. These vast economic benefits may be the primary explanation for the predominant "regulation through taxation" policy and the largely de facto legalization (i.e., very weak enforcement) of opium-related activities across the history of Imperial China. However, once the delirious effect of opium on China's trade balance with the Great Britain and India was fully recognized in the mid-nineteenth century (e.g., the silver famine under the the Qing government), legal prohibitions on importing opium became more prevalent.

Box 5.2 Functions of Drug Law in Imperial China

- Symbolic function
  - Opium smoking as cultural rituals and status symbols in Imperial China
  - The largely de facto legalization throughout Imperial China due to economic interests and political weaknesses

- Instrumental function
  - Opium prohibition law used to resolve the "silver famine" crisis and balance the trade
  - Regulation through taxation aimed at increasing revenue for the Qing government

The Opium Wars of the mid-nineteenth century epitomized the confluence of economic and political interests surrounding the regulation of opium. Unequal treaties that removed the Qing's legal prohibitions on opium importation and opened up more Chinese ports for foreign commerce served both the economic and political interests of Western imperialism (led by the British government). It also exposed the ineffectiveness of the political governance of the late Qing dynasty. However, this foreign intrusion into China's economic and political life had direct bearing on further regulation and control of opium-related activities. In particular, the repeal of bans on opium cultivation and the subsequent policies of regulation through taxation were functional for the Qing government for several reasons, including the improvement of China's trade balance (by replacing opium imports with domestic cultivation), averting a fiscal collapse from the "silver famine" produced by the opium trade, and maintaining a crucial source of the government revenue through the taxation on domestic cultivation and production of opium.

In terms of its symbolic functions, the use and regulation of opium has been shrouded with cultural meaning and symbolism throughout China's history. Opium was first used as a medical remedy for various health problems and smoking opium was later transformed into a leisure activity. The leisure smoking of opium began among the royal court and nobles, symbolic of a type of cultural decadency because of opium's status as a foreign luxury item. The social rituals and routines surrounding opium smoking further added to its cultural value as a symbol of social status. For peasants and laborers in Imperial China, opium smoking offered a public forum for conspicuous consumption and a temporal respite from the pains of everyday life. In addition, as discussed in Chapter 2, both Confucianism and Taoism, two dominant philosophies in the Chinese history, exhibited a high degree of tolerance toward opium smoking in comparison to other social disorderly behaviors (e.g., alcohol abuse). The acceptance of opium smoking based on cultural norms under the influence of these two dominant philosophies helped the spread of opium use in Chinese society as a whole.

As a tool for social engineering, legal prohibitions on opium-related activities in Imperial China served several instrumental and symbolic functions. For example, royal edicts against the opium trade were often merely symbolic gestures (e.g., public posturing about the intrusion of Western "barbarians") because they were often pronounced at the same time when the government maintained a "regulation by taxation" policy on these activities. The great debate on opium legalization organized by Emperor Daoguan (discussed in Chapter 2) was such a perfect example, showing a complex decision-making process where multiple concerns had to be addressed at the same time by the Qing government. However, when the opium trade became a serious economic problem in the nineteenth century, the strict enforcement of prohibitive laws against importation functioned as a direct instrumental means of eliminating this problem.[2] The weakening of prohibitions against domestic cultivation in this period also served an instrumental goal of enhancing economic resources through legalization and taxation.

Functions of Narcotic Drug Laws in the Republic Era

Although covering a relatively short historical period (1911–1949), the Republic era was one of the most politically volatile times in China's history. Civil wars, revolutions, foreign invasions, and fundamental changes in the economic, intellectual, and cultural life were rampant social problems in this era. Legal rules and their abolition served multiple purposes to deal with opium-related activities and other social problems.

One of the first approaches used by the Nationalist government to legally regulate opium focused on the establishment of a government monopoly on this drug. Established in 1928, this Nationalist government's monopoly involved the strict enforcement of prohibition laws, management of the government-controlled supply of drugs to addicts, and collection of taxes from government-controlled drug sales. The dual function of this monopoly policy was to control opium-related activities and increase revenue for the military. For various reasons (e.g., corruption, resistance from local merchants), this plan for regulation and control through a government monopoly has been viewed by most commentators as a failure (see Su 1997, 294–310; Jiang and Zhu 1996, 252–320).

---

2   The confiscation of opium and British troops during the Arrow incident that precipitated the Second Opium War was a clear example of this instrumental role of legal prohibitions. However, even in this case, the symbolic significance of the conflict as it related to the principles of British imperialism and China's sovereignty cannot be underestimated.

Box 5.3 Functions of Drug Law in the Republic Era

- Symbolic function
  - Strong anti-opium law out of mounting public pressure – law used symbolically to pacify public

- Instrumental function
  - Opium control as government monopoly – regulation through taxation to increase revenue for the military
  - Narco-chemical policy used by the Japanese military in its controlled territories in China during the Sino-Jananese war to pacify resistance

The next major drug control strategy in the Republic era involved the passage of the 1928 Criminal Law that prohibited multiple types of drug-related offenses, including the manufacturing, selling, smuggling, cultivating, smoking, and injecting of narcotic drugs. This criminal code was augmented in the same year by other laws prohibiting opium smoking and detailing how to implement this ban. While mounting public pressure to take a strong anti-drug position was the apparent impetus for these laws, the lucrative revenues that derived from the legal regulation and taxation of narcotics served as major impediment in the actual achievement of this objective. In fact, given how opium-generated taxes and revenues supported the military actions of warlords in this time period, these anti-drug laws are probably best characterized as a symbolic reform to pacify public sentiments rather than a concerted effort to eradicate drug-related activities.

The repeal of the narcotic drug laws in the Japanese-controlled territories of China in the 1930s represented a relatively unique function of law for purposes of social engineering. In this particular context, the Japanese government carried out a narcotic trading campaign and suspended all prohibitive laws for purposes of using these drugs to pacify resistance from the Chinese population.[3] This type of narco-warfare involved a wide variety of activities, including the release of drug addicts and peddlers from prison, permitting retail shops to sell opium, and rewarding farmers to grow narcotic plants. Estimates of a rising number of drug addicts in cities like Tianjin and Qingdao that were directly affected by these pro-drug practices offered some empirical support for the efficacy of this campaign in achieving its primary function (Su 1997, 404–419).

---

3   A similar narco-chemical campaign of pacification was used in the Vietnam War of the 1960s. In this context, the wide availability of both heroin and marijuana was used by the North Vietnamese to weaken the resolve and combat readiness of U.S. soldiers. For a review of this history of heroin and other narcotics in Southeast Asia, see McCoy (1973 and 2004).

Functions of Narcotic Drug Laws in the People's Republic of China

Similar to other historical periods, narcotic drug laws were enacted and enforced in the People's Republic of China (PRC) for various purposes. Specific eradication efforts were designed to resolve particular problems associated with drug-related activities. However, many of the anti-drug prohibitions in the PRC's history also had strong symbolic significance regardless of their effectiveness in controlling these drug-related activities.

When the Communist Party gained political power from the Nationalist government in 1949, the newly-formed PRC inherited serious and multi-faceted drug problems. The physical dimensions of these drug problems involved an estimated 20 million drug addicts, 600,000 drug dealers and smugglers, and 10 million farmers who planted opium poppies (Su and Zhao 1998, 384). However, the lingering historical association of opium with Western imperialism and Japanese occupation also added a particularly poignant dimension of symbolic significance to the eradication of these drug problems under the PRC (e.g., getting rid of one's addiction was equated to showing one's patriotism).

In its early years, the PRC adopted a diverse array of anti-drug initiatives for purposes of eliminating the problems of drug trafficking, cultivation, and consumption. By all accounts, the anti-drug campaigns in the 1950s were widely successful in transforming China into a "drug free" nation (see Wang 2004, 158 166; Su 1997, 294–310). Subsequent efforts in the post-reform era (post-1978) have been far less effective.

Box 5.4 Functions of Drug Law in the PRC

- Symbolic function
  - "Drug free" nation as symbol of an independent nation throughout the 1950s and the 1970s
  - Drugs as symbol of social evil during the reform era of the 1980s and onward

- Instrumental function
  - Drug prohibition law to achieve order maintenance
  - To reduce crime
  - To foster socialist morality and value

The anti-drug campaigns in the PRC's early history involved drug suppression laws of both a national and regional scope. The particular elements of these laws that may have enhanced their functions in drug eradication included: (1) lighter criminal sanctions for offenders who turned themselves in, confessed, and showed remorse, (2) severe punishments (e.g., death sentences) for those who committed more serious drug offenses (such as transporting narcotics with arms or cultivation/ manufacturing of drugs), and (3) leaving the content of drug-related laws and decrees vague and brief to allow huge discretionary powers for local authorities to mete out punishment. Other critical aspects of these drug eradication efforts involved extensive "mass-line" propaganda campaigns, the mobilization of the general public to identify drug users, the mandatory registration of drug addicts, demands for participation in drug rehabilitation centers, and the establishment of neighborhood committees for purposes of drug surveillance and education. The anti-drug propaganda served as symbolic crusades that emphasized the connection of drugs to "evil" foreign influences, whereas the policies of mandatory registration and neighborhood surveillance empowered the people to take major constructive steps to reduce the opportunity for drug-related activities in their communities.

After Mao's death in 1976, China experienced dramatic changes in its social, economic, legal, and political structures. The economic reforms and the "open door" policy were especially important in the emergence of international drug trafficking. To respond to a variety of drug problems, China again passed various drug laws and increased its effort to gain international cooperation and support for combating its domestic war on drugs. "Strike hard" campaigns that rigorously attacked various social problems (e.g., ethnic unrest, economic corruption) were also employed for drug eradication purposes.

While large numbers of people are arrested and convicted for drug offenses in contemporary China, most commentaries believe that the "people's war" on drugs is now less effective and complete in eradicating drug addicts, cultivators, and traffickers. This is the case because other social, economic, and political issues have replaced the "drug problem" as more pressing concerns in China's participation in a global world system (for a study of the PRC's globalization progress and its impact on China's legalization, see Liang and Lauderdale 2006).

Causes and Consequences of Changes in Narcotic Drug Laws

As described throughout this book, China's narcotic drug laws have gone through major changes over time. Royal decrees and prohibitive laws were present in some periods of Imperial China but these bans were lifted or largely unenforced at other times. A similar volatility in the retention and abolition of narcotic drug laws was found in the Republic era. In contrast, a more uniform trend of legal prohibitions against drug-related activities is evident in the history of the PRC. However, even in this latest period of China's history, the relative attention given to the "drug problem" by the PRC government has vacillated over time. The obvious question is what accounts for this variability in China's drug laws over time?

Chambliss' theory of structural contradictions has been used to describe the causes and consequences of law making and legal change in a variety of different socio-political contexts (see Chambliss 1979; Chambliss and Zatz 1993). This theory has been most widely applied in the study of the conflicts and dilemmas that emanate from the fundamental contradictions in capitalism (e.g., between the bourgeois class who have the means of economic production and the working class who do not have the means of economic production). However, previous research has also extended this approach to study the structural contradictions in fundamental social relations within socialist countries (Chambliss 1993; Curran 1998; Gaylord and Levine 1997; Zatz and McDonald 1993). Consistent with these previous applications, we believe that Chambliss' theory is especially relevant for describing the causes and consequences of lawmaking and legal changes in the nature of China's drug laws over time.

The theory of structural contradictions assumes a dynamic relationship between law and the economic, political, and ideological structures within a society at a particular time and place. Under this theory, contradictions refer to "the conditions inherent in a particular historical period that produce conflicts and dilemmas which, in turn, necessitate the alteration of existing social relations" (Curran 1998, 264). Laws and legal change in this context are a common means for resolving particular conflicts and dilemmas, but these legal solutions often create future conflicts and dilemmas that require subsequent legal changes as remedial actions. This dialectic process involving conflicts, dilemmas, and resolutions is typically perpetuated over time in most societies because the resulting legal solutions do not address the core or fundamental contradictions that are inherent in the economic, political, and ideological structures of the particular society.

Box 5.5 Theory of Structural Contradiction

- There is a dynamic relationship between law and the economic, political, and ideological structures within a society's particular time and place.
- Contradictions are conditions inherent in a particular historical period that produce conflicts and dilemmas.
- Laws and legal change are means for resolving these conflicts and dilemmas, yet in the process of doing so, they create new conflicts and dilemmas that require new legal changes.
- This dialectic process involving conflicts, dilemmas, and resolutions is perpetuated over time in most societies because contradictions are inherent in the economic, political, and ideological structures of a particular society.

When applied to China's history of narcotic laws, there are numerous examples of the dynamic interrelationship between laws and the particular social conditions within each major historical period that generated conflict, dilemmas, and subsequent legal changes. Descriptive accounts of the explicit causes and consequences of these changes in China's narcotic laws in each historical period that are consistent with the basic ideas of the theory of structural contradiction are summarized below.

Box 5.6 Drug Laws and Structural Contradictions in Imperial China

- Contradictions
  - The Qing government's desire to maintain its political authority and control through a self-sufficient, agrarian economy that lacked technological innovation

- Conflicts and dilemmas
  - Lack of technological development and rapid population growth
  - Central government and local protectionism
  - Corrupt bureaucracy and vast territory
  - Rise of European power and ignorance and the closed door policy of the Qing government

- Law, legal change, conflicts, and dilemmas
  - Deregulation, taxation, prohibition, criminalization, and de facto legalization were some of the legal responses to the changing conflicts and dilemmas involving opium trade and the particular economic, political, and ideological structures of particular historical periods of time

Drug Laws and Structural Contradictions in Imperial China

Throughout the history of Imperial China, the passage and repeal of narcotic drug laws had been both a cause and a consequence of basic contradictions in the prevailing socio-economic and political conditions. For much of this time period, the main contradictions involved the Qing government's desire to maintain its political authority and control through a self-sufficient, agrarian economy that lacked technological innovation.

The political and economic structure of the Qing dynasty became increasingly problematic in achieving its basic goals due to the vast territory within China's physical boundaries, rapid population growth, inherent conflicts between the central government and local protectionism, and the corrupt bureaucracy that managed daily governmental operations. The primary external dilemma that threatened the Qing government involved the rise of European influences. This Western threat turned out to be both ideological (e.g., challenging China's sovereignty and its feelings of superiority) and economical (e.g., opening Chinese markets for a more favorable trade balance through the use of their superior technology, better-equipped military, and as a result unequal treaties). Opium and its trade was a major source of these conflicts and dilemmas.

When opium was first introduced into China by Turkish and Arab traders in the sixth century, it was used in its raw form for medical purposes, especially for the treatment of diarrhea and as a general pain reliever. Opium was a small but steady trade commodity for medical use until the 1500s.

Both the form of opium use and its purpose shifted dramatically in the 1500s. In particular, an increasing number of nobles and wealthy merchants began smoking opium as a leisure activity. Similar to China's preexisting cultural symbols of tea drinking and tobacco smoking, social rituals and routines became linked with opium smoking. The fact that opium was a foreign luxury item surrounded in smoking rituals gave it a particular cultural significance for demonstrating one's social standing. In a relatively short period of time, opium smoking became a fashionable leisure activity in Chinese society. Even peasants and farmers could participate in the conspicuous consumption of this drug by smoking the ashes and residue of previously consumed opium in public opium dens.

The conflicts and dilemmas that arose from the shift of opium from medicine to a leisure drug were wide and diverse. One immediate consequence of this shift was an increased demand for opium, providing foreigner traders an increasingly lucrative trade commodity and the Chinese government a major source of revenue through taxation on opium imports. At the same time, however, there appeared to be growing concerns about opium abuse and the foreign influence that derived from the opium trade. To respond to these sometime contradictory problems, the imperial governments (such as the Tang and Yuan dynasties, and most conspicuously the Qing dynasty) at various times used royal decrees to ban opium importation and further ban opium use (i.e., use by only particular groups such as royal palace guards, eunuchs, and military but not use by the general public), or simply made the opium-related activities legal through taxes and non-enforcement of legal violations.

The importance of conflicts and dilemmas in economic relations on lawmaking and legal changes in China's drug laws was clearly revealed in opium's role in the trade balance between China and other countries in the nineteenth century. The confluence of the following socio-economic conditions led to dramatic changes in China's laws on opium-related activities:[4]

- European traders discovered that many Chinese products (e.g., spices, teas, and silk) could be sold profitably in their homelands. However, other than precious metals (e.g., gold and especially silver), Europe had very

---

4   See Chambliss 1993, 66–68 for an extended discussion of these social forces underlying the opium trade.

little to offer in trade value to the Chinese. China's self-sufficient, agrarian economy made it difficult to find a demand for European goods in China.

- The accumulation of gold and silver reserves was a principal measure of a nation's wealth (Chambliss 1993, 66). Having strong gold and silver reserves was critical for European capitalist countries to support their militaries and enhance their colonial expansion. Due to their enormous trade imbalance with China, European countries (especially Great Britain, Holland, and Portugal) faced the serious problem that acquiring Chinese products in exchange for gold and silver would seriously deplete these reserves.
- As the popularity of opium grew in China, the foreign opium trade (e.g., using British companies and merchants to subsidize and transport India-cultivated opium to China) provided a resolution to the British trade imbalance with China. Over the nineteenth century, the costs of opium imports exceeded China's exports, creating a serious threat of a "silver famine" for the Chinese government.
- The successful resolution of the European trade deficiency required a high Chinese demand for opium and the absence of strong legal prohibitions against opium trade or consumption. The Opium Wars from 1839 to 1842 and from 1856 to 1860 occurred in a large part to preserve and protect these foreign economic interests.
- From the perspective of the Chinese government, the basic conflicts and dilemmas surrounding opium involved the growing trade imbalance, the large government revenue generated by opium taxes, and the ideological implications of the foreign intrusion into China's sovereignty. The problem of foreign intrusion in China through the opium trade was mediated through the combined efforts of increased taxation on opium imports, the growth of domestic cultivation of opium poppies, and the legal prohibition of all opium-related activities at the end of the nineteenth century and the beginning of the twentieth century.

Drug Laws and Structural Contradictions in the Republic Era

The major structural contradictions in the Republic era derived from the efforts of a weak Nationalist government to seek an independent identity and authority in a context of political turmoil and economic change. The political conflict included territorial battles among the warlords, the Sino-Japanese war, and the civil war between the Nationalists and the Communists. The fundamental economic change involved the transition from an agricultural-based economy to an emerging capitalist, free market-oriented economy. Opium played a major role in these conflicts and dilemmas that characterized this larger political and economic context of the Republic era.

Box 5.7 Drug Laws and Structural Contradictions in the Republic Era

- Contradictions
  - A weak Nationalist government seeking an independent identity and authority in a context of political turmoil and economic change

- Conflicts and dilemmas
  - The political conflict included territorial battles among the warlords, the Sino-Japanese war, and the civil war between the Nationalists and the Communists.
  - The fundamental economic change involved the transition from an agricultural-based economy to an emerging capitalist, free market-oriented economy
- Opium laws and repeal during this historical period of time served both as a cause and a consequence of these conflicts and dilemmas

Upon taking the reigns of national power in 1928, the Nationalist government announced a plan to ban opium through taxation. Citing the need to strengthen the government and the military (e.g., the Nationalists were fighting the wars against the warlords, and later the Communists, and trying to strengthen its control over the vast territory after a decade of warlordism following the collapse of the Qing dynasty), the Nationalist government relied on local bandits and drug dealers to collect fees and taxes on opium. The official banning of opium became a way to collect fines and taxes on the banned goods, making the government lose its authority and credibility. This inherent contradiction of collecting fees in the name of prohibiting opium resulted in an epidemic of opium sale and consumption and made the public even more cynical about the true intent of the law.

Opium laws and their repeal were both a cause and a consequence of other conflicts in the Republic era. For example, to subsidize the military of warlords in the 1920s, peasants were coerced to cultivate opium poppy despite its ban by the central government. The custom of military protection and coercion of opium cultivation continued through the secret societies and organized groups that controlled the drug trade even after this warlord period. Similarly, Japan's narco-chemical policy of pacification through the lifting of bans on opium-related activities and the encouragement of the use of narcotics in their occupied regions of China is another example of opium's role in the basic conflicts of this era. It shouldn't be surprising that the tumultuous political and economic change in this historical period was the backdrop for the dramatic ebb and flow of legal prohibitions against narcotic drugs across the Republic era.

Drug Laws and Structural Contradictions in the PRC

The People's Republic of China (PRC) established a new government that was isolated from the international community for about 30 years from 1949 and 1978. During this period, a major goal of the Chinese government was to support the development of an independent and self-reliant nation dictated by the proletarian class led by the working class. This goal was in direct contradiction with the legacy of centuries of oppression that the Chinese people, especially the working class (e.g., farmers), had to endure at the hands of Western imperialism and corrupt dynastic rule, and the more recent tumultuous decades of warlordism, civil war, and the Japanese invasion, which resulted in the characterization of China as being a "semi-colonial and semi-feudal" society. Within this context, the PRC government was resolute to eliminate the stigma of being the "sick man of Asia", a symbolic image that derived from opium's impact on the body and mind of the Chinese people.

Box 5.8 Drug Laws and Structural Contradictions in the PRC

- Contradictions
  - Rebuilding an independent and self-reliant nation with the legacy of "semi-colonial and semi-feudal" society.

- Conflicts and dilemmas
  - Completely different political, economic, and ideological structures in socialist China
  - Confronted with conflicts and dilemmas different from other previous dynasties and governments

- Opium prohibition laws utilized to achieve the goals of nation building and elimination of stigma of "sick man of Asia".

Because the Communist ideology adopted by the PRC represented a complete departure from the past Chinese governments in aspects of politics, economy, and society, the conflicts and dilemmas faced by previous governments in fighting the war on drugs (e.g., economic profits derived from opium vs. its social and economic costs; local interests vs. national interests; an open boarder policy for trade vs. smuggling of drugs) by and large no longer existed under the new PRC government.

To eliminate the "poisonous" influence of opium and other narcotics on the Chinese people, the PRC government took dramatic measures on all fronts of trade, cultivation, and consumption. In the aspect of opium trade and smuggling, instead of profiting from the taxation of opium trade, the PRC government cut off all trade with Western nations and closed its borders, cracked down on local bandits and secret societies, and mobilized intense community surveillance to control opium trade and smuggling.

With regard to cultivation of opium poppy, the Chinese government utilized the land reform to transform the land ownership from private to collective and adopted the policy of a planned economy so that the rural economy was planned in every stage of the agricultural production involving planting, harvesting, purchasing, and distribution. Compared to policies in the past, this policy of collective land ownership and planned economy removed the conflicts and dilemmas between the national and local interests, the government and farmers' interests, and regional economic conflicts.

The problem of drug consumption was addressed through the mandatory registration of drug addicts, the policies of mandatory detoxification and rehabilitation programs, rewards for voluntary compliance, and severe punishments for noncompliance. Similar to the various detoxification programs and punishment schemes utilized in the late Qing dynasty and the Republic era, the measures adopted by the PRC also aimed at addressing the conflicts and dilemmas surrounding drug consumption; for example, treating drug addition as evil but not drug addicts, and implementing policies of phased out treatment programs and mandatory detoxification for those who refused to comply with the law. Nevertheless, PRC policy exhibited some fundamental differences from the previous laws and policies in dealing with drug use. For example, instead of focusing on addiction as an individual problem that may lead to stigmatization and demonization of the individual, PRC policy called for massive educational campaigns about the harm that opium and other narcotic drugs may have on human health, family, and the nation. This step-up of the national dialog about narcotic drugs in turn helped mobilize individuals to voluntarily quit their habit and/or to report family members and neighbors for their drug use.

The current post-1978 war on drugs in the Reform era, however, has been fought in a completely different political, social, and legal context. Politically, China has been increasingly integrated into the world system with its membership in major international organizations such as the United Nations and the World Bank. Economically, China has been engaging in an "open door" policy and a market-oriented economy that promotes free trade (especially after it joined the World Trade Organization in 2001). Because of its economic reforms, China has quickly improved its modernization, industrialization, and urbanization process over the past 30 years, resulting in increasing diversity and plurality in social, ideological, and cultural lives. In the aspect of law, formalism and professionalism have been advocated for decades to achieve a rule by law nation so as to protect the economic interests and facilitate further economic development.

Within this large structural context, new inherent contradictions arise, including most noticeably the need for the continued economic development versus the need for preserving the fundamental Chinese traditional values and ways of life (e.g., social harmony, order, close-knit family and community, and status of authority). These conflicts and dilemmas are manifested in different dimensions of Chinese society. First, a conflict is looming between formal and informal social control. Second, a dilemma involves how to preserve local norms and customs within the "open door" policy and free market economy. Third, a similar conflict involves the need to preserve family and community in the face of massive migration due to employment opportunities and change of economic structure. Finally, there is a conflict between the need to prevent social evils (i.e., gambling, prostitution, drug use) and the need to improve people's living standards.

Drug laws and policies in the Reform era of the PRC have been inevitably shaped by these new political, social, economic, and legal developments. For example, the war on drugs in this new era has been more and more likely to be fought by formal law, not by the Party's or official policies. The passage of the drug prohibition law in 2008 is indicative of the PRC government's resolution to subject governmental (anti-drug) actions to the law. Technically, the differential classification of criminal sentences afforded to a variety of drug-related offenses under China's criminal law demonstrates a more rational and legitimate lawmaking towards the emerging drug problem (e.g., subjecting drug traffickers to the death penalty, not drug addicts; dealing with drug problems with judicial rather than extra-judicial means). In contrast to the increasing formal control, informal control struggled but is still alive. For example, the mass-line policy favored and used as an effective tool by the PRC in the past continued to be used from time to time in the new era of the PRC (e.g., in the forms of "strike-hard campaigns"). Nevertheless, this grassroots campaign-style policy will probably be reduced and replaced gradually by formal legal process. Public educational campaigns about narcotic drugs remain a regular fixture in this large scheme of the war on drugs in the PRC. Drug use in modern China has been labeled as one of the social evils (along with gambling and prostitution). However, drug use is now rarely being connected to the fate of the nation (in a form of nationalism) or Western imperialism as was seen in the 1950s.

Given these developments, the current PRC's official stance on drugs has also been adjusted. In particular, drugs are viewed as a grave social problem and must be dealt with. However, drugs do not represent the most acute social problem or conflict that deserves the sacrifice of other political, economic, and social goals. These other goals, such as the principles of harmony and order protected by law, improving people's living standards with continued economic development, free market, and open trade, have been clearly recognized as the top priority.

The Effectiveness of China's Narcotic Drug Laws

Whether or not China's narcotic drug laws were effective at various historical periods depends on their specific purposes. When their purposes were largely symbolic (e.g., decrees/edicts to placate public demands for strong drug control, policies to mobilize public outrage including educational campaigns that emphasized the link between drugs and "evil" foreign influences), it is difficult to discern their effectiveness.

The effectiveness of drug laws is more easily evaluated when the specific goals of the drug laws aim at the reduction or eradication of particular drug-related activities (i.e., trade, cultivation, and consumption). In this particular case, our analysis involves comparisons of the relative prevalence of these activities before and after the implementation of a particular legal action. While factors other than the legal action may explain a rise or fall in particular historical periods, this pre- and post-law comparison is nonetheless a common analytic strategy to provide some preliminary assessment of the relative effectiveness of these laws in reducing various types of drug-related activities.

For purposes of assessing the effectiveness of drug laws, we explore trends in estimated levels of drug addiction, drug transportation, and opium poppy cultivation over time. These trends are then compared with patterns of legal prohibition of these drug-related activities over time. These results are described below and summarized in Figures 5.1–5.4.

Drug Addiction and Legal Prohibitions

One measure of the severity of the problem of drug consumption involves the estimated number of drug addicts over time. These estimates will provide only gross approximations of the magnitude of this problem for various reasons (e.g., the scarcity of reliable and comprehensive historical data, definitional ambiguity surrounding the term "drug addicts", the political sensitivity of drug addiction). However, even with the problems of extant data, it is still important to examine the extent to which the level of reported drug addiction comports to the legal prohibitions of drug consumption over China's history. Accordingly, Figures 5.1 and 5.2 display historical patterns of drug addiction over two different time periods (i.e., 1840–1949; 1982–1995).[5] These patterns and their association with particular periods of legal prohibition and tolerance of drug activities are summarized below.

---

5   These figures were taken from Su 1997, 8–16. Su estimated these patterns of opium consumption, cultivation and trade based on customs reports and various historical documents and accounts. As he acknowledged in his book, it was very difficult to figure out the exact pattern of these drug activities because of the nature of drug trade and consumption.

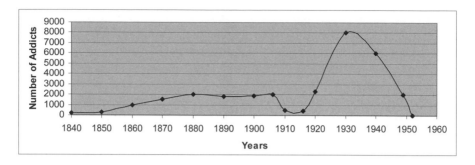

**Figure 5.1 Estimated Number (in 10,000s) of Drug Addicts in China
              from 1840 to 1952**
Source: Based on data presented in Su 1997, 14.

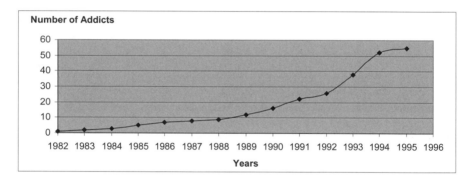

**Figure 5.2 Estimated Number (in 10,000s) of Drug Addicts in China
              from 1982 to 1995**
Source: Based on data presented in Su 1997, 16.

As shown in Figure 5.1, the estimated number of opium addicts in China was around 2 million in 1840 and increased to about 20 million by 1880. It stayed between 15 million and 20 million until the early 1900s, when the estimated number of opium addicts dropped to about 4 million at the end of the Imperial era in 1911. However, the estimated number of narcotic addicts increased dramatically to 80 million by the mid-1920s and early 1930s before a precipitous drop to 20 million at the beginning of the PRC era in 1949 and an additional drop to a virtually "addict free" level by 1952.

Assuming that these estimated numbers are somewhat reflective of the nature of drug consumption in this time period, the pattern of changes in the number of drug addicts over time may be explained by both legal actions and social forces during these particular historical periods. The context-specific effects of particular legal and social factors that may underlie these changes in the number of drug addicts include the following:

- Opium smoking had been legally prohibited by various royal decrees between 1813 and 1842. The Qing government in 1839 issued one of its most comprehensive anti-drug laws that mandated serious punishment for opium use and other drug-related activities. While the deterrent effect of this "get tough" legal mandate may have caused a temporary reduction in the number of drug addicts by 1840, several social conditions in China at this time period would have severely impeded the effectiveness of any legal prohibition. These social conditions included the vast territorial boundaries of China that made the dictates of its central government far removed from its diverse and expanding population, the vested economic interests surrounding opium-related activities in almost all walks of lives (from the royal palace to governmental officials, to opium merchants, and to farmers in the rural area), local protectionism and the inability of the order of the central government to penetrate effectively into the local political groups and customs, widespread corruption in enforcement practices, and the emergence of opium smoking as a cultural ritual.
- Due to the aftermath of the Opium Wars (1839–1842, 1856–1860) and weak enforcement of existing drug bans, opium smoking was essentially (de facto) legal from 1843 to 1905. Once adjustments were made for increases in China's population, there would be no compelling evidence to suggest that the de facto legalization of opium smoking dramatically increased the rate of opium addiction in this period. In fact, some research suggested that only between 1% and 3% of the Chinese population were either heavy or regular opium addicts between 1879 and 1906 (See Su and Zhao 1998; Newman 1995).
- The decrease in the estimated number of drug addicts from around 1906 to the mid-1910s occurred in the same general period in which several royal edicts (1906, 1909) and a criminal code (1907) reaffirmed and stipulated the legal prohibition of opium use. During this last decade of its rule, the Qing government was under great internal and external pressures for political and institutional changes. Within this context, the passage and enforcement of laws against opium use may have been a more sincere than symbolic reform, thereby resulting in actual reductions in the number of opium addicts.
- The drastic rise in the estimated number of drug addicts from the mid-1910s to the early 1930s corresponded to a time period of major social and legal changes in China. The "needle culture" rose dramatically in this period where opium and its derivatives (e.g., morphine, heroin) were being injected as a more addictive, relatively inexpensive, and convenient alternative to opium smoking. Political and military conflicts (e.g., the Nationalist revolution in the 1910s, the turmoil of warlordism in the 1920s) were major social forces that created a general sense of anomie and civil unrest among the Chinese population. The widespread use of opium and its cultivation in this context may have served as a coping mechanism for

the millions of farmers who relied upon opium for economic survival and personal comfort. One major legal response to this growing problem of drug addiction was the effort by President Sun Yat-sen in 1924 to establish a government monopoly on opium in order to: (1) enforce prohibition laws, (2) manage the "controlled" supply of drugs to addicts, and (3) collect taxes from drug sales. Unfortunately, this plan of "suppression through taxation" failed to alleviate this drug problem because of rampant corruption, resistance by local merchants, and the inherent conflicting interests of trying to control opium at the same time as using opium sales proceeds to increase revenue for the military. It is this combination of social changes and ineffective legal prohibitions that offers the best explanation for the precipitous increase in the estimated number of drug addicts in this period of the Republic era.

- The steep decline in the estimated number of drug addicts from the mid-1930s to the early 1950s may also be attributed to several social and legal changes. For example, the Nationalist government in 1935 passed a criminal code that increased the penalties for various drug-related activities and established a "six-year plan" for drug prohibition. The penalties for convicted addicts (morphine and heroin addicts, in particular) were increased from five years (or more) of incarceration to life imprisonment or the death penalty. Under the six-year plan, addicts were required to register, opium smokers were required to purchase a permit to use drugs legally, the country was divided into drug-free zones and gradual reduction zones (where smoking was permitted under particular conditions but would eventually phase out), and opium detoxification centers were established wherever possible. Other plans by the Nationalist government to further control narcotic consumption (e.g., through enlisting the military court to enforce these bans) in the 1940s were circumvented by internal corruption, local resistance, and political conflicts. After the civil war between the Nationalists and Communists (1945–1949), the effective use of the mass educational campaigns to mobilize local efforts to control drug-related activities was the primary strategy associated with the apparent reduction in drug addiction in the early period of the PRC.

During the post-Reform era of the PRC, the estimated number of drug addicts has increased from far less than 5,000 in 1982 to about 520,000 in 1995 (see Figure 5.2). Figure 4.1 in Chapter 4 recorded the most recent official data on the number of registered drug addicts in the new era. The data basically reaffirmed the growth of narcotics use, where the number of registered drug addicts increased from 50,000 in 1988 to 937,000 in 2007. The Chinese government has continued to use legal sanctions as a mechanism of social control for drug addiction, especially as it relates to a series of "strike hard" campaigns against drug abuse and other types of deviance in the 1980s and 1990s. However, in the current context of major social and economic reforms in China within a global market, the problems of drug consumption and drug addiction, in particular, have been given far less attention than other social problems.

Narcotic Drug Transportation/Importation and Legal Prohibitions

Figure 5.3 displays the estimated quantity of opium and other narcotic drugs transported into China from 1800 to 1949. These data were derived from customs reports and other historical documents and accounts (Su 1997, 8–10). Many of the social and legal changes used in the explanation of temporal changes in the number of drug addicts are also relevant to this measure of the supply side of opium and other narcotics in China's history.

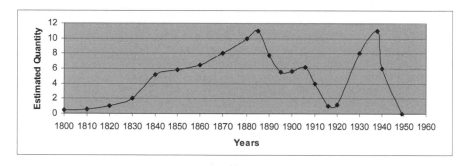

Figure 5.3 Estimated Quantity (in 10,000s of chests) of Opium and other Narcotic Drugs Transported in China from 1800 to 1949
Source: Based on data presented in Su 1997, 9.

The estimated quantity of opium transported through China's ports increased steadily from 1800 to its peak of about 100,000 chests in 1880, followed by a sharp and general decline until the mid-1910s. Similar to the temporal pattern for the number of drug addicts, the transported supply of opium and other narcotics rose drastically from the late 1910s to 1930. The estimated amount of narcotics then dropped from 1930 to a reported "drug free" level by 1952.

The Qing government issued legal prohibitions on multiple types of opium-related transportation activities (e.g., sale, importation, manufacturing, operating opium dens) at various times in the mid-1800s (e.g., in 1839, 1843, and 1854). However, the rather steady rise in opium transportation shown in Figure 5.3 in this period suggests that these legal bans had no noticeable impact on the supply side. These bans may have been ineffective for a variety of reasons, including their circumvention through political corruption, local protectionism, and widespread smuggling. Given the Qing government's vested economic interests that derived from opium import taxes, the existing legal bans may also have been primarily symbolic gestures rather than specific sincere attempts to eliminate this drug problem.

The general decline in opium transports from 1880 to the mid-1910s occurred at about the same time as when increases in opium taxes and domestic cultivation made foreign imports a less attractive trade venture. Various edicts and decrees that banned opium-related activities in the early twentieth century (e.g., in 1906 and 1907), as well as a subsequent agreement in 1911 by the Qing and the British governments to stop opium exports from India by 1917, were legal prohibitions that may have further reduced the attractiveness of opium-related activities, especially in the volatile times at the end of the dynastic rule in China.

During the first half of the Republic era (1911–1930), the rise in opium transportation may be attributed to various social and legal factors, including the use of opium for military financing and the ill-advised "suppression through taxation" policy to establish a government monopoly on opium distribution and sales. The subsequent declines in opium transportation within the last half of the Republic era (1930–1949) were also influenced by various legal interventions, including the six-year plan that mandated serious penalties for drug trade activities and several specific legal bans on the opium trade in the Communist controlled regions in the pre-PRC period.

In the early years of the PRC, eradication of opium was one of the first priorities of the new PRC government. This focus was not solely because opium represented Western imperialism and aggression. Instead, the elimination of opium would also signal to the world that China could once again gain political and economic independence and self-reliance through dramatic reform of its political, economic, and social systems. The mass educational programs and community mobilization efforts (coupled with the adoption of a closed-door trade policy and a collective, planned economy) were the primary vehicles in which opium-related trade activities were largely eliminated in the early years of the PRC.

The Reform era of the PRC has experienced a dramatic rise of drug smuggling first from its southwestern boarder next to the Golden Triangle region, and then from all major ports of its coastal areas. Table 4.2 in Chapter 4 presented the information on illegal drug seizures by the Chinese authorities from 1983 to 2005, and it indirectly reconfirmed the dramatic rise of drug smuggling in the Reform era of the PRC. For example, a mere 5.2 kilograms of opium were seized by the Chinese authorities in 1983, but this number reached 2,820 kilograms by 2001; heroin, the number one reported narcotic consumed by the Chinese addicts, showed a very similar path, and its official seizure increased from five kilograms in 1983 to 10,836 kilograms by 2004. The "open door" and free trade policies adopted by the current PRC government are the demand of its economic development policy. Within this context of the market economy, drug smuggling activities are unlikely to be completely and effectively suppressed despite the PRC government's border patrol and enforcement efforts, and its increased cooperation with the international drug enforcement agencies.

Opium Poppy Cultivation and Legal Prohibitions

Figure 5.4 displays the estimated area of opium cultivation in China from the mid-1800s to the early 1950s. The physical space dedicated to domestic opium cultivation increased slowly from 1840 until about 1870, increased more rapidly until 1880, and stayed relatively stable during the early 1900s. Domestic cultivation decreased from about 1906 until the mid-1910s, followed by a dramatic increase in these activities until about 1930. The estimated area of opium cultivation declined drastically between 1930 and the early 1950s.

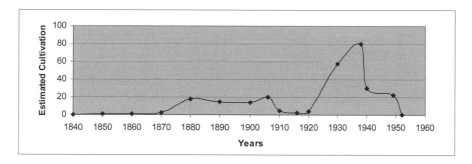

Figure 5.4 Estimated Area (in millions of *mu*) of Opium Poppy Cultivation in China from 1840 to 1952
Source: Based on data presented in Su 1997, 12.

The social and legal factors associated with drug consumption and importation were also found in patterns of domestic cultivation. For example, during the late Qing dynasty and early Republic era from 1906 to 1917, the international pressure on drug prohibition had intensified. Great Britain and the United States launched opium prohibition campaigns partly due to the declining economic interests in the opium trade and partly due to the anti-opium sentiments expressed by their people. This opium suppression movement was further precipitated by the 1909 International Opium Commission held in Shanghai that aimed at regulating the production, sale, and use of opium and other narcotic drugs. Within this broad international context of opium suppression, the Qing government launched a series of drug eradication campaigns to appease the reformists and salvage the Qing government. By all accounts, these campaigns brought quick and impressive results in areas of consumption, cultivation, and trade.[6] In the aspect of cultivation,

---

6   Reins stated that even the most suspicious foreign observers had to admit that the Qing government's opium prohibition efforts had achieved unexpected positive results. Nevertheless, he stated that opium prohibition lost its momentum in China soon because: (1) the central government found it difficult to coordinate its reform program with the local

poppy cultivation almost stopped in Sichuan and Shanxi, was reduced by three-fourths in Yunnan and Guizhou, and more than 80% of all poppy farms were converted to food crop producers by early 1911 (Spence 1975, 173; Bastid-Bruguiere 1980, 598–599).

However, the brief success was followed by a period of the most massive influx of poppy cultivation in the 1920s, a tumultuous time of political unrest and the legal policy of "suppression through taxation" that encouraged domestic cultivation as a source of revenue. In addition, given the weak political power of the Nationalist central government, rampant official corruption, and other more pressing political and military conflicts at the time, the war on opium was doomed to fail.

In contrast, the most extreme decline in the estimated physical space for domestic poppy cultivation was in the early 1950s. Concerted efforts by the PRC government at the eradication of domestic cultivation involved the use of severe punishments for these drug-related activities and the mass-line, educational policies of the early PRC that mobilized the public and neighborhood groups to fight these "evil" activities in their community. Moreover, the fundamental change of the economic structure (e.g., from private ownership to collective ownership of the land) and the incentives for farming essential crops (e.g., through the planned economy) all consolidated and sustained the initial success of the poppy eradication campaigns during that time period.

In the Reform era of the PRC, domestic production of narcotic drugs took a variety of forms including plant cultivation and the manufacture of synthetic, chemical-based narcotic drugs. Because of its underground nature, drug labs are more difficult to detect and eradicate. This difficulty is further precipitated by the privatization of land and free enterprises. Take the most recent drug case cracked by the Guangzhou public security bureau as an example. In particular, the Guangzhou public security bureau on August 6, 2008, announced its success in cracking a significant drug case with the assistance with other authorities. In addition to arresting 13 offenders and seizing 1.7 tons of precursor chemicals, the Chinese officials uncovered four manufacturing plants (including one measuring 4,000 square feet) in multiple cities such as Zhujiang and Fujian. Based on the official report, these offenders covered their narcotics manufacturing with legal licenses, got rid of the waste of production with advanced equipment, ordered raw materials online, and stored narcotics in Guangzhou. It took the official authorities over a year to conduct investigations and collect evidence before they took actions (see the *Guangzhou Daily*, October 27, 2008). With today's

---

governments due to the large profit that opium trade brought to the local governments' revenue; (2) the attempted mobilization of public opinion was circumvented due to the fear of arousing anti-Western sentiment and nurturing a Nationalist sentiment that may have turned the Hans against the Manchurians and the Qing government; and (3) ultimately, the Republican revolution ended the Qing dynasty and its opium suppression programs (Reins 1991, 101–142).

technology of communication and transportation, eradication of drugs becomes far more challenging because drug trafficking has evolved into an international phenomenon. Any national effort at trying to eliminate the supply or demand end of the trade may be impeded by the complex and global nature of this trafficking activity.

Legal Impact Studies and the Effectiveness of China's Narcotic Drug Law

Western socio-legal studies have found that certain conditions, if met, would facilitate the enforcement and the effectiveness of laws. These conditions include that: (1) law derives its authority from a legitimate, authoritative, and prestigious source; (2) law embodies values compatible with existing social norms; (3) the proposed changes have successful precedents; (4) the changes are intended to be made in a relatively short time; and (5) the new law has positive and negative sanctions that are precise enough to be enforced.

Our review and analysis of China's narcotic history and its legal control seem to lend ample support for many of these claims. For example, the success of the early PRC's drug war served as a direct contrast to the failed attempts of the Qing government and the Nationalist government. These efforts failed in a large part because of the lack of legitimacy and authority of these previous governments due to their inherent corruption, weak political leadership and military power, and non-responsiveness to the public's needs. The top-down approach taken by the previous governments of the Qing dynasty and the Republic era was especially ineffective because of this legitimacy crisis and the lack of support from the public. In contrast, the grassroots, bottom-up approach used by the early PRC government may have been more effective due to its endorsement of these principles.

The success of the early PRC's effort in eradicating opium also helps explain the importance of the compatibility of law and social norms. The massive educational campaigns launched in the early 1950s were designed to arouse the public's consciousness and to increase the public's understanding of the harmful effects of narcotic drugs on the body and mind of the individual, on the structure and organization of the family and community, and on the national economy, polity, and spirit. Without this basic understanding, resistance will inevitably occur because recreational use of opium had been intertwined with Chinese culture of tea drinking and tobacco smoking for centuries. Even though both the Qing government (particularly in its last years) and the Nationalist government tried to mobilize the public on the grounds of the "opium crisis" (e.g., the image of the "sick man of Asia"), the Chinese Communist Party was the only entity that succeeded in reaching and utilizing public participation in its anti-drug campaigns.

It took less than five years for the PRC to completely eradicate the opium problem; from 1949 to 1954. In this regard, the assumption that the intended result of the law needs to be made in a relatively short period of time may be correct. In addition, Chinese laws of punishment and rewards were remarkably specific, not just in the early PRC era but in the late Qing dynasty and the Republic era as well, as shown throughout this book. It is arguably true that the more precise the laws are, the easier they are to be enforced. In the context of the war on drugs, however, this condition is certainly not sufficient to warrant a successful result.

As to the claim that law is likely to be successful when it evolves from a successful model or precedent, the Chinese case seemed to cast doubt on this idea. What successful legal reform required in China's case was a comprehensive plan that addresses all aspects of the conflicts raised by the drug problems, similar to the approach used by the PRC government in its early history. However, this early PRC policy of all-around intensive eradication campaigns at all costs resulted in unintended and collateral consequences that in turn minimized the positive impact of legal reforms. For example, even though it is widely acknowledged that China achieved a "drug free nation" in the early 1950s, it paid a hefty price for it. During the eradication campaigns of the early 1950s, the impact of the full-scale mass-line campaign and education movements was unimaginable to a Western audience. The use of high-pressure power, extensive arrests and targeted executions, and the pressing call for (drug addicts') self-surrender and disclosing drug use of friends and family members to the authority were all unprecedented. In addition, the economic, political, and social policies adopted by the PRC government between the 1950s and the 1970s had a long-lasting impact. The closed-door policy isolated China from the world for almost four decades; class struggle, lawlessness, and political campaign style governance made the building of a formal legal system impossible and directly led to the disastrous Cultural Revolution (1966–1976). A national planned economy did not improve economic productivity as predicted, individuals' (especially farmers in the rural area) living standards did not improve and they suffered greatly during a three-year period of natural disaster and famine (1959–1961); strict management and control of population movement as part of the planned economy and the household registration system (*hukou*) hindered economic productivity and limited freedom of individual movement. Only after the Chinese government initiated its reforms in the 1980s were these problems addressed and improved gradually. Unfortunately, the Chinese government now faces new dilemmas that arise from the resurgence of drug problems and the inability of the current system of social control to maintain its crime-control function.

Western socio-legal studies also suggest that the enforcement of a new law will inevitably meet with resistance. The resistance may come from a variety of individuals, groups, and other social forces. For example, as discussed in Chapter 1, previous studies indicate that law enforcement agencies such as the police, prosecutors, and judges, often serve as filtering agents and are believed to have a great impact on mediating and moderating the impact of law. Depending on their personal beliefs, identification, and understanding of the new law, they may interpret the law differently or selectively enforce the law. In addition, a new law may meet with resistance from the target population due to a variety of social, psychological, economic, or cultural reasons.

Our review and analysis of China's narcotic drug laws and their enforcement showed that even though the effectiveness of a law may have something to do with the clarity of the law, its effectiveness is largely dependent upon the enforcement of the law. In different historical periods within the Qing dynasty and the Republic era, drug laws were not effectively enforced because the enforcement agents (e.g., local government officials) were unwilling to sacrifice their economic interests related to opium and other narcotics (e.g., through taxation and bribery). The target population, such as farmers and drug addicts, also resisted the drug laws because they saw threat (financial, social, and psychological) of these laws on their future wellbeing and families (e.g., depriving them of economic opportunities). It is thus imperative to have an effective educational campaign as well as an incentive mechanism for drug addicts and cultivators. This would make the enforcement of law much more effective, as witnessed in the early PRC era.

Summary

This chapter has examined several questions about law and the structure of society. It has explored the basic principles underlying theories about legal evolution and societal complexity, the instrumental and symbolic functions of laws, the causes and consequences of legal change, and the facilitators and constraints on the effectiveness of law.

Our application of these ideas to the study of China's history of narcotic drug laws reveals several patterns of consistency and divergence with previous theoretical formulations. For example, little evidence was found to support the claim that the transition to modern society is characterized by a shift from repressive to restitutive sanctions. We also found little evidence of the basic principles of Black's theory about the quantity of law and its particular form. As a tool for social engineering, several examples across China's history were noted in which the passage or repeal of drug laws served both instrumental and symbolic purposes. Among theories of the causes and consequences of legal change, Chambliss' theory of structural contradictions was viewed as especially useful in describing how basic dilemmas and conflicts in political and economic structures have led to legal resolutions that, in turn, have generated further contradictions, conflicts, and dilemmas. Finally, China's drug laws were interpreted as being effective in some cases and ineffective in others in achieving the purpose of reducing the magnitude of a particular drug problem. Legal prohibitions against opium-related activities were especially effective during the early years of the PRC, when the mass-line, educational campaigns (combined with political and ideological campaigns) and efforts at public mobilization were used to identify and control particular drug problems in their neighborhoods. In contrast, drug laws and regulations adopted by the Qing government and the Nationalist government to a large extent failed to achieve meaningful results due to a combination of reasons (e.g., the confluence of economic interests and weak political governance).

Chapter 6
Fighting Narcotic Drugs in a Global Context

A century has passed since the opening of the International Opium Commission in 1909 in Shanghai. The Shanghai Opium Commission was a true milestone as it represented one of the very first steps towards international drug prohibition. The fact that China hosted this meeting both acknowledged the opium struggle that China experienced by the early twentieth century and showed an important role that China had to play in joining the international arena. As recently summarized by the United Nations Office on Drugs and Crime (UNODC), this past century has been a century of international drug control (UNODC 2008). Now in the twenty-first century, China and the rest of the world still face significant drug problems (e.g., cultivation, production, trafficking, and consumption). Ironically, China was both the nation of major drug problems and the nation of most successful drug control, often exemplified as a perfect case (McCoy 2004, 24). How we study China's drug history and drug regulations is a critical question to be addressed, as we attempted in this book.

In this concluding chapter, we first summarize all substantive chapters and emphasize our analytical approach of studying opium and other narcotics regulations in their historical context and focusing on the political, economic, social, and cultural conditions within each historical period. Second, we link China's drug prohibition efforts to the global context, and pay special attention to how China struggled with its drug control in the eighteenth and nineteenth centuries when the "free trade" policy was practiced and imposed onto China by foreign powers, and then how China tried to cooperate and catch up with international drug control efforts in the twentieth century when the world entered into a drug prohibition era, and finally how China actively reached out and sought cooperation with other nations in fighting its arising domestic drug problems by the end of the twentieth century and in the new twenty-first century. Lastly, we discuss challenges and obstacles faced by the Chinese government in the new era, and draw some historical lessons from China's case.

China's Drug History and Drug Control

Significance of China's Narcotics History

Opium and other narcotics drugs did not originate in China but there is no doubt that they had a significant impact and dramatically changed the course of China's history. The nature of China's drug history is represented by the following summary observations:

- China was the very first nation to regulate opium activities (e.g., opium dealing, smuggling, cultivation, importing, and smoking). From 1729, when Emperor Yongzheng issued the first royal edict that penalized opium dealers and opium den-keepers, to 1952 when the Chinese Communist government declared its anti-drug campaign victory, China experienced the world's longest narcotics history, covering a total of 223 years.
- From 1729 to the present day, over 500 laws, regulations, legal documents, and local rules were enacted and published with regard to opium and other narcotics, placing China as the country with the most narcotics regulations in the world (Qi and Hu 2004, 422–423).
- At one time in its history, China was the largest opium importer, consumer, and producer in the world, and the image of the "sick man of Asia" in the late nineteenth century and the early twentieth century became a symbol of Chinese people who were addicted to opium. This stereotyped image of "opium fiends" even affected Chinese immigrants in other regions of the world (e.g., McMahon 2002).
- The long historical struggle with opium from the eighteenth century to the early twentieth century was remembered by the Chinese as a period of national humiliation. The drug-free status finally achieved by the Chinese Communist government in the 1950s was hailed as an unprecedented success. After 30 years, however, the reemergence of drug problems in China after China initiated its economic reforms and adopted the "open door" policy in the 1980s seemed to have shattered the Communist myth at a very fast pace and in a very short period (Zhou 1999, 173). The agony and joy that opium brought to the Chinese society and Chinese people over the last three centuries is simply beyond imagination.

Given this vast history of China's drug-related activities, the basic premise of this book is that China's experiences have been a key component of the world drug control history. Knowing what has happened throughout China's diverse history is also important for understanding the current global context of drug control policies and practices.

Table 6.1 A Comparison of Economic, Political, Social, and Cultural Conditions and Drug Prohibitions in Major Historical Periods

Various conditions	Imperial era (pre-1911)	Republic Era (1912–1949)	PRC: pre-Reform era (1949–1978)	PRC: Reform era (1978–present)
Economic structure	Self-sufficient agrarian economy, low technology level	Semi-feudal and semi-capitalist, still dominantly agrarian society	Planned, self-sufficient economy, public and collective ownership	Economic reform, market-oriented economy, privatization,
Political structure	Unified political system, centralized power in the Emperor, no separate judicial system, strong local control	Weak central government, judicial system separate but not independent; warlordism, civil wars	CCP's leadership, people's dictatorship; no separate and independent judiciary	Legal reform: rebuilding of judiciary, formalism and professionalism
Social condition and social control	Close-knit, highly structured family and community life: social control through *Baojia* or *Lijia* system	Old social structure still present; subject to military rules	Mass-line policy and movement; class struggle; neighborhood registration & committee	Urbanization, population migration, increasing inequality, neighborhood registration system facing challenge
Cultural condition	Strong influence under Confucianism & Taoism	Clash between traditional value system and Western influence (e.g., *New-Life movement*)	New socialist ideology, Mao's thought, opium use denounced and linked to patriotism;	Socialist ideology challenged and fading; cultural diversity & tolerance
Foreign policy	(1) Pre-Opium Wars: Closed-door policy, limited foreign trade (2) Post-Opium Wars: unequal treaties, legalized opium trade, establishment of foreign concessions	Strong foreign influence; Japanese invasion	Isolation, Cold-War ideology	"Open-door" policy, globalization process, Western influence

Table 6.1 continued

Various conditions	Imperial era (pre-1911)	Republic Era (1912–1949)	PRC: pre-Reform era (1949–1978)	PRC: Reform era (1978–present)
Drug laws and regulations	(1) prior to 1729: little regulation (2) 1729–1857: Gradual regulation over opium trafficking, dealers, business, importation, cultivation and use (3) 1857–1905: Legalization of opium trade, domestic cultivation; regulation through taxation (4) 1906–1911: new opium prohibition	(1) Nationalists: *de jure* drug regulation, but *de facto* legal (e.g., monopoly, taxation) (2) Japanese (1937–1945): narco-chemical policy (3) Communists: strict regulation	Strict prohibition through anti-drug campaigns, people's war on drugs waged	Strict prohibition, increasingly formal and comprehensive, "strike-hard" campaigns continued
Drug prohibition outcome (a) and major reasons (b)	(a) failure in general despite minor achievements (b) lack of effective enforcement at the local level, official corruption, lucrative opium trade; Western imperialism, tolerance by cultural norms; opium use as a cultural & social symbol	(a) regulation with little effect (b) economic interest, official corruption, local resistance, weak central government and enforcement, Japanese invasion, civil war, warlordism	(a) unprecedented success (b) unified polity, strong central and local control; strict prohibition, mass-line campaign and education; little corruption; supporting economic and political efforts; international isolation	(a) prohibition facing challenge and becoming less effective (b) increasing international drug trafficking; fading ideological and social control; "Open Door" policy; privatization

Study of China's Drug Control: Focusing on Historical Conditions

Using a comparative and historical approach, our study examined patterns of drug consumption and its regulations in China over time. Specifically, we focused on opium (and other narcotics in more recent decades) use, importation, cultivation, and smuggling in three historical periods (the Imperial era, the Republic era, and the PRC era), and discussed drug regulations, enforcement, and their effectiveness over the years. A primary goal of this study was to explore how various political, economic, social, and cultural conditions at particular historical periods affected the nature of drug activities and their regulations.

Table 6.1 summarizes the key features of the historical context in these major periods. It also identifies the major drug regulations, their outcome on drug-regulated activities, and reasons for their relative success and failure. As we suggested in previous chapters, particular historical conditions played a significant role in each period. Some social, political, and economic factors were critical to drug-related activities in some periods, but had no discernable impact at other times.

Increasing Opium Consumption and the Qing Prohibition   While historical records indicate that opium was available in China since 600 A.D., opium use was not considered a serious problem until the late eighteenth century. The spread of opium use and its status change from medicine (*yao*) to drug/poison (*du*) was a critical turning point in its emergence as a social problem in Chinese society in this historical period. A number of reasons were identified by scholars that could have potentially explained such a transition.

First of all, the introduction of a new method of opium ingestion (i.e., smoking) at the end of the seventeenth century presented greater addiction potential than the traditional method of eating opium. Social customs and rituals surrounding smoking tobacco and tea consumption were also adopted in opium smoking, further increasing its use as leisure activity. As a response to this growing problem, Emperor Yongzheng's effort in 1729 to ban opium dealing merely slowed down the spread of opium use, and inadvertently led to the beginning of opium smuggling.

Second, increasing opium importation (e.g., via the triangular trade among India, the United Kingdom (UK), and China), especially in the second half of the eighteenth century and the early nineteenth century, circumvented the Qing dynasty's powerless efforts at opium control (e.g., Emperor Jiaqing's edicts in 1796 and 1810s). When the opium price dropped significantly by the 1830s after the British East India Company started losing its monopoly in opium trade, a larger proportion of the Chinese population fell to opium and became addicts. When the Qing government tried desperately to stop opium smuggling and enacted new prohibition laws in the 1830s (e.g., Emperor Daoguang's edict in 1831), Britain (and other foreign powers) turned to its superior military force. After two Opium Wars, China's door was forced open, opium importation became legalized, and opium flooded the Chinese market. In 50 years, the estimated number of opium users in China increased dramatically from 2 million in the 1830s to 20 million in the 1880s (Hsu 2000, 171–173; Su and Zhao 1998, 193–194).

Third, the Qing government by the nineteenth century had deteriorated considerably in terms of its power and control. The low-skill agricultural economy, centralized but weakened political structure, and its closed-door Sino-centric policy all made the Qing government ill-prepared for dealing with the opium problem and aggressive Western forces. After conceding defeat in the two Opium Wars, the Qing government had no other option but to adopt a new legalization policy – a policy that encouraged domestic cultivation to fight off foreign importation (*yitu diyang*) and regulated opium activities through taxation (*yujin yuzheng*). By most historical accounts, this new policy actually worked in that it both effectively slowed down foreign import and increased revenues for the government. The downside of this policy, however, was that the skyrocketing levels of domestic poppy cultivation were linked to dramatic increases in China's opium consumption. By the early twentieth century, domestic production reached a record high of 35,000 metric tons, the estimated number of opium smokers passed 20 million and reached as high as 40 million based on some estimates, and China was consuming between 85% and 95% of the global opium supply.[1] When China became the largest opium producer and consumer besides the largest importer, an opium epidemic became virtually unstoppable.

Fourth, as we suggested in Chapter 2, opium consumption also grew over the years as part of China's unique cultural traditions. Neither Confucianism nor Taoism, two dominant philosophies in China, seriously denounced opium use during this period. The use of opium, instead, became part of the consumption culture, spreading from the royal palace, governmental officials, and military soldiers to urban working class and rural peasants (see Dikotter, Laamann and Xun 2002). The consumption of opium, in various forms, became a means of showing off one's social class in society and facilitating social interactions. By the nineteenth century, opium use was so entrenched that it became part of everyday life for people from all walks of life.

Given these internal and external factors, it seems clear that the Qing dynasty's opium control policies largely failed for most of its history. Only in the last years of its reign did the Qing government return to opium prohibition policies due to a changing domestic environment (e.g., increasing calls for opium prohibition from governmental officials, various anti-drug associations, and students who studied abroad), a changing international environment (e.g., declining profits in foreign opium trade, increasing anti-drug efforts in Great Britain and the U.S.), and the passage of international agreements (e.g., the 1907 Anglo-Chinese treaty to phase out opium importation). Despite this initial progress in its final stages, the collapse of the Qing dynasty in 1911 quickly nullified its brief success.

---

1   See UNODC (2008, 176–77). The Chinese production of 35,000 metric tons of opium was "enormous" in 1906, as pointed out by the UNODC Report, in comparison to 9,000 metric tons produced by Afghanistan in 2007 (over 95% of the world's illicit opium in that year).

Domestic Struggles, Unstable Authority, and the Republican's Drug Prohibition

Despite a favorable international environment (entering into the prohibition era) and increasing domestic denouncement of opium use as evil, succeeding governments after Qing (e.g., the Beiyang government (1912–1928), the Nationalist government, the Wang Jingwei government (1940–1945)) all struggled with opium control after their official establishment. The two most salient internal factors during this historical period, as identified by Slack (2001), were the narco-economy and warlordism, both of which interacted with each other and dominated the economic and political conditions of this period.

Economically, opium activities (e.g., cultivation, trade) proved to be so deeply imbedded in Chinese society that it quickly bounced back and reached a new level in the 1920s and 1930s, rendering obsolete the progress made by the Qing government in its last years. At the Geneva opium conferences in 1924–1925, the International Anti-Opium Association of Beijing reported that China was growing at least 15,000 tons of opium annually, accounting for 88% of global production (Slack 2001, 6).

Despite the labor-intensive nature of opium growing and the high taxes,[2] farmers cultivated and stored opium for two major reasons. First, growing poppies earned them more profits than other crops. The average net profit of opium per *mu* was USD 38.50 in 1929, in comparison to USD 12.72 for rice, USD 12.99 for glutinous rice, and USD 3.73 for wheat. In addition, opium was often traded and exchanged as a "hard currency" from time to time, especially when the official currency struggled and faced increasing inflation during this period. Second, farmers were often encouraged or coerced by local authorities to grow poppies when regional warlords fought fiercely over the control of opium trade and tried to extract the maximum opium taxes from farmers. In Chongqing, Sichuan province, for example, warlord Liu Chengxun ordered that the county must devote 100,000 *mu* of land to opium growing (Slack 2001, 11). Local authorities in some cases disguised the forced cultivation of opium in the form of increased taxes. When the taxes reached too high a level, however, farmers had no other options but to grow poppies to generate enough income and pay the taxes (Slack 2001, 11). In short, opium cultivation had become a necessary living means for many rural peasants, and peasants' resistance to opium eradication was recorded from time to time (see Bianco 2000; Wong 2000). The estimate of annual opium spending in the 1920s and 1930s ranged from USD 1–2 billion, more than 5% of China's estimated gross domestic product at that time (about USD 29 billion) (Slack 2001, 32–33).

Politically, China in the 1920s and 1930s was decentralized, fragmented, and at times chaotic, largely due to the rise of warlords and warlordism at the expense of a civilian-dominated central government. Not long after the 1911 Revolution, Yun Shikai of the Beiyang government replaced civilian governors of the provinces with military ones, abandoned the democratic system, and named

---

2   The average land tax for opium was USD 8 per *mu* (and it could be as high as USD 25), in comparison to just USD 1 to USD 3 for wheat and rice (Slack 2001, 13).

himself an emperor. After his death in 1916, regional powers quickly severed their strained bonds with the Beijing government. From 1916 to 1937, Chinese politics was characterized by continual warfare between competing military factions and regional warlords. In 1916, there was an estimate of 500,000 soldiers in the republic, and an estimate cost of USD 153 million to maintain the army. By 1928, the size of the army reached 2.2 million, which required USD 800 million maintenance cost (Slack 2001, 66). Generating revenues from the opium activities became a significant means of subsidizing the military expense by all authorities, including the Guomindang (Kuomintang) and the Communist Party. As Slack (2001) pointed out, on the one hand, the warlord system brought the Republican narco-economy to life and sustained the narco-economy; on the other hand, the high level of revenue generated from the opium trade made possible the sustained military conflict among warlords, the Guomindang and the Communist Party.

The opium policy of the Nationalist government struggled therefore in the context of the warlord system and the narco-economy. Despite its ostensible efforts to deal with opium (and other narcotics) use and trade (e.g., prohibition law in 1928, the "six-year" plan in 1935), its regulation achieved no real effect at the national level despite some regional success and progress. The dominant policy against drugs adopted by the Nationalist government indeed was to establish a governmental monopoly and to regulate drugs through taxation (*yujin yuzheng*). Various opium suppression offices and bureaus were established at different times to eliminate local control and monopolize opium regulation. Even so, the implementation of such a monopoly policy was rifled with serious problems, including issues surrounding strong local control and resistance, official corruption, and involvement of the underworld organizations and foreign concessions. As Slack (2001) pointed out, the brittle central government, which often relied upon regional militarists and armies to unite the nation for a brief period of time, exacerbated the situation by appointing many of these warlords and their military commanders to important positions in the party and in national and local governments. In addition, the Republic government failed to reform the structure of local financial system. As a result, the government itself heavily relied upon opium taxes to sustain and fight a series of wars against the warlords (e.g., in the Northern Expedition (*Beifa*)), the Communists, and the Japanese.

From 1934 to 1937, the amount of income derived from the opium suppression and monopoly by the Nationalist government, based on the official report, was USD 26 million, USD 25 million, USD 32.9 million, and USD 30 million respectively. In contrast, unofficial data, often viewed as more reliable, put the estimate well above USD 100 million per year, and the annual estimate accounted for roughly 10% of the total revenues received by the government (Slack 2001, 147–148). Such an inherently contradictory policy (both relying upon and denouncing opium trade), though bombarded as morally reprehensible and unacceptable by patriotic civil associations, was no doubt determined by its historical conditions. The Japanese invasion and occupation in the late 1930s and early the 1940s and its practice of "narco-chemical" policy in its occupied territories in China further aggravated the opium problems in China (Brook 2000; Kobayashi 2000b).

Anti-Drug Campaigns in the 1950s and Reemergence of "Old Problems" in the New Era

The unprecedented drug war success achieved by the Chinese Communist government in the 1950s was a significant but unique experience in the hundreds of years of drug control and regulation in the Chinese history. As detailed in Chapter 4, the success was accomplished through a series of political, economic, and social transformations under its historical conditions.

First, the Chinese Communist Party was able to build a strong social control system after it unified mainland China, which centralized power into the hands of Communist party members and allowed the will of the government to be fully extended into local communities. A series of social control mechanisms such as neighborhood committees, public security committees, the household registration system, and mandatory drug addict registration were established nationwide, restrained free movement of the populace in general and drug addicts and traffickers in particular, and cut off trafficking routes effectively. In anti-drug campaigns, these social control mechanisms also helped promulgate public education and mobilize public participation in uncovering drug addicts and traffickers. In comparison to the inability of the Nationalist government in the Republic era to reach and control local authorities, the Communists' ability to enforce drug law and regulation at the basic level guaranteed significant outcomes despite the fact that opium and narcotics laws and regulations adopted during this time were rather simple and vague.

Second, the centralized national economy and collectivized private sectors both in urban and rural areas significantly affected opium cultivation and manufacturing. Land reform in the early 1950s facilitated the reduction of poppy-cultivation as the redistribution of lands weakened the ability of big landowners to engage in mass cultivation of opium poppies. In addition, the socialist planned economy both in urban industrial and rural farming sectors offered rural farmers incentives and means to plant crops others than poppies.

Third, politically, a series of movements during the early years of the new nation such as the Three-Anti Campaign in the 1951 and the Five-Anti Campaign in the 1952 continuously built up momentum for anti-drug campaigns, and drug traffickers were quickly rounded up, punished, and sometimes executed as counterrevolutionaries. Harsh punishment such as the death penalty was also made available in both the Qing era and the Republic era. However, the nationwide and sweeping political pressure and the grassroots mobilization during the anti-drug campaigns in the 1950s turned out to make social control efforts far more effective during this historical period.

Fourth, though there was evidence that the Chinese Communist Party also profited from drug trade both before and after it took the power (see Slack 2001, 154–155), the Party took a strong stance openly and officially against drug use and trade. Utilizing propaganda, the CCP masterfully linked its anti-drug campaign to China's unique history, adopted a strong rhetoric to blame opium use as the evil of the feudal Qing society and foreign nations' imperialism, and argued that to build a new communist society meant to get rid of the image of the "sick man of Asia". Emphasizing several contrasts such as the old China versus the New China, the Nationalists versus the Communists, and the imperialists versus the Chinese people, the government effectively mobilized the public to participate in anti-drug campaigns and tied its anti-drug campaigns to the notion of nationalism and patriotism. Fighting opium and other narcotics was therefore being patriotic and revolutionary, while resisting the campaign would be unpatriotic, antirevolutionary, and be punished and/or reformed.

Lastly, due to the Cold War ideology, Communist China after 1949 became largely isolated from the rest of the world. Its economic self-sufficiency policy and its isolation cut off potential routes for opium trade and international trafficking, and allowed China to remain "drug free" from the 1950s to the 1970s. By all historical accounts, the Communist government's success in the 1950s was rare and unique and made possible under its particular social, political, and economic conditions. Such a success, though highly praised both by the Chinese government itself and international anti-drug organizations, would be very difficult to replicate, as partially witnessed by the reemergence of drug problems in the Reform era. In fact, the resurgence of drug problems after the 1980s occurred when China was experiencing various types of dramatic economic, political, social and cultural changes that were linked to its economic reforms and adoption of an "open door" policy.

First, economic reforms both in urban and rural areas were propelled by increasing privatization and marketization. The once dominant state-owned economy and collective enterprises faced increasing challenges from other forms of non-public economies and lost their dominant positions in the national economy. Getting rich in this new China was no longer shameful but glorious, and people are now willing to take any means to be rich, including committing crimes such as drug trafficking. In addition, local governments gained more and more economic and administrative powers in the process of economic reform. Fierce competition gave local authorities more control but at the same time bred conditions for power abuse and corruption, which, in turn, facilitated drug trafficking and trade.[3]

Second, China's "open door" policy ended its isolation and its increasing integration into the global economic system further made China an important component of the world system and a new target for drug trafficking at the same time. As drug trafficking resumed and escalated quickly, China became a new trafficking route for major drug producing regions such as the Golden Triangle and the Golden Crescent. In recent years, China also became a major producer and

---

3   As pointed out by Swanström and He (2006), though corruption is getting worse in China, narcotics-related corruption is indeed rarely reported. Most cases of reported narcotics related corruption in China involve low-level officials in the border provinces, and no senior PRC official has been connected to narcotics money so far.

exporter of precursor chemicals that are often used to manufacture illegal drugs (see DEA 2004; Li 1994; Navarro 2007; Swanström and He 2006; Zhou 2000).

Third, with ongoing dramatic social transformations such as increasing urbanization, population migration, and widening social inequality, China's old social control system and mechanisms began to face challenges. The zeal of building a socialist nation and mobilizing grassroots support as in the 1950s is no longer present in contemporary China. Instead, the government may have to turn to formal lawmaking and the formal legal system to fight drug problems. Under this approach, appropriate legal procedures have to be spelled out and followed in order to hold people accountable for their actions (e.g., *Drug Control Law of PRC* in 2007). These requirements, to a large extent, have changed the nature of the people's war on drugs in the new era.

Fourth, with increasing Western influence, the socialist ideology began waning. New conditions in the post-Reform era have fostered an environment of greater tolerance of diversity and deviance. Old vices such as drug use, prostitution, and gambling are no longer viewed as problematic by some people, despite of the government's propaganda. Many drug addicts view their actions as personal leisure and do not accept the patriotism lesson that was used for gaining popular support in the 1940s and 1950s. This de-politicized and individualized nature of drug offenses is indicative of a clear demarcation from the highly politicized drug-control practices in the old golden days.

In sum, the contrast between the Communist success of drug suppression in the 1950s and the resurgence of drug problems in the Reform era shows to a large extent exactly how changing economic, political, and social conditions in different historical periods could have brought very different results to the same problem. These changes in the effectiveness of drug-control practices occurred, even though the same political party and authority carried out the same drug war (and did so in the latter period with a more formalized and professionalized legal system that is widely endorsed from a Western perspective).

Testing Western Theories of Law

In Chapter 5, we illustrated how major Western theories of law would apply to the study of China's drug laws. We focused on theoretical arguments about legal evolution, the instrumental and symbolic functions of law, the causes and consequences of legal change, and the effectiveness of law.

First of all, our historical analysis of China's drug laws over time failed to lend support to either Durkheim or Black's contentions about legal evolution. Rather, our analysis suggests that the assumption of monotonic or linear transformation from repressive to restitutive laws over time does not adequately represent the nature of the legal evolution in the Chinese context. Instead, the nature and content of China's drug laws is far more dynamic, non-linear, and context-specific than is conveyed by this conventional Western image of law and society. For instance, draconian laws (e.g., the death penalty) were enacted in each of the three major historical periods against drug offenders but carried seemingly different effects. Restitutive measures were also found present in drug laws adopted by the late Qing government (e.g., detoxification program in the 1906 decree), the Nationalist government (e.g., use of fines and treatment in the 1928 *Temporary Criminal Law*), and the PRC government, not necessarily following the progression suggested by these theories. Similarly, the lawmaking process in all three periods did not follow clear patterns in terms of both quantity or style change, as suggested by Black, as we witnessed more nuanced lawmaking in each historical period, often targeting specific groups.

Second, we explored multi-functions served by China's drug laws over time, based on suggestions from Western literature such as the conflict and the functional models. Our historical analysis of China's drug laws suggests that these laws were used for various functions over time. Depending upon the particular historical period and the type of drug-related activity, these laws served both instrumental and symbolic purposes. For instance, the Qing dynasty's very early opium regulation attempts (e.g., Yongzheng's edict in 1729) targeted addiction problem as potential danger to morality and community harmony. By 1830s, however, the main concern was shifted to the looming "silver famine" as a result of unbalanced triangle trade; after two Opium Wars, the Qing government could no longer enforce opium prohibition and had to adopt the legalization approach to encourage domestic cultivation and regulate it through taxation. Though the symbolic function of the Qing dynasty's opium regulation always existed (and arguably became more salient in the last years of its reign when the government returned to strict prohibition), the Qing dynasty's opium policy was clearly modified to tackle its immediate needs, therefore serving instrumental functions. In the Republic era, the Nationalist government's opium monopoly and regulation through taxation policy was not much different. The national narco-economy and the warlord system were so intertwined and embedded in Chinese society at the time that any real effort by the central government to tackle opium problems proved to be unrealistic. Indeed, we witnessed vacillation in the Nationalist government's drug policies from insisting strict opium and narcotics regulation to relying upon opium trade revenues for its military expense. As a result, its drug laws (e.g., 1928 and 1935) often contained ostensible and implicit messages and carried out both symbolic and instrumental functions. In the PRC era, the Communist government adopted strong anti-drug campaigns to rid of drug problems; at the same time, the government also deliberately delivered symbolic messages to the nation through its patriotism propaganda and by claiming its unprecedented drug suppression success to the world (e.g., it was only made possible under the Communist leadership). All these observations suggest that China's (drug) lawmaking process often embraced multiple messages and tried to serve multiple functions, though some factors may have had more salient effects than others in a specific time.

Third, in examining the changes of China's drug laws over time, we found that Chambliss' theory of structural contradictions is most relevant to the Chinese case. Chambliss' theory of structural contradictions assumes a dynamic relationship between law and the economic, political, and ideological structures within a society at a particular time and place. When applied to China's history of narcotic laws, there are numerous examples of dynamic interrelationships between laws and the particular social conditions within each major historical period that generated conflicts, dilemmas, and subsequent legal changes. In the Qing era, for example, opium use and trade became a major source of increasing conflicts and dilemmas domestically and internationally. Domestically, rapid population growth, backward agrarian economy, inherent conflicts between the central government and local protectionism, sporadic peasant uprising, and corrupt bureaucracy all made the Qing government ill-prepared for the increasing opium problems. Abroad, the Qing government faced unprecedented threats from Western powers, led by the British government, both ideologically (e.g., challenging China's sovereignty and its sense of superiority) and economically (e.g., forcing open the Chinese market for opium trade). After the defeat in the Opium Wars, the Qing government was forced to adjust its opium policy (through legalization) to fight off foreign import but only led to an opium epidemic. The years of opium struggle witnessed changes in the Qing government's opium laws and policies and also the collapse of a giant dynasty. In similar fashions, as we detailed in Chapter 5, structural contradictions in both the Republic era and the PRC era also determined to a large extent the content and the effectiveness of their drug laws.

Lastly, we took on the issue of effectiveness of China's drug laws over time. Specifically, we assessed the effectiveness of drug laws in three areas, drug addiction (measured by the number of estimated drug addicts over time), drug trade (measured by opium importation over time), and cultivation (measured by the estimate of opium poppy cultivation). Our examination exhibited very similar patterns in all three subjects: despite the Qing dynasty's prohibition efforts in the eighteenth and nineteenth centuries, drug problems/activities gradually escalated over the years and peaked around 1880. Then, various drug estimates started declining until they spiked again in the late 1910s and reached a new level by the late 1920s and early 1930s. Afterwards, all these drug problems precipitated drastically and were officially "eliminated" by the early 1950s after the Communist government completed its anti-drug campaigns. Only in the new Reform era did China witness the resurgence of drug problems, when drug use and trafficking increased steadily over the years but it was far from reaching the epidemic level as seen before.

These consistent patterns suggest that the effectiveness of drug laws was very much determined by their economic, political, social, and cultural conditions. From a lawmaking perspective, the law could be imperial or modern, simple or complex, specific or general. Whatever its form, however, the effectiveness of the law in this context depended largely upon the enforcement by the authority. Our study of China's case also lent support to some propositions about the effectiveness of law enforcement based on Western socio-legal studies (e.g., law derives its authority from a legitimate, authoritative, and prestigious source; law embodies values compatible with existing social norms) but failed to do so in others (e.g., the proposed legal changes have successful precedents; the new law has positive and negative sanctions that are precise enough to be enforced).

In short, China's long history of opium struggle and control provides us with rich and invaluable information in testing Western theories of law and legal impacts. Our examination shows how complex the issue is and suggests that any drug law in the Chinese history was deeply rooted in its historical conditions, which also had played a determinative role in the enforcement of the corresponding law. Only in this way can we understand and appreciate the hundreds of years of opium problems that plagued the Chinese society and Chinese people and the unique nature of the rare success achieved by the Communist government in the 1950s.

China's Drug Prohibition in the Global Context

The Free Trade Era, the Prohibition Era, and the Global Context

In his critical review of the history of the global narcotics trade, McCoy (2004) carefully examined two successive policy regimes toward narcotics – free trade in the nineteenth century and the prohibition in the twentieth century. In the free trade era, European powers deployed coercion, market, and military in Asia both to promote opium production for trade and opium consumption for colonial revenues and to prohibit local cultivation that weakened their monopolies. During this period, opium (just like tea) became an important commodity in the global merchandise system, produced and traded to the extent, as McCoy argued, that its economic scale and social ramifications laid solid foundations to resist suppression in the next Prohibition era. At its peak, opium trade reached 41,000 tons in 1906 while China alone produced 35,000 tons (McCoy 2004, 26).

The tide, however, began to change and moved to gradual but steady prohibition by the late nineteenth century and such prohibition efforts accelerated in the early twentieth century. In 1907, the British government helped advocate a new Anglo-Chinese treaty to phase out India's opium exports to China; around the same time, the United States outlawed opium use in its Philippine colony. In 1909, the International Opium Commission was convened in Shanghai. Though the Shanghai Opium Commission came short on drafting international opium regulation, it laid solid groundwork for the Hague International Opium Convention in 1912. The Hague Opium Convention of 1912 and Geneva Conventions of 1925 signified a full scale of prohibition efforts in the global context and extended drug control from opium to many others such as morphine, cocaine and heroin. After World War II, the United Nations inherited and continued the drug control legacy of the League of Nations, negotiated a succession of conventions to expand the scope of drug prohibition, and raised the number of prohibited drugs from 17 in 1931 to 245 by 1995 (McCoy 2004, 27). Among these international conventions, the *United Nations Single Convention on Narcotic Drugs of 1961*, the *United Nations Vienna Convention on Psychotropic Substances of 1971*, and the *United Nations Convention Against Illicit Traffic in Narcotics Drugs and Psychotropic Substances of 1988* were the most noticeable and important.

Table 6.2 Development and Control of Opium and Other Narcotics: China vs. World

Years	China	World
Seventh–sixteenth centuries	• Around 600 AD: Opium was brought into China by Arab traders in the Tang dynasty, mainly used as medicine (legal) • Around fifteenth century: recreational use (e.g., as aphrodisiac) appeared • In 1589, opium became a taxable commodity	• Opium was widely used in many places, mainly as medicine; • No recorded regulation
Seventeenth century	• 1630s–1640s: Brief ban of tobacco smoking encouraged smoking of opium in the Ming dynasty	• 1640s: The Dutch East India Company (VOC) dominated the India-China opium trade
Eighteenth century	• 1729: Yongzheng's opium prohibition, first royal edict; penalized opium dealers and opium den keepers • 1735–1796: Qianlong's prohibition, banned opium smuggling • 1796: Jiaqing's prohibition, banned opium imports and domestic cultivation	• Triangle trade system: Indian opium and cotton to China; Chinese tea to Britain, British textiles and machinery to India • The British East India Company dominated China's opium trade: e.g., opium exports raised from 13 tons in 1729 to 2,588 tons in 1858
Nineteenth century	• 1813: Jiaqing's prohibition, banned opium smoking • 1831, 1839: Daoguang's prohibition, comprehensive regulation • 1839–1942: First Opium War; Treaty of Nanjing opened the Chinese market (i.e., five ports) for European merchants; paid an indemnity to Britain, and ceded Hong Kong; in the supplementary Treaty of Bogue, the Qing government also recognized Britain as an equal to China and gave British subjects extraterritorial privileges in treaty ports • 1856–1860: Second Opium War, Treaty of Tianjin, opium legalized • 1858–1906: Legalization of opium, domestic cultivation to counter opium importation; regulation through taxation	• American competition: increased opium shipments from 102 chests in 1805 to 1,428 in 1830 • the British East India Company lost monopoly in 1834; informal regulation collapsed • First Opium War • Second Opium War, ten new ports forced open, permission for foreigners (including Protestant and Catholic missionaries) to travel throughout the country, and indemnities of 3 million ounces of silver to Great Britain and 2 million to France • 1870s: Protestant churches of England and the U.S. launched moral crusades against the opium trade

Table 6.2 continued

Years	China	World
Twentieth century (first half)	• 1906–1907: (Emperor Guangxu) Qing's effort to resume opium suppression and cultivation eradication (e.g., the new *Criminal Code*) • 1912: Regulation by the Beiyang government (e.g., the *Temporary Criminal Code*) • 1925–1940s: the Republican prohibition, e.g., the Nationalist government's new *Criminal Code* (1928); the Nationalist's *Criminal Code* (1935) and its "six-year" drug prohibition plan • 1930s–1940s: Japanese invasion and its "narco-chemical" policy in China	• 1907: the Anglo-Chinese Treaty reached to phase out Britain shipments of Indian opium • 1909: International Opium Convention at Shanghai, launching a global antinarcotics diplomacy • 1909: *Smoking Opium Exclusion Act* of the U.S. prohibited importation, possession and use of "smoking opium" • 1911–1912: International Opium Convention at the Hague, restricting opium to medical use • 1914: U.S. passed the *Harrison Narcotics Act* • 1920: U.K. passed the *Dangerous Drugs Act* • 1925: the League of Nations approved International Opium Conventions (Geneva) • 1931: the League of Nations approved *Convention for Limiting the Manufacture of Narcotic Drugs* (compulsory control over production and sale of narcotics) • 1936: the *Convention for the Suppression of the Illicit Trafficking in Dangerous Drugs* was approved

Table 6.2 continued

Years	China	World
Twentieth century (second half)	• 1950s: The Communists' anti-drug campaigns • 1950s–1970s: "drug-free" • 1980s–1990s: Resurgence of drug use, trafficking, • 1982: The State Council issued an *Emergency Notice on Banning Opium*; the Standing Committee of the NPC issued a *Decision on Severely Punishing Those who Disturb the Economy* • 1990: The Standing Committee of the NPC passed the *Resolution on Prohibiting Narcotics Drugs* • 1995: The State Council issued a *Measure on How to Carry out the Forced Detoxification* • 1997: Revision of the PRC's *Criminal Law* (1997) to strengthen narcotics control	• 1950s: The rise of the "Golden Triangle" • After WWII, influence of the Cold War • 1961: *United Nations Single Convention on Narcotic Drugs* • 1971: *United Nations Vienna Convention on Psychotropic Substances* • 1970s: Nixon's drug wars in the U.S. • 1970s: The rise of the "Golden Crescent" • 1988: *United Nations Convention Against Illicit Traffic in Narcotics Drugs and Psychotropic Substances* • 1980s: Reagan and Bush's "war on drugs" in the U.S. • 1980s: rise of new narcotics regions, e.g., Afghanistan and Colombia • 1997: U.N. established the United Nations Office on Drugs and Crime (UNODC) to supervise international drug control • 1998: A special session of the United Nations General Assembly (UNGASS) took place in New York
Twenty-first century	• 2005: the State Council issued *Regulations on Administration of Precursor Chemicals*; and *Regulations on Administration of Narcotic Drugs and Psychotropic Substances* • 2007: the NPC passed the PRC's first comprehensive *Anti-Drug Law*	• 2000: *United Nations Convention Against Transnational Organized Crime*

A century has now passed since the Shanghai Opium Commission, and the prohibition effort will seemingly continue (and probably intensify) in the twenty-first century. In 1909, merely 13 nations attended the Shanghai Opium Commission; a century later, over 180 nations (about 95% of all United Nations members) ratified the 1961 Single Convention on Narcotic Drugs, the 1971 Convention on Psychotropic Substances, and the 1988 Convention (UNODC 2008). The world prohibition has been literally extended to cover the whole globe.

In what follows, we will focus on China's role in the global prohibition movements and discuss its relation with the global drug system. In Table 6.2, we listed major drug development and control events, in parallel timelines, by both China and other major countries in the global system.

China's Drug Prohibition in the Global Context

China's drug prohibition efforts in the global context could be divided into three periods. These periods are described below.

First, from the eighteenth century to the end of nineteenth century, the Qing government of China appeared to be the lone drug (opium) fighter in the whole world, after it adopted a number of royal edicts regulating opium activities. The Qing prohibition, however, struggled domestically, and more importantly, was circumvented by free trade policies practiced and imposed onto China by foreign powers (led by the British empire). This is the only historical period when China's drug policy of practicing prohibition diverged from that of the powers of the world (i.e., their philosophy of promoting "free trade"). The debacle of the Qing dynasty's regulations led to opium legalization and also an epidemic of consumption by the late nineteenth century.

Second, from the beginning of the twentieth century to the end of the 1980s, China, despite a succession of various governments, entered into a new round of drug prohibition along with the emerging and growing anti-drug efforts worldwide. During this period, China resumed its prohibition policies, and tried to cooperate and catch up with international drug control movements in the twentieth century. Such efforts were periodically disrupted due to domestic turmoil and changes of governments but they were very much coexisting with the global prohibition movements in the Prohibition era.

Third and most recently, from the 1990s to the present, the PRC entered a new phase of drug prohibition and began actively reaching out and seeking cooperation with other nations in fighting its arising domestic drug problems. Although covering a short period, this new phase witnessed a significant transition of the PRC from a passive player who was defending its own border to a progressive player who sought increasing roles in drug prohibition movements in both Asia and the rest of the globe.

China as a Lone Fighter in Free Trade Era   After opium was brought into China by the Arab traders during the Tang dynasty, it had been used mainly as medicine. Despite a major functional transformation of opium from medicine to aphrodisiac in the fifteenth century, its new "recreational" function was limited to a small group of people who were able to afford it. By the time when opium first became a taxable commodity in 1589, it was taxed as medicine. Near the end of the seventeenth century, the introduction of the new opium smoking method into China significantly increased opium use due to its greater addiction potential. Though the Qing government carefully controlled and limited its contact with Western nations, it did not adopt any measure to regulate opium activities in the seventeenth century.

The 1729 royal edict issued by Emperor Yongzheng banned opium dealing and opium dens and started the Qing dynasty's opium prohibition era. As revealed by available historical records, Yongzheng was mainly concerned about opium smoking's deleterious effects on sexual desire and promiscuity, opium smokers' personal health, and their withdrawal from family and society (Su and Zhao 1998, 151). These concerns were based on Confucian virtues and opium's potential destruction of family structure. It was noticeable that Yongzheng's royal edict did not penalize either opium users or opium imports. The use of opium for medicinal purposes was also exempted from this legal mandate. Over the years, however, the Qing government gradually but steadily broadened its regulation to include various opium activities such as Emperor Qianlong's edict to ban opium smuggling, Emperor Jiaqing's edict to ban both opium imports and domestic cultivation, and Jiaqing's 1813 decree to regulate opium smoking by officials, soldiers, and civilians. Similar to that of the 1729 edict, most historical interpretations of these early laws emphasized the deleterious effect of opium on basic Confucian principles of morality and on the well-being of the individual and society as the primary motivation for these legal prohibitions (Su and Zhao 1998, 536–541). In a way, it shows that the Qing government still believed in its self-sufficient economy and its closed-door foreign policy, and did not take into account seriously (or at least underestimated) the impact of foreign commerce and foreign powers within the global system. These laws essentially failed to stop the spread of opium use, and led to the increasing opium smuggling.

At the same time, the world system had witnessed a full-fledged development of a free trade system in the seventeenth and eighteenth centuries, particularly with regard to opium exporting to China first led by the Dutch East India Company (VOC) and the Portuguese and then dominated by the British East India Company. After the 1757 Battle of Plassey and 1764 Battle of Buxar, the British East India Company established its monopoly on opium production in India, and its opium trade to China steadily increased over the years. The illegal sale of opium became one of the world's most valuable single commodity trades. In 1836, for instance, the Chinese bought USD 18 million worth of opium from the British, yet only sold USD 17 million worth of tea and silk to the British (Hsu 2000, 173). Opium provided more than 5% of the British East India Company's revenue in India in 1826–1827, 9% in 1828–1829, and 12% in the 1850s (Hsu 2000, 172–173). The opium trade received another boost in the early nineteenth century when other growing powers joined the free trade competition. Among them, the most noticeable were American merchants, whose opium shipments increased from 102 chests in 1805 to 1,428 in 1830.[4] Such a global free trade system eventually cost the British East India Company its monopoly in 1834 but at the same time it also cost the Qing government its informal control over opium importation through the triangle trade system with Britain. As a result, the illegal opium trade became more rampant.

One direct impact to the Qing government's fiscal system was the continuous outflow of silver caused by the opium trade. Recognizing this "silver famine" problem, the Qing government decided to reexamine illegal drug imports. Bolstered by the moralistic arguments, the Daoguang administration initiated sweeping enforcement campaigns to strictly carry out the 1939 opium prohibition regulation. This inevitably precipitated the clash between the Qing government and Western powers. The First Opium War (1839–1842) resulted in the 1842 Treaty of Nanjing, which forced open the Chinese market to Western powers, required the Qing government to pay monetary compensation to Western powers, and the cession of Hong Kong.[5] What was unsettled was the status of opium trade. On the one hand the Qing government did not abandon its official position stated in the opium prohibition law. For example, it tried to stress the importance of the opium ban on several occasions (e.g., Daoguang's 1843 edict, Xianfeng's 1854 resolution). On the other hand, because of its weak political and military power, the Qing government had little sanctioning power over the opium trade and this practice became de facto legal after 1843.[6]

The outbreak of the Second Opium War (1856–1860) is a good example of how the Qing government's prohibition against the opium importation was doomed to clash with the free trade system. The War began with the *Arrow incident* in 1856, in which Qing officials boarded a Chinese-owned ship, the *Arrow*, to inspect opium smuggling and arrested 12 suspects. Quickly the British officials in Canton demanded the release of these sailors and claimed that the ship was recently British-registered and therefore protected under the Treaty of Nanjing. To strengthen their arguments, the British further insisted that the ship had been flying a British flag and the Qing soldiers insulted the flag. Refuted by the Chinese, negotiations broke down and the British resorted to its superior military force once again, and were later joined by the French. Plagued by domestic turmoil (e.g., uprisings), the Qing government put up little resistance before it conceded another defeat. As a consequence, the Treaty of Tianjin (Tientsin) in 1858 forced the Qing government to open up 10 more ports along with other provisions and formally legalized the

---

4   For a detailed study of American opium trade to China in the nineteenth century, see Stelle 1981.

5   See Wakeman 1978, 211–12; Gentzler 1977, 29–32.

6   For example, opium exports from India (only Bombay and Kolkata) increased from 42,699 chests in 1843 to 58,681 chests in 1860 and the destination was mainly China (Su and Zhao 1998, 161).

opium trade.[7] By 1860, all previous edicts by the Qing government banning the opium growth and trade were repealed (Candlin 1973). The two Opium Wars not only accelerated the Qing's downhill collapse in the nineteenth century but also led to the debacle and the end of Qing's lonely fighting against opium in the free trade global system. Facing stronger and growing Western powers, all problems with the Qing's political, economic, and foreign policies had become more acute and eventually cost them their prohibition efforts.

China's Renewed Prohibition in the Global Prohibition Era   Once China's door was forced open and opium importation became legalized, opium flooded the Chinese market. Available records indicated that the amount of imported opium increased steadily from 46,000 chests in 1848 to 80,000 chests by 1880, started declining afterwards due to increasing competition from China's domestic opium production, and ultimately dropped to approximately 50,000 chests per year and continued that trend until 1905 (Blue 2000; Su and Zhao 1988, 161). Forced to abandon its prohibition, the Qing government had no other option but to reconsider legalizing domestic opium production.

Provincial authorities took the first step to permit and tax domestic cultivation despite the fact that such cultivation was kept officially illegal by the central government until 1890 (UNODC 2008). By 1860, domestically cultivated opium started to gain popularity among the Chinese due to technological innovations and enhanced farming skills. The annual domestic harvest was estimated at 50,000 chests in 1866, and further increased to 70,000 chests by 1870, surpassing for the first time the amount of opium imported at that time. By the turn of the twentieth century, poppy cultivation flourished in China and the annual harvest reached 300,000 piculs, approximately six times more than that of the imported from India (Candlin 1973).

The Qing government's new decriminalization and legalization policies not only increased domestic cultivation and effectively fought off foreign imports (*yitu diyang*) but also garnered invaluable revenues through duties and taxes on opium production, transportation, and importation (*yujing yuzheng*). For instance, duties on opium imports and transit taxes on foreign opium amounted to about 5–7% of the Qing government's total revenue over the 1887–1905 period; after the Qing government consolidated taxes on both foreign and domestic opium in 1906, income further tripled and accounted for 14% of the central government's annual income (UNODC 2008). Ironically, the Qing government's free trade policy beat out its foreign counterparts but only led to an opium epidemic nationwide. In 50 years, the estimated number of opium users in China increased dramatically from 2 million in the 1830s to 20 million in the 1880s. By the early twentieth century, due to record-high domestic production, the estimated number of opium smokers passed 20 million and reached as high as 40 million based on some estimates, and China was consuming between 85% and 95% of global opium supply (UNODC 2008, 176–177).

---

7   See Fairbank, 1978b, 251. For a detailed study of the Second Opium War, see Wong 1998.

By the late nineteenth century and the early twentieth century when China deeply struggled in the mire of the opium crisis (i.e., it was the world's largest opium importer, consumer and producer), prohibition movements began to take charge both within China and more importantly in the global arena. Domestically, there had been increasing calls for new prohibitions from governmental officials, various anti-drug associations, and students who studied abroad. The Qing government already realized the significance of the opium crisis and the importance of taking on political, economic, military, and social reforms to rid of the image of the "Sick Man of Asia". Internationally, on the one hand, declining profits in foreign opium trade (partially due to China's domestic competition) tipped the economic leverage that foreign powers once enjoyed; on the other hand, anti-drug efforts were stepping up worldwide, especially in Great Britain and the U.S. (in the former, the British Liberal Party won the election in 1906 and held a strong anti-opium stand on moral grounds; in the latter, Congress in 1905 adopted an Opium Committee's recommendation to progressively prohibit importation or sale of opium in its Philippine colony) (see UNODC 2008). Given that China was the main focus of opium/drug problems at that time, the pressure had been mounting to take actions.

One major change made by the Qing government towards its new prohibition in the new century was to adjust its approach when dealing with foreign powers from confrontation to diplomacy. Through negotiations, Qing was able to secure cooperation from Western powers one by one, and the most noticeable was the 1907 Anglo-Chinese treaty, in which the British agreed to gradually reduce its opium exports to China by 10% annually and eventually phase out opium exports by 1917. At the same time China promised to cut back its domestic opium cultivation under the same terms. Once it gained foreign support, the Qing government wasted no time in carrying out a new round of prohibition. New laws such as the *1907 New Criminal Law* and the *1909 Opium Smoking Prohibition Decree* were quickly enacted and adopted to cover various opium offenses such as manufacturing, selling, stocking with the intention of sale, smuggling, manufacturing, and providing shelter for opium smoking, cultivating opium, and opium smoking. It was not difficult to discern the modern nature of these new regulations – for instance, for the first time in the Chinese history, fines were imposed as punishment for some opium-related offenses and the penalties for all offenses were much lighter than that of the earlier eras (Su and Zhao 1998, 540–541).

Another major contribution by the Qing government before its collapse was the convening of the Shanghai Opium Commission in 1909. During this meeting, the Chinese delegation reported its recent achievements on domestic drug campaigns, appealed to foreign governments to control their concessions in China and to cooperate with the Qing government's campaign, and urged all nations to take measures to control the manufacture and distribution of morphine (itself a growing problem in China). Though the 13 attending nations failed to reach agreements on drafting regulations with binding power to the signatories, the meeting carried a significant symbolic meaning for international cooperation on drug prohibition, prompted other drug prohibition movements worldwide (e.g., the *Smoking Opium*

Exclusion Act in the U.S.), and laid solid groundwork for the Hague International Opium Convention. Three years later, in 1912, the Hague Convention witnessed the world's first international drug control treaty, and it included two new substances, cocaine and heroin (in addition to opium and morphine), given the increasing abuse of both. Despite the fact that the outbreak of World War I prevented the implementation of the Convention, the Convention provided further impetus for growing anti-drug movements worldwide, including the 1914 *Harrison Act* in the U.S. and the 1920 *Dangerous Drugs Act* in the United Kingdom.

The unstable situation and political turmoil in China really complicated and disrupted China's anti-drug campaigns during this time. As detailed in Chapter 3, succeeding governments after the Qing such as the Beiyang government and the Nationalist government no longer enforced previous strict prohibitions. Instead, they turned to a policy that focused on establishing an official opium monopoly and regulation through taxation as the means of drug control. Such policies were equivalent to legalizing opium activities and indeed made opium more common.

Despite China's struggle, the global prohibition regime continued to grow after the World War I and with the creation of the League of Nations in 1920. From November 1924 to February 1925, two back-to-back conferences were held and two Geneva Conventions were concluded. While the first Convention targeted opium-producing nations and proposed signatories to adopt the British import/export authorization model (through governmental monopolies), the second one intended to impose global controls over many substances (including the newly added cannabis) and proposed to set up statistical reporting systems along with key international organizations such as the Permanent Central Board, the forerunner of the International Narcotics Control Board (INCB) (UNODC 2008). However, due to the inability of the delegates to come to an agreement on reductions in opium production, the U.S. delegation as well as the Chinese delegation withdrew from the conference and did not sign and ratify the 1925 Convention. In the subsequent years of the League of Nations, more meetings were convened and more conventions (e.g., the *1931 Convention for Limiting the Manufacture and Regulating the Distribution of Narcotic Drugs*, the *1936 Convention for the Suppression of the Illicit Trafficking in Dangerous Drugs*) were adopted, though the practical importance of these conventions were rather limited due to the failure to reach agreements among leading powers especially on the brink of World War II.

During the same period (1920s and 1930s), China continued to ride the roller coaster on drug prohibition with occasional strict prohibition at some time and in some regions (e.g., the 1928 and 1935 *Criminal Code*) and legalized regulations at other time and in other regions. Such practices were to a large extent determined by China's narco-economy, political turmoil (e.g., the warlordism), and strenuous foreign relations with leading powers (e.g., the U.S., U.K., and Japan). Despite its domestic struggle, China tried to keep up with the pace of the global movements and participated in various international meetings. In 1935, for instance, Hu Shize, the Chinese representative, presented a report to the League of Nations Opium Advisory Committee at its twentieth session based on preliminary results of the

Republican government's efforts in combating narcotics under Chiang Kai-shek's "six-year plan". Based on the reported achievements, the League's Anti-Opium Information Bureau issued a statement lauding Chiang and his government for the "unmistakable progress" they made against the scourge of narcotics on May 24 (Slack 2001, 109). Ironically, the governmental monopoly and regulation through taxation approach was the internationally sanctioned method for dealing with the opium problem embodied in the 1925 Geneva Convention that China had refused to sign. In the second half of the 1930s, members of the League of Nations Opium Advisory Committee continued praising the Nationalists' anti-drug campaign, and, after the Japanese invasion, began to condemn Japan's "narco-chemical" policy which turned Manchuria and Rehe into huge poppy fields and flooded northern China and Fujian with opium, heroin, and morphine. In this new atmosphere, the Nanjing government signed the 1925 Geneva Convention. As Slack (2001, 112) put it, the international approval of Chiang's opium suppression by means of monopoly system at least allowed the Nationalists to achieve parity with foreign powers. It is fair to say that during this period, China tried hard to comply with international drug control requirements; however, its domestic struggle to a large extent doomed such efforts until the Chinese Communist Party gained control in the late 1940s.

After World War II, the newly established United Nations (U.N.) assumed drug control functions and responsibilities formerly carried out by the League of Nations. In the second half of the twentieth century, the U.N. dedicated itself to the drug control and adopted a series of Conventions, among which the most noticeable include the *United Nations Single Convention on Narcotic Drugs of 1961*, the *United Nations Vienna Convention on Psychotropic Substances of 1971*, and the *United Nations Convention Against Illicit Traffic in Narcotics Drugs and Psychotropic Substances of 1988*. The 1961 Single Convention superseded all previous international conventions, protocols and treaties, codified them into one single document, streamlined international drug control machines (e.g., restructure of key organizations such as INCB), and extended drug control scope into new areas (e.g., regulation over cultivation of plants grown as raw material for drug manufacturing and prevention of non-medical drug consumption). The 1971 Convention on Psychotropic Substances for the first time placed psychotropic substances under control such as amphetamine-type stimulants, hallucinogens, sedative hypnotics, anxiolytics, and many others. The 1988 Convention emphasized and targeted illicit production of narcotics drugs and psychotropic substances, given that illicit drug production and trafficking started dominating the world black market and becoming the major drug sources in the 1980s (after legal drug production and manufacture were brought down and under control). The 1988 Convention obliged members to make drug trafficking activities "criminal offenses" and further extended international drug control to cover precursor chemicals. All these conventions, along with major drug wars waged by key nations such as the U.S., witnessed the full-scale development of anti-drug movements during this historical period. The consensus was built, the agreements were reached, and the prohibition actions were taken but the effects were not as fruitful and promising, especially given the elasticity of international narcotics supply and the rising of new drug producing regions (e.g., the Golden Triangle in the 1950s, the "Golden Crescent" in the 1970s, Afghanistan and Columbia in the 1980s) in replacement of others.[8]

Despite the general frustration experienced by the global prohibition community, China enjoyed its most successful history of drug control by having three decades of being "drug-free" after the Communist government launched its anti-drug campaigns in the early 1950s. It is interesting to notice that such a success, often cited by the U.N. as an example of effective drug control, was achieved by dissociating China itself from the global system. During this period, the Chinese Communist government unified the nation, built a strong government and effective social control mechanisms (e.g., the neighborhood committee, the household registration system), centralized the national economy, adopted self-sufficient policies, and remained "isolated" from Western influences (to some extent due to the "Cold War" ideology). Such an independent stance allowed the Chinese government to take effective measures (e.g., harsh penalty, public education) to deal with domestic drug problems and cut off potential international drug trafficking routes. Though China's success was achieved without much help from the international prohibition regime, its anti-drug campaigns did change the configuration of the world drug problems significantly (e.g., driving drug dealers and producers to other regions indirectly). In any event, China's change from the world's largest drug problem nation to the largest drug-free nation delighted the Chinese people and impressed the whole world.

The reemergence of drug problems in the 1980s after China initiated its economic reforms and adopted its "open door" policy once again rang the bell of the Chinese government and Chinese people (see Chapter 4). Struggling to curb the worsening drug problems, the Chinese government stepped up its legislation (e.g., the 1990 *Resolution on Prohibiting Narcotics Drugs* by the Standing Committee of the NPC, the 1997 revised *Criminal Law*) and official crackdown (e.g., the "strike-hard" campaigns) on various drug offenses.

However, in this recent period of increased drug problems, China also turned to the help of international organizations and re-embraced the global drug prohibition system. In the mid-1980s, China began to send delegations to attend international drug control meetings held by key organizations such as the United Nations, the International Criminal Police Organization, and the World Health Organization. In 1985, China acceded to both the United Nations 1961 Single Convention and the 1971 Convention on Psychotropic Substances. In 1988, China actively participated in the draft and enactment of the United Nations 1988 Convention Against Illicit Traffic in Narcotic Drugs and Psychotropic Substances, and acceded to the Convention next year, becoming one of the very first member countries (see Table 6.3). After dissociating itself from the international anti-drug regime for over three decades, China sprinted to regain its connections before it assumed more proactive roles in the international arena in the 1990s and in the new twenty-first century.

---

8   See McCoy 2004 for a summary of such struggles.

Table 6.3 China's Increasing Roles in International Cooperation in the New Era

Year	Major events
1984	China began to send delegations to attend international drug control meetings held by the United Nations, the International Criminal Police Organization, the World Customs Organization, and the World Health Organization.
1985	China acceded to the United Nations 1961 Single Convention on Narcotic Drugs and 1971 Convention on Psychotropic Substances, and started to work together with the United Nations.
1987	The Chinese and the U.S. governments signed the Sino-U.S. Memorandum of Cooperation in Narcotic Drugs Control.
1988	China actively participated in the draft and enactment of the United Nations Convention Against Illicit Traffic in Narcotic Drugs and Psychotropic Substances.
1989	China acceded to the United Nations Convention Against Illicit Traffic in Narcotic Drugs and Psychotropic Substances, becoming one of the first member countries.
	In October, China held the Asian Region Anti-Drug Seminar in Beijing.
1990	The Ministry of Public Security of the PRC sent delegations twice to visit Burma and Thailand.
	In February, the Chinese government sent delegation to take part in the Seventeenth United Nations General Assembly special session on drug control.
1991	The United Nations held a special Convention on drug prohibition in Tokyo. The United Nations Drug Control Programme (UNDCP) proposed cooperation in the "Golden Triangle" region based on the agreement between China, Burma, and Thailand.
	In May, the National Narcotics Control Commission (NNCC) hosted the first meeting of senior officials of China, Thailand, Myanmar and the United Nations Drug Control Programme (UNDCP) in Beijing, to discuss the proposal on multilateral cooperation against drug abuse in the sub-region.
1992	A joint project between China, Burma and Thailand was signed, and it signified the formal cooperation among Asian multi-lateral cooperation.
	In June, China, Myanmar and the UNDCP signed the China/Myanmar/United Nations International Drug Control Program (UNDCP) Joint Cooperation Project on Drug Control in Rangoon, Myanmar.
1993	In October, China, Myanmar, Thailand, Laos and the UNDCP signed the *Memorandum of Understanding (MOU) on Narcotic Drugs Control*, which stressed keeping contacts between high officials to further the cooperation in drug control in the sub-region.
1995	The Chinese government and the United Nations Commission on Narcotics Drug held a ceremony on the second phase of cooperation. The second phase runs for three years, and the Chinese government agreed to invest 50 million RMB to strengthen the equipment and manpower in the fight against the drugs.
	In May, China, Vietnam, Laos, Thailand, Myanmar, Cambodia, and the UNDCP convened the first minister-level meeting on cooperation in sub-region drug control in Beijing. The meeting adopted the Beijing Declaration and signed the Sub-region Drug Control Program of Action.

Table 6.3 continued

Year	Major events
1996	China signed a cooperation treaty with India and Pakistan.
	In April, China and Russia signed an Agreement on Cooperation Against Illicit Trafficking and Abuse of Narcotic Drugs and Psychotropic Substances.
	In November, China hosted the International Stimulant Specialists Meeting in Shanghai.
1997	The heads of China and the U.S. signed the Sino-U.S. Joint Statement containing contents on cooperation in drug control, which upgraded this cooperation between the two countries to a new level.
1998	In June, the Chinese government sent delegation to take part in the Twentieth United Nations General Assembly special session on drug control.
	The heads of state of China, Kazakhstan, Kyrgyzstan, Russia, and Tajikistan signed a joint statement, taking cracking down drug-connected and transnational crimes as major contents in cooperation among the five countries.
1999	The Chinese government sent delegations to attend the sub-region minister-level meetings in Japan and Laos to continue to promote enthusiastic cooperation in drug control in the sub-region.
2000	In March, China attended the Forty-third session of U.N. Commission on Narcotic Drugs in Vienna.
	In July, the fifth ICPO-Interpol Heroin Conference was held in Beijing.
	In October, China and the Association of Southeast Asian Nations (ASEAN) approved the ASEAN and China Cooperative Operations in Response to Dangerous Drugs.
	In November, China attended the Twenty-fourth meeting of Heads of National Drug Law Enforcement Agencies (HONLEA) of Asia and Pacific Region in Rangoon, Myanmar.
2001	In March, China attended the Forty-fourth session of U.N. Commission on Narcotic Drugs in Vienna.
	In May, China attended the Sub-Regional Senior Officials Meeting on Drug Control (MOU) in Rangoon, Myanmar.
	In August, China held a four-nation ministers' meeting on drug control with Laos, Myanmar and Thailand, and reached an agreement, titled "Beijing Declaration" to strengthen joint actions against narcotics activities.
	In October, China attended the Twenty-fifth meeting of Heads of National Drug Law Enforcement Agencies (HONLEA) of Asia and Pacific Region in Sydney, Australia.

Table 6.3 continued

Year	Major events
2002	In March, China attended the Forty-fifth session of U.N. Commission on Narcotic Drugs in Vienna.
	In May, China hosted the MOU Senior Officials Committee Meeting on sub-regional drug control cooperation in Beijing.
	In October, Chinese and U.S. officials held a first Sino-U.S. Narcotics Control Strategic Intelligence Sharing Conference.
2003	In April, China attended the Forty-sixth session (Ministerial segment) of U.N. Commission on Narcotic Drugs in Vienna.
	In July, China, India, Laos, Myanmar, and Thailand held a meeting in Chiang Rai, Thailand, and agreed on cross-border cooperation to fight drugs.
	In September, China attended the Sub-Regional Senior Officials Meeting on Drug Control (MOU) in Hanoi, Vietnam.
2004	In March, China attended the Forty-seventh session of U.N. Commission on Narcotic Drugs in Vienna.
	In April, China attended the Twenty-second International Drug Enforcement Conference in Lima, Peru.
	In May, China attended the MOU Senior Officials Committee Meeting on sub-regional drug control cooperation in Thailand.
	China, along with Afghanistan, Iran, Pakistan, Tajikistan, Turkmenistan, and Uzbekistan, signed the *Kabul Good Neighborly Relations Declaration on Drug Control.*
	In October, China attended the Twenty-eighth meeting of Heads of National Drug Law Enforcement Agencies (HONLEA) of Asia and Pacific Region in Bangkok, Thailand.
2005	In February, the Bureau of Narcotics of the Ministry of Public Security of China and the Drug Enforcement Agency of the U.S. signed a *Memorandum of Intent* to raise the level of cooperation.
	In May, China attended the MOU Senior Officials Committee Meeting on sub-regional drug control cooperation in Cambodia.
	In October, ASEAN and China held a second meeting in Beijing and reaffirmed the ASEAN and China Cooperative Operations in Response to Dangerous Drugs and sought opportunities to expand cooperation.
	In November, the first Ministerial Conference of the Sino-Russian Cooperation in Drug Control was held, and an anti-drug cooperation protocol was signed.

Table 6.3 continued

Year	Major events
2006	In March, China attended the Forty-ninth session of U.N. Commission on Narcotic Drugs in Vienna.
	In May, China and Myanmar reached an agreement on enhancing cooperation in drug control.
	In November, China attended the Thirtieth meeting of Heads of National Drug Law Enforcement Agencies (HONLEA) of Asia and Pacific Region.
2007	In February, China attended the Twelfth Asia-Pacific Operational Drug Enforcement Conference (ADEC) in Japan.
	In March, China attended the Fiftieth session of U.N. Commission on Narcotic Drugs in Vienna.
	In May, China attended the Twenty-fifth International Drug Enforcement Conference (IDEC) in Madrid, Spain.
	In May, China hosted the MOU Senior Officials Committee Meeting on sub-regional drug control cooperation in Beijing.
	In November, China attended the Thirty-first meeting of Heads of National Drug Law Enforcement Agencies (HONLEA) of Asia and Pacific Region in Thailand.
2008	In December, the Fourth meeting of the Sino-Russian cooperation in drug control was held in Sanya, Hainan.

Source: *Liaowang* 1997, 18, 19; Narcotics Control in China (governmental white paper, 2000); Statement by Mr. Xie Bohua, Counselor of the Chinese Mission to the U.N., at Third Committee of the GA Fifty-ninth Session on Crime Prevention, Criminal Justice and Narcotic Control (Item 96, 97); Xinhua News, August 28, 2001; October 29, 2002; Emmers, 2007; Narcotics Control in China (annual reports, 2000–2008); news posted on www.cpd.com.cn, December 3, 2008;

China as an Active Player in New Prohibition Era   In 1998, a special session of the United Nations General Assembly (UNGASS) took place in New York. It was an effort by the U.N. to address the problem of drugs globally, raise the profile of the issue, and set the agenda for drug control in the coming era. The UNGASS unanimously adopted a political declaration to reaffirm its "unwavering determination and commitment to overcoming the world drug problem through domestic and international strategies to reduce both the illicit supply of and the demand for drugs".[9] The declaration emphasized a number of key items such as

---

9   The first operative paragraph of the Political Declaration, cited in *2008 World Drug Report*, United Nations Office on Drugs and Crime, 208.

"shared responsibility", "balanced approach" (between prevention of drug use and reduction of adverse consequences), "sovereignty and territorial integrity", and "human rights", and adopted a number of action plans targeting key issues such as eradication of illicit drug crops, combating illicit manufacture and trafficking, control of precursors, promotion of judicial cooperation, and countering money laundering. In addition, the declaration for the first time linked drug production/ trafficking and terrorism. In 2000, the *United Nations Convention Against Transnational Organized Crime* was enacted and provided another weapon against drug problems in the global setting. All of these activities indicate clearly that the global prohibition movement will continue (and probably intensify) in the twenty-first century.

In such an environment, China has sped up its globalization process and has begun to play an increasing role and assume more responsibilities in both Asia and the world since the 1990s (see Table 6.3). Such a transition is evident in several aspects.

First, after China acceded to the key United Nations Conventions in the 1980s, it has become actively involved in various international drug control meetings. For example, China continuously sent its delegation to take part in the United Nations General Assembly special sessions on drug control (e.g., in 1990 and 1998); from 2000 to 2007, China continuously attended sessions of United Nations Commission on Narcotic Drugs (UNCND) in Vienna; in November 1996, China hosted an International Stimulant Specialists meeting in Shanghai; in 2000, China hosted the fifth International Criminal Police Organization (ICPO)-Interpol Heroin Conference in Beijing; in 2004 and 2007, China attended the twenty-second and the twenty-fifth International Drug Enforcement Conferences. Besides attending these meetings, China also sought various opportunities to work with international organizations on drug control issues. In 1995, for instance, the Chinese government and the UNCND kicked off their second phase of cooperation, during which the Chinese government agreed to invest 50 million Yuan (RMB) to strengthen the equipment and manpower in its fight against drugs in the next three years.

Second, China has begun to reach out to neighboring nations and exert a leading role in fighting drug trafficking and production. As early as the 1990s, the Ministry of Public Security of the PRC began to send delegations to visit Burma and Thailand to discuss action plans to combat drug problems. Two years later in 1992, a joint project between China, Burma, and Thailand was signed and it signified the establishment of formal cooperation. In subsequent years, with the help of the United Nations International Drug Control Programme (UNDCP), China managed to hold frequent minister-level meetings and sign the *Memorandum of Understanding (MOU) on Narcotic Drugs Control* with a growing list of nations (including Myanmar, Thailand, Laos, Vietnam, and Cambodia) in South Asia.

On its north and west borders, China engaged in similar efforts with its neighbors. In April 1996, China and Russia signed an *Agreement on Cooperation against Illicit Trafficking and Abuse of Narcotic Drugs and Psychotropic Substances*. In 1998, China along with Kazakhstan, Kyrgyzstan, Russia, and Tajikistan signed a joint statement to crack down on drug connected and transnational crimes. In 2004, China along with Afghanistan, Iran, Pakistan, Tajikistan, Turkmenistan, and Uzbekistan signed the *Kabul Good Neighborly Relations Declaration on Drug Control*. In 2005, the first Ministerial Conference of the Sino-Russian Cooperation in Drug Control was held, and an anti-drug cooperation protocol was signed between the two nations. Most recently, in December 2008, China hosted the fourth meeting of the Sino-Russian cooperation in drug control in Sanya, Hainan.

All these actions showed that China has already realized that it cannot fight drug problems alone any more as it did decades ago. Instead, China has extended its defense line by working with its neighbors. In recent years, China has also delivered necessary resources and sent experts to countries such as Burma and Laos to help train local officials. By the end of 2004, the Chinese government had already spent more than RMB 500 million (USD 63 million) for this purpose (Swanström and He 2006). These observations suggest that China has definitely become more assertive and tried to fight narcotics more aggressively not only in its own territory but in neighboring nations.

Third, China also began to exert a leading role in working with regional associations. As early as 1989, China had already held an Asian Region Anti-Drug Seminar in Beijing. In May 1991, the National Narcotics Control Commission (NNCC) of China hosted the first meeting of senior officials of China, Thailand, Myanmar, and the UNDCP in Beijing to discuss proposals on multilateral cooperation against drug abuse in the sub-region. Since 2000, China has actively participated in meetings of Heads of National Drug Law Enforcement Agencies (HONLEA) of Asia and Pacific Region. In 2000, China and the Association of Southeast Asian Nations (ASEAN) approved the ASEAN and China Cooperative Operations in Response to Dangerous Drugs (ACCORD). In 2005, ASEAN and China held a second meeting in Beijing and reaffirmed the ACCORD and sought opportunities to expand cooperation. As Emmers (2007) pointed out, it is still premature to claim the ACCORD as a working regional regime because actions within the ACCORD framework have been national and bilateral so far rather than multilateral and collective efforts. China's leading role in the sub-regions of Asia, however, is very clear and expected to continue to grow in the future.

Fourth, despite China's focus on sub-regions of Asia, China continued to increase its ties with leading powers in other regions such as the U.S., the European Union, and Australia. Take Sino-U.S. cooperation as an example. Besides active involvement by both nations in key regional and international meetings, there has been increasing interaction and communication between the two countries. In 1987, the Chinese and the U.S. governments signed a Sino-U.S. Memorandum of Cooperation in Narcotic Drugs Control. The heads of China and the U.S. governments in 1997 signed a joint statement that contained important contents on cooperation in drug control and as a result upgraded cooperation between two countries to a new level. In October 2002, Chinese and U.S. officials also held the first Sino-U.S. Narcotics Control Strategic Intelligence Sharing Conference, a strong indicator of willingness by both nations to crack down drug trafficking based on joint efforts. The Bureau of Narcotics of the Ministry of Public Security of China and the Drug Enforcement Agency (DEA) of the U.S. in 2005 signed a *Memorandum of Intent* to further raise the level of cooperation. In May 2006, a joint inquiry by the U.S. DEA and customs agents in Hong Kong and mainland China uncovered a network of Colombian drug gangs and criminals, seized over 300 pounds of cocaine (a record bust then) and arrested nine suspects including two Colombians. This case marked the first time that Chinese customs has worked with U.S. authorities on a drug investigation.[10]

In sum, China's drug control has always been an important part of the global drug control history. While Western powers exported opium as a merchandise commodity to China during the free trade era, China fought opium problems single-handedly in the eighteenth and nineteenth centuries. It eventually gave in to the stronger foreign powers. Only after the global prohibition movements gained momentum by the end of the nineteenth century and in the early of the twentieth century, did China get another chance to deal with its opium epidemic domestically. Unfortunately, the narco-economy, political turmoil, and the Japanese invasion in the first half of the twentieth century all prevented China from effectively eradicating drug problems.

The unprecedented success achieved by the Communist government in the early 1950s was very unique given its historical conditions. It was also accomplished largely independent of the world system. Once China faced the challenge of drug problems again in the 1980s, it began to rejoin the global anti-drug movements and assumed increasing roles and responsibilities in both sub-regions and the world in general after the 1990s.

Drug Control in Twenty-First Century: Challenges and Lessons

Challenges in the New Century

A century has passed since the Shanghai International Opium Commission in 1909, and the global prohibition movements continued to grow in the twentieth century and the new twenty-first century. Despite the strong consensus and coalition built through the years, drug problems, as acknowledged by the United Nations Office on Drugs and Crime (UNODC), have only been contained. The fundamental objectives of the U.N. conventions (i.e., restricting the use of drug and psychoactive substances under international control to medical and scientific use) have not yet been achieved. At the same time, the UNODC identified a number of 'unintended consequences' as the result of the global control efforts, including the creation of a black market, policy displacement (in which law enforcement approach takes over and trumps the public health approach), geographical displacement, substance displacement, and marginalization of drug addicts (UNODC 2008, 216). It is now well-acknowledged

---

10   News reported by the Associated Press, May 9, 2006.

that drug problems (e.g., production, trafficking, and consumption) are deeply intertwined with political, economic, social, and cultural dimensions, and intersect many different domains such as law, criminal justice, human rights, development, public health and the environment (UNODC 2008, 218). This is exactly what we have witnessed in China's case throughout our study.

Besides common problems faced by all nations today (Ghodse 2008), China has to deal with a number of unique challenges due to its history, geographic location, political-legal system, economic reform, and its increasing integration into the global system. These challenges are illustrated below.

First, China has been experiencing dramatic changes (economic, social, cultural, and political-legal) in the last three decades, and the impact of these changes is far-reaching. In many ways, this transitional period has bred the conditions for people's consumption of drugs and alcohol (e.g., culture clash, diversity and tolerance, new recreation, avoiding frustration in reality), and also opened up opportunities for illegitimate business such as drug trafficking and running entertainment centers where drugs could be offered. Due to their illegal status and addictive nature, drug consumption, cultivation, transportation, and smuggling turned out to be so lucrative despite the high-risks associated with these activities. Information on market price changes in various locations showed that one kilogram of heroin, which is worth about USD 1,250 in Burma (the originating place), could be sold in Yunnan province at a price from USD 3,000 to USD 6,000; the price further jumped to the USD 37,500–62,500 range in Guangzhou city, Guangdong province, and to more than USD 100,000 in Hong Kong; and it reaches USD 1 million in the U.S. (a price 800 times as high as in Burma) (see Table 6.4). The basic demand-supply principle essentially dominates and determines the resistance by drug dealers in the global anti-drug movements, and casts serious doubt on the effectiveness of national and international drug regulations (McCoy 2004). Within this context, China is no exception.

Table 6.4 Price and Profit Changes for One Kilogram of Heroin in Various Regions

Region	RMB	US$	Gross Profit
Burma (Myanmar)	10,000	1,250	
Baoshan (in Yunnan)	17,000–25,000	2,130–3,130	1.7–2.5 times
Dali (in Yunnan)	30,000–35,000	3,800–4,500	3–3.5 times
Kunmin (in Yunnan)	40,000–45,000	5,000–6,300	4–4.5 times
Guangzhou (in Guangdong)	300,000–500,000	37,500–62,500	30–50 times
Hong Kong	900,000–1 million	100,000–200,000	80–160 times
U.S.	8 million	1 million	800 times

Source: Su 1997, 509; see also Deng 2002, 103; Yao and Xue 2004, 259; Zhao and Zhang 2004, 196.

Second, the geopolitical conditions of China in the global system present a tough challenge after China further opens its doors and integrates into the world system. China is in the center of this Eurasian narcotic nexus with North Korea in the Northeast, the "Golden Triangle" in the south, the "Golden Crescent" of Afghanistan, Pakistan, and Iran in its east, and Central Asia in the northwest. Major drug trafficking routes run through China's long border line and infiltrate into China through adjacent provinces such as Yunnan, Guangxi, and Xinjiang. Fifty years ago, China managed to win its domestic war on drugs but drove off drug problems into other regions in Asia. However, 50 years later, these drug problems have come back and now China has to learn how to work with its neighbors in order to defend its own territory.

Third, the nature of narcotic drugs has changed. It was opium that plagued China for centuries and led to an epidemic in the past. Currently, other narcotics such as heroin and methamphetamine are the drugs that addict Chinese consumers. These new drugs, more addictive and more difficult to rehabilitate, presented another tough challenge to the Chinese government. Moreover, these new drugs are not related to China's "drug history" as opium was, and the "patriotism" arguments against opium are largely irrelevant today against other drugs. Granted, the Chinese government always uses the failure of Qing dynasty's and the Republic's regulations as a lesson and praises Lin Zexu's heroic efforts in its drug education. From this perspective, the goal is to equate new narcotics with opium and revamp the people's war on drugs, but the rhetoric does not seem to be working (as least not as effectively as it was before). For example, the messages that drug use is a foreign practice and drug crimes are driven by Western materialism no longer match with the reality of current practices. As a result, the Chinese government has lost a strong ideological weapon in its drug war.

Fourth, China's system of social control including the household registration system and neighborhood committees has faced increasing challenges in the process of dramatic transitions. The weakened functions of these informal social control mechanisms inhibited the government's war on drugs in many meaningful ways such as surveillance, persuasion, assistance to policing, and rehabilitation. China has tried in recent years to strengthen its formal legal system and step up its legislation. However, this transition from informal to formal control represents a relatively new type of war on drugs, and its impact remains unknown.

Finally, beyond its geographical challenge, China has to learn how to implement its new war on drugs within a growing global system. As we have noted, China's drug control history has always been a key component of the global movements, and in recent years China has definitely increased its role in both the sub-region of Asia and the world in general. China's drug control history is, no doubt, an asset for China's further drug regulation. Nevertheless, its Communist political and legal systems still draw suspicion and criticism when other issues (e.g., human rights) are entangled with its anti-drug campaigns. For example, China's quick and heavy utilization of the death penalty in its anti-drug campaigns was often denounced by human rights groups and organizations.[11] China's crackdown on separatism, extremism and terrorism especially in minority regions, based on a claim that there is a close relationship between international drug trade and these extreme groups, also has received global scrutiny (Swanström and He 2006). How to succeed in the global drug prohibition movement without compromising its current political system is another challenge for the Chinese government.

Lessons from China's Experience

Despite the ongoing challenges, looking forward to the future, we can offer a few lessons from China's past experiences with regard to both China's domestic drug control and drug control in a global context.

First, to reiterate, drug problems are complex social problems and deeply embedded in previous and current political, economic, social and cultural conditions within the country and the global system itself. The ebb and flow of drug problems in China's history proved exactly such a lesson. Given this complexity, any attempt at looking for an easy fix would most likely end up in vain. It is true that drug problems could be significantly curtailed and suppressed in the case of a "perfect coercion" (to borrow McCoy's term) as witnessed in the success of China's anti-drug campaigns in the 1950s. Such coercion, however, usually turned out to be short-lived and carried other collateral consequences or damages. As we have emphasized several times, China's success in the 1950s was very unique, and it is unlikely to replicate such an experience even in China (and its struggle with the resurging drug problems in the reform era seems to validate this claim). Even if it was effective within China, the focus on the elimination of one country's drug problem may also simply exacerbate the drug problems elsewhere through the processes of geographical and substance displacements.

Second, with regard to China's most recent struggle with reemerging drug problems and its "war on drugs", there seems to be both good news and bad news. The good news is that the "new" drug problems are very unlikely to become as onerous as the opium "epidemic" of China's nineteenth and twentieth centuries because this problem was the result of unique confluence of social, political, and economic conditions. The current political, economic, social, and cultural conditions in China would seem to prevent the development of a drug problem of similar magnitude. However, the bad news is that it is also very unlikely for the Chinese government to completely eradicate drug problems today (as did in the 1950s) and it has to be prepared to deal with drug problems in many years to come. Nonetheless, it appears that the Chinese government is currently managing

---

11   See, for example, reports on China's death penalty practice by the Amnesty International.

its drug problems at home and increasing its role in the global response to drug-related issues.[12]

Third, from a law-making and enforcement perspective, China's history of drug control calls into question any simple theory of law and society that has been offered by some Western scholars. Drug laws often served multiple purposes and often catered to different interests and concerns that varied and evolved over time. The form of these laws could be imperial or modern, simple or complex, and specific or general. Regardless of their form, however, the effectiveness of these drug laws was inevitably affected by the prevailing economic, political, social and cultural conditions of the times. It is interesting that the Chinese government seems to always point to its inadequate legislation as a major reason for the arising drug problems that it faces in contemporary society (see Li et al. 2002), even though the success of the anti-drug campaigns in the 1950s was not achieved through modern, advanced law-making. Given the increasingly global nature of the anti-drug movement (e.g., increasing approval of international conventions, protocols and treaties), it appears that any future attempts at effective containment of global drug problems must focus on the enforcement and adherence to these principles, instead of the mere passage of formal preventive laws per se.

Finally, as acknowledged by the UNODC (2008), building an effective drug control system requires taking on multiple functions simultaneously including enforcement of the laws, prevention of drug abuse, treatment of drug addicts, and mitigation of potential negative consequences of drugs. China's success in the 1950s, a comprehensive effort, seemingly lent support for this multi-function task. Unfortunately, although China has tried to emphasize all of these key elements in its latest war on drugs, serious questions have emerged about the harm reduction approach taken by the Chinese government, especially given the nature of China's political-legal system and its previous practice in drug wars (e.g., the strike-hard campaign, stigmatization of drug addicts) (Aldrich 1992). In addition, the Chinese government has only recently taken some measures to help ease the rehabilitation and treatment process (e.g., the adoption of methadone maintenance therapy program and a clean needle/syringe exchange program in 2003) (Swanström and He 2006). As these examples illustrate, China still has many lessons to learn from its own drug control history and from other nations in a global world.

---

12   It should be noted that China's rate of addiction today is lower than the world average. See Swanström & He (2006). The most recent data disclosed by the NNCC showed that the increase rate of new heroin users declined from 30% to 5.6% in the last three years. News reported at www.cpd.com.cn, June 25, 2008.

Appendix 1

All Narcotic Drugs Related Laws Passed after 1978*

1	Drug Control Law of the People's Republic of China 中华人民共和国禁毒法	2007.12.29
2	Anti-money Laundering Law of the People's Republic of China 中华人民共和国反洗钱法	2006.10.31
3	Amendment VI to the Criminal Law of the People's Republic of China 中华人民共和国刑法修正案(六)	2006.06.29
4	Decision of the Standing Committee of the National People's Congress on Ratifying the Treaty of Good-Neighborliness and Friendly Cooperation between the People's Republic of China and the Islamic Republic of Pakistan 全国人大常委会关于批准《中华人民共和国和巴基斯坦伊斯兰共和国睦邻友好合作条约》的决定	2005.08.28
5	Law of the People's Republic of China on Penalties for Administration of Public Security 中华人民共和国治安管理处罚法	2005.08.28
6	Amendment III to the Criminal Law of the People's Republic of China 中华人民共和国刑法修正案(三)	2001.12.29
7	Law of the People's Republic of China on Prevention of Juvenile Delinquency 中华人民共和国预防未成年人犯罪法	1999.06.28
8	Revision of the Criminal Law of the People's Republic of China 中华人民共和国刑法(97修订)	1997.03.14
9	Law of the People's Republic of China on Control of Guns 中华人民共和国枪支管理法	1996.07.05
10	Regulations of the People's Republic of China on Administrative Penalties for Public Security (Amended in 1994) (expired) 中华人民共和国治安管理处罚条例(1994修正)[失效]	1994.05.12

11	Legislative Committee of the National People's Congress on the Understanding and Execution of Certain Laws and Regulations (regarding Guangdong province's regulation on seven types of people including planting, using, and trafficking narcotic drugs) 全国人大常委会法制工作委员会关于如何理解和执行法律若干问题的解答(四)	1992.04.01
12	Law of the People's Republic of China on Protection of Minors 中华人民共和国未成年人保护法	1991.09.04
13	Decision of the Standing Committee of the National People's Congress on the Prohibition Against Narcotic Drugs (expired) 全国人民代表大会常务委员会关于禁毒的决定[失效]	1990.12.28
14	Law of the People's Republic of China on the Protection of Wildlife 中华人民共和国野生动物保护法	1988.11.08
15	Supplementary Provisions of the Standing Committee of the National People's Congress Concerning the Punishment of the Crimes of Smuggling (expired) 全国人民代表大会常务委员会关于惩治走私罪的补充规定[失效]	1988.01.21
16	Customs Law of the People's Republic of China 中华人民共和国海关法	1987.01.22
17	Regulations of the People's Republic of China on Administrative Penalties for Public Security (expired) 中华人民共和国治安管理处罚条例[失效]	1986.09.05
18	Decision of the Standing Committee of the National People's Congress Regarding the Severe Punishment of Criminals Who Seriously Sabotage the Economy 全国人大常委会关于严惩严重破坏经济的罪犯的决定[失效]	1982.03.08
19	Criminal Law of the People's Republic of China (1979) 中华人民共和国刑法	1979.03.14

Note: * All search results of keywords "du pin" (narcotic drugs) in the database of "fagui zhongxin" (law center) on the website of Beijing University Center for Legal Information at http://law.chinalawinfo.com/newlaw2002/chl/index.asp?jd=1, retrieved on December 29, 2008.

Appendix 2

All Narcotic Drugs Related Administrative Regulations Issued after 1978*

1	Notice by the State Council on the Action of "Eleventh Five-Year Plan" of Prospering Frontier and Enriching People 国务院办公厅关于印发兴边富民行动"十一五"规划的通知	2007.06.09
2	Civil Administration Regulations 行政机关公务员处分条例	2007.04.22
3	Notice by the State Council on the Action of "Eleventh Five-Year Plan" of Minority Businesses 国务院办公厅关于印发少数民族事业"十一五"规划的通知	2007.02.27
4	Notice by the Office of the State Council on Circulating the Guidelines of Public Safety Education in Primary and Secondary Schools Issued by the Ministry of Education 国务院办公厅关于转发教育部中小学公共安全教育指导纲要的通知	2007.02.07
5	Notice by the Office of the State Council on Publishing China's Containment and Prevention of AIDS Action Plan (2006–2010) 国务院办公厅关于印发中国遏制与防治艾滋病行动计划（2006－2010年）的通知	2006.02.27
6	National Long and Mid-term Scientific and Technological Development Program (2006-2020) 国家中长期科学和技术发展规划纲要（2006－2020年）	2006.02.09
7	Notice by the State Council on Publishing the Program of Popular Science and Quality Action Plan (2006–2010–2020) 国务院关于印发全民科学素质行动计划纲要（2006－2010－2020年）的通知	2006.02.06
8	Regulation on the Prevention and Treatment of HIV/AIDS 艾滋病防治条例	2006.01.29
9	Ordinance of Entertainment Venues Management 娱乐场所管理条例(2006)	2006.01.29
10	National Contingency Plan For Environmental Emergencies 国家突发环境事件应急预案	2006.01.24

11	Notice by the Office of the State Council on Publishing the State Council's Opinion and Plan on 2006 Legislation 国务院办公厅印发关于做好国务院2006年立法工作的意见和国务院2006年立法工作计划的通知	2006.01.05
12	Regulation on the Administration of Precursor Chemicals 易制毒化学品管理条例	2005.08.26
13	Notice by the State Council on Strengthening HIV Prevention and Control 国务院关于切实加强艾滋病防治工作的通知	2004.03.16
14	Notice by the State Council on Circulating 2003-2007 Education Development Action Plan by the Ministry of Education 国务院批转教育部2003－2007年教育振兴行动计划的通知	2004.03.03
15	Opinions by the CCP Central Committee and State Council on further Strengthening and Improving Juveniles' Ideological and Moral Education 中共中央、国务院关于进一步加强和改进未成年人思想道德建设的若干意见	2004.02.26
16	People's Republic of China Regulations on the Management of River Traffic Safety 中华人民共和国内河交通安全管理条例	2002.06.28
17	Measures for the Administration of Chinese Citizens Overseas Travel 中国公民出国旅游管理办法	2002.05.27
18	Regulations on the Safety Administration of Dangerous Chemicals 危险化学品安全管理条例	2002.01.26
19	China Child Development Outline (2001–2010) 中国儿童发展纲要（２００１－２０１０年）	2001.05.22
20	Notice by the Office of the State Council on Circulating Primary Responsibilities of Main Units of the National Narcotics Control Commission 国务院办公厅关于转发国家禁毒委员会成员单位主要职责的通知	2001.01.05
21	Ordinance of Entertainment Venues Management (expired) 娱乐场所管理条例[失效]	1999.03.26
22	Notice by the State Council on Publishing General Administration of Customs Functions of Configuration, Internal Structure and Staffing 国务院办公厅关于印发海关总署职能配置内设机构和人员编制规定的通知	1998.08.10
23	Industrial Catalog for Foreign Investment (expired) 外商投资产业指导目录[失效]	1997.12.31

24	Answer by the State Council to the Provisional Administration Regulation on China Citizens' Self-Paid Overseas Travel (expired) 国务院关于《中国公民自费出国旅游管理暂行办法》的批复[失效]	1997.07.01
25	Measure on How to Carry Out Forced Detoxification 强制戒毒办法	1995.01.12
26	Notice by the CCP Central Committee and the State Council on Restructuring and Regulating Publications and Audio-Visual Market, and Cracking Down on Crimes 中共中央办公厅、国务院办公厅关于整顿、清理书报刊和音像市场，严厉打击犯罪活动的通知	1989.09.16
27	Notice by the State Council on Strengthening Administration of the Customs 国务院关于加强海关工作的通知	1988.03.10
28	Provisional Regulation on Management of Urban and Rural Individual Industrial and Commercial Businesses 城乡个体工商户管理暂行条例	1987.08.05
29	Notice by the State Council on Approving Dalian City's Plans on Further Opening-Up, Energy and Transportation Construction 国务院批转关于大连市进一步对外开放和能源、交通建设等问题的会议纪要的通知	1984.09.25
30	Notice by the State Council on Prohibiting Opium 国务院关于重申严禁鸦片烟毒的通知	1981.08.27

Note: * All search results of keywords "du pin" (narcotic drugs) in the database of "fagui zhongxin" (law center) on the website of Beijing University Center for Legal Information at http://law.chinalawinfo.com/newlaw2002/chl/index.asp, retrieved on December 29, 2008.

Appendix 3

All Narcotic Drugs Related Judicial Interpretations Issued after 1978*

1	Notice of the Supreme People's Court, the Supreme People's Procuratorate and the Ministry of Public Security on Printing and Distributing the Opinions on Several Issues Concerning the Application of Law in Handling Drug-related Criminal Cases 最高人民法院、最高人民检察院、公安部关于印发《办理毒品犯罪案件适用法律若干问题的意见》的通知	2007.12.18
2	Strengthening national trial work on major criminal cases to provide strong judicial guarantee for harmonious and stable development of economic society (excerpt of a speech given by Vice President of the Supreme People's Court Xiong Xuanguo) 全国加强刑事大案要案审判工作为经济社会和谐稳定发展提供有力司法保障(最高人民法院副院长熊选国讲话节录)	2007.06.15
3	Notice by the Supreme People's Procuratorate on issuing the revised "Regulation on Disciplinary Punishments of Prosecutor (Trial)" (2007) 最高人民检察院关于印发修改后的《检察人员纪律处分条例(试行)》的通知(2007)	2007.05.14
4	Notice of the Supreme People's Court on Printing and Distributing Some Opinions of the Supreme People's Court about Providing Judicial Protection for the Construction of Socialist Harmonious Society 最高人民法院印发《最高人民法院关于为构建社会主义和谐社会提供司法保障的若干意见》的通知	2007.01.15
5	Notice by the Supreme People's Procuratorate on issuing "Opinions by the SPP on Implementing the Combination of Lenience-Severity Criminal Trial Policy in Procuratorial Work" 最高人民检察院关于印发《最高人民检察院关于在检察工作中贯彻宽严相济刑事司法政策的若干意见》的通知	2007.01.15
6	Decision of the Supreme People's Court on the Exclusive Exercise of the Power to Review Death Penalty Cases 最高人民法院关于统一行使死刑案件核准权有关问题的决定	2006.12.28
7	Speech given by President of the Supreme People's Court Xiao Yang at the Criminal Judges' Conference of the SPC (excerpt) 最高人民法院院长肖扬在最高人民法院刑事法官大会上的讲话(节录)	2006.12.15

8	Strengthening criminal trial work to provide strong judicial guarantee for harmonious and stable development of economic society (excerpt of a speech given by President of the Supreme People's Court Xiao Yang at the fifth National Criminal Trial Conference) 全面加强刑事审判工作为经济社会和谐发展提供有力司法保障——最高人民法院院长肖扬在第五次全国刑事审判工作会议上的讲话(节录)	2006.11.07
9	Provisions on the Seizure and Freeze of Money and Property by the People's Procuratorates 最高人民检察院关于印发《人民检察院扣押、冻结款物工作规定》的通知	2006.03.27
10	Notice by the Supreme People's Court on Issuing "the Platform of the Second Five-year Reform of the People's Courts" 最高人民法院关于印发《人民法院第二个五年改革纲要》的通知	2005.10.26
11	Opinion of the Supreme People's Court on Application of Laws for the Trials of Criminal Cases Involving Robbery or Seizure 最高人民法院印发《关于审理抢劫、抢夺刑事案件适用法律若干问题的意见》的通知	2005.06.08
12	Some Opinions of the Supreme People's Court on Enhancing Judicial Capacities and Improving Judicial Proficiency 最高人民法院关于印发《关于增强司法能力、提高司法水平的若干意见》的通知	2005.04.01
13	Notice by the Supreme People's Procuratorate on Issuing the "Regulation on Disciplinary Punishments of Prosecutor (Trial)" 最高人民检察院关于印发《检察人员纪律处分条例(试行)》的通知	2004.06.21
14	Notice by the Supreme People's Procuratorate on Implementing the Spirit of the National Crackdown on Smuggling Conference and Severely Cracking Down on Smuggling Activities 最高人民检察院关于认真贯彻全国打击走私工作会议精神依法严厉打击走私犯罪活动的通知	2003.08.14
15	Notice by the Investigation and Supervision Office and the Public Prosecution Office of the Supreme People's Procuratorate on Intensifying Crackdown on Drug-Related Crimes 最高人民检察院侦查监督厅、公诉厅关于进一步加大对毒品犯罪打击力度的通知	2003.08.13
16	Answer by the Research Office of the Supreme People's Court on Ketamine as a Type of Narcotics 最高人民法院研究室关于氯胺酮能否认定为毒品问题的答复	2002.06.28
17	Opinion by the Supreme People's Procuratorate on Carrying out a Special Campaign on Prosecuting and Investigating Evil Forces 最高人民检察院关于开展"打黑除恶"立案监督专项行动的实施意见	2002.04.12

18	Decision by the Supreme People's Procuratorate on Abolition of some Judicial Interpretations and Regulatory Documents (2) 最高人民检察院关于废止部分司法解释和规范性文件的决定（2）	2002.02.25
19	Interpretation of some issues by the Supreme People's Court on Hearing Criminal Cases in Traffic Accident and Specific Application of Law 最高人民法院关于审理交通肇事刑事案件具体应用法律若干问题的解释	2000.11.15
20	Opinion by the Supreme People's Procuratorate on Giving Full Play to the Procuratorial Functions on Active Service for the Western Development 最高人民检察院关于充分发挥检察职能积极为西部大开发服务的意见	2000.11.06
21	Interpretation by the Supreme People's Court on Sentencing Standards in Drug-related Cases 最高人民法院关于审理毒品案件定罪量刑标准有关问题的解释	2000.06.06
22	Notice by the Supreme People's Court on Issuing "Minutes of the National Court Criminal Trial Work Conference for Safeguarding Stability in Rural Area" 最高人民法院关于印发《全国法院维护农村稳定刑事审判工作座谈会纪要》的通知	1999.10.27
23	Notice by the Supreme People's Procuratorate on Issuing "the Platform of Five-Year Development of Procuratorial Work" 最高人民检察院关于印发《检察工作五年发展规划》的通知	1999.02.08
24	Notice by the Supreme People's Court, Supreme People's Procuratorate, Ministry of Public Security, Ministry of Justice, and the General Administration of Customs on Investigative Organs' Application of Criminal Procedure in Handling Smuggling Cases 最高人民法院、最高人民检察院、公安部、司法部、海关总署关于走私犯罪侦查机关办理走私犯罪案件适用刑事诉讼程序若干问题的通知	1998.12.03
25	Notice by the Supreme People's Court on Further Carrying out Crackdown Campaign on Smuggling 最高人民法院关于深入开展严厉打击走私犯罪专项斗争的通知	1998.07.27
26	Decisions on some issues by the Supreme People's Court, Supreme People's Procuratorate, Ministry of Public Security, Ministry of State Security, Ministry of Justice, and the Legislative Affairs Committee of the Standing Committee of the National People's Congress on Application of Criminal Procedural Law 最高人民法院、最高人民检察院、公安部、国家安全部、司法部、全国人大常委会法制工作委员会关于刑事诉讼法实施中若干问题的规定	1998.01.19

27	Opinion by the Supreme People's Procuratorate on Applying Criminal Charges in Criminal Law Provisions 最高人民检察院关于适用刑法分则规定的犯罪的罪名的意见	1997.12.25
28	Decision by the Supreme People's Court on Implementing Established Criminal Charges of the Criminal Law of the People's Republic of China 最高人民法院关于执行《中华人民共和国刑法》确定罪名的规定	1997.12.11
29	Notice by the Supreme People's Court on Authorizing People's High Courts and Military Courts to Approve Death Sentences in Certain Cases (expired) 最高人民法院关于授权高级人民法院和解放军军事法院核准部分死刑案件的通知［失效］	1997.09.26
30	Notice by the Supreme People's Court on Authorizing the High Court of Guizhou Province to Approve Death Sentences in Certain Drug-related Cases (expired) 最高人民法院关于授权贵州省高级人民法院核准部分毒品犯罪死刑案件的通知［失效］	1997.06.23
31	Notice by the Supreme People's Procuratorate on Strengthening Prosecution and Arrest of Drug-related Crimes 最高人民检察院关于加强毒品犯罪批捕起诉工作的通知	1997.06.10
32	Notice by the Supreme People's Court on Taking Care of Trials of Drug-related Crimes in Anti-Drug Campaign 最高人民法院关于认真抓好禁毒专项斗争中审判工作的通知	1997.04.25
33	Notice by the PRC State Planning Commission, Supreme People's Court, Supreme People's Procuratorate, and the Ministry of Public Security on Issuing "the Management Measures of Evaluating Seized, Recovered or Forfeiture Goods" 国家计委、最高人民法院、最高人民检察院、公安部关于印发《扣押、追缴、没收物品估价管理办法》的通知	1997.04.22
34	Answer by the Supreme People's Procuratorate on dihydroetorphine hydrochloride as a Type of Narcotics and Application of Relevant Laws 最高人民检察院关于盐酸二氢埃托啡是否属毒品及适用法律问题的批复	1996.11.28
35	Notice by the Supreme People's Procuratorate on Issuing "the Ninth Five-year Plan of Procuratorial Work and the Guideline of Long-Term Goals for 2010" 最高人民检察院关于印发《检察工作"九五"计划和２０１０年远景目标纲要》的通知	1996.08.16
36	Notice by the Supreme People's Court on Issuing "Administrative Measures of Legal Documents of the People's Courts" 最高人民法院关于印发《人民法院公文处理办法》的通知	1996.04.09

37	Notice by the Supreme People's Court on Authorizing People's High Courts in Guangxi Zhuang Autonomous Region, Sichuan Province and Gansu Province to Approve Death Sentences in Certain Drug-related Cases (expired) 最高人民法院关于授权广西壮族自治区、四川省、甘肃省高级人民法院核准部分毒品犯罪死刑案件的通知〔失效〕	1996.03.19
38	Answer to some issues by the Supreme People's Court on Applying Laws in Drug-related Criminal Cases 最高人民法院关于办理毒品刑事案件适用法律几个问题的答复	1995.11.09
39	Notice by the Supreme People's Procuratorate on Issuing "Provisional Regulations on Training of Prosecutors", "Provisional Regulations on Examination of Prosecutors", "Provisional Regulations on Prosecutors' Resignation and Retirement", and "Provisional Regulations on Prosecutors' Disciplinary Actions" (expired) 最高人民检察院关于印发《检察官培训暂行规定》、《检察官考核暂行规定》、《检察官辞职、辞退暂行规定》、《检察官纪律处分暂行规定》的通知〔失效〕	1995.09.21
40	Interpretation of some Issues by the Supreme People's Court on Implementation of "the Decision on Narcotics Control by the Standing Committee of the National People's Congress" 最高人民法院关于执行《全国人民代表大会常务委员会关于禁毒的决定》的若干问题的解释	1994.12.20
41	Notice by the Supreme People's Court and Supreme People's Procuratorate on Abolition of some Joint Judicial Interpretations Published Prior to 1993 最高人民法院、最高人民检察院关于废止１９９３年底以前联合发布的部分司法解释的通知	1994.08.29
42	Notice by the Supreme People's Court on Authorizing People's High Court in Guangdong Province to Approve Death Sentences in Certain Drug-related Cases (expired) 最高人民法院关于授权广东省高级人民法院核准部分毒品犯罪死刑案件的通知〔失效〕	1993.08.18
43	Interpretation of a number of issues by the Supreme People's Court and the Supreme People's Procuratorate on Applying Specific Laws in Theft Cases 最高人民法院、最高人民检察院关于办理盗窃案件具体应用法律若干问题的解释	1992.12.11
44	Answer by the Supreme People's Court on Applying Laws to Minors who are older than 14 years old but younger than 16 years old and involved in Smuggling, Selling, Transporting, and Manufacturing Narcotics 最高人民法院关于已满十四岁不满十六岁的人犯走私、贩卖、运输、制造毒品罪应当如何适用法律问题的批复	1992.05.18

45	Telephonic Answer by the Research Office of the Supreme People's Court on How to Correctly Understand and Apply Article 13 of "the Decision on Narcotics Control by the Standing Committee of the National People's Congress 最高人民法院研究室关于正确理解和执行全国人大常委会《关于禁毒的决定》第十三条规定的电话答复	1992.01.11
46	Notice by the Supreme People's Court on Studying, Promoting and Applying "Law of the People's Republic of China on Protection of Minors" 最高人民法院关于学习宣传贯彻《中华人民共和国未成年人保护法》的通知	1991.12.24
47	Notice by the Supreme People's Court on Issuing a Speech Given by Vice President of the SPC Zhu Mingshan at the Second National Court Records Work Conference and the "Management Measures of People's Court Records" 最高人民法院关于印发祝铭山副院长在第二次全国法院档案工作会议上的讲话及《人民法院档案管理办法》等规章制度的通知	1991.12.24
48	Minutes of the Supreme People's Court on Trial Work Conference of Drug-related Crimes by People's Courts in 12 Provinces and Autonomous Regions 最高人民法院关于十二省、自治区法院审理毒品犯罪案件工作会议纪要	1991.12.17
49	Notice by the Supreme People's Court on Authorizing People's High Court in Yunnan Province to Approve Death Sentences in Certain Drug-related Cases (expired) 最高人民法院关于授权云南省高级人民法院核准部分毒品犯罪死刑案件的通知［失效］	1991.06.06
50	Answer by the Supreme People's Procuratorate on How to Examine Issues on Sale of Counterfeit Narcotics in Drug-related Cases 最高人民检察院关于贩卖假毒品案件如何定性问题的批复	1991.04.02
51	Notice by the Supreme People's Procuratorate on Strict Enforcement of the "Decision on Narcotics Control" and "Decision on Punishing Criminals Who Smuggle, Manufacture, Traffic, and Disseminate Pornographic Materials" by the Standing Committee of the National People's Congress 最高人民检察院关于严格执行全国人大常务委员会《关于禁毒的决定》、《关于惩治走私、制作、贩卖、传播淫秽物品的犯罪分子的决定》的通知	1991.01.05
52	Notice by the Supreme People's Court on Strict Enforcement of the "Decision on Narcotics Control by the Standing Committee of the National People's Congress" and Severely Punishing Criminals 最高人民法院关于严格执行《全国人民代表大会常务委员会关于禁毒的决定》严惩毒品犯罪分子的通知	1991.01.03

53	Decision by the Supreme People's Court and the Supreme People's Procuratorate on Treating Illegal Cultivation of Poppies as Manufacturing Illegal Narcotics (expired) 最高人民法院、最高人民检察院关于非法种植罂粟柰构成犯罪的以制造毒品论处的规定［失效］	1990.07.09
54	Telephonic Answer by the Supreme People's Court to Issues on Confiscating Narcotics 最高人民法院研究室关于如何处理没收毒品问题的电话答复	1990.05.09
55	Notice by the Supreme People's Court on Assisting Public Security Organs in Carrying out the Anti-Six-Evils Campaign 最高人民法院关于配合公安机关开展除"六害"工作的通知	1989.11.13
56	Minutes of the National High People's Court Forum 全国高级人民法院院长座谈会纪要	1989.05.11
57	Answer by the Supreme People's Procuratorate on Applying Laws to Criminals who sell to others Opium or other Narcotics inherited from Fathers or Grandfathers (expired) 最高人民检察院关于向他人出卖父辈祖辈遗留下来的鸦片以及其他毒品如何适用法律的批复［失效］	1988.08.12
58	Telephonic Answer by the Research Office of the Supreme People's Court on Issues with regard to Drug-related Offenses 最高人民法院研究室关于毒品犯罪问题的电话答复	1988.01.03
59	Answer by the Supreme People's Court on Death Penalty Sentencing Standards of Drug Trafficking 最高人民法院关于《贩卖毒品死刑案件的量刑标准》的答复	1987.07.15
60	Notice by the Supreme People's Court, Supreme People's Procuratorate, Ministry of Health, and Ministry of Public Security on Issuing "Cases of Selling Coffee Sodium Drugs" 最高人民法院、最高人民检察院、卫生部、公安部关于印发《贩卖安钠咖毒品罪的案例》的通知	1986.03.05
61	Notice by the Supreme People's Court, Supreme People's Procuratorate, Ministry of Public Security, and Ministry of Justice on Severely Cracking Down Manufacturing and Selling Counterfeit Drugs, Narcotics and Toxic Food that Seriously Endanger People's Lives and Health 最高人民法院、最高人民检察院、公安部、司法部、关于抓紧从严打击制造、贩卖假药、毒品和有毒食品等严重危害人民生命健康的犯罪活动的通知	1985.07.12
62	Notice by the Supreme People's Court on Forwarding from the Ministry of Finance "the Notice on Reiterating that the Country will turn over to the Treasury income confiscated" 最高人民法院关于转发财政部《关于重申国家罚没收入一律上缴国库的通知》的通知	1985.04.13

63	Notice by the Supreme People's Court and the National Archives on Issuing "Measures on Filing Lawsuit Documents of the People's Court", "Management Measures on Filing Records of the People's Court", and "Custodial Statutory Limitations of Filing Records of the People's Court" 最高人民法院、国家档案局颁发《人民法院诉讼文书立卷归档办法》、《人民法院诉讼档案管理办法》和《关于人民法院诉讼档案保管期限的规定》的通知	1984.01.04
64	Notice by the Supreme People's Procuratorate on Forwarding "the State Council's Approval of the Ministry of Public Security's Resolution on Cracking down Criminals who write letters to and communicate with the KMT's secret services" 最高人民检察院转发《国务院批转公安部关于坚决打击向国民党特务机关写信挂钩的犯罪分子的通知》的通知	1981.09.14
65	Notice by the Supreme People's Court on Issuing "Minutes of the Work Conference by some People's Courts on Drug-related Trials 最高人民法院印发《全国部分法院审理毒品犯罪案件工作座谈会纪要》的通知	Date not available
66	最高人民法院印发《全国部分法院审理毒品犯罪案件工作座谈会纪要》的通知 (same as above)	Date not available

Note: * All search results of keywords "du pin" (narcotic drugs) in the database of "fagui zhongxin" (law center) on the website of Beijing University Center for Legal Information at http://law.chinalawinfo.com/newlaw2002/chl/index.asp, retrieved on December 29, 2008.

Appendix 4

Selected Texts of Narcotics Drug-Related Laws Passed after 1978

Drug Control Law of the People's Republic of China

(Adopted at the Seventh Meeting of the Standing Committee of the Sixth National People's Congress on September 20, 1984; revised at the Twentieth Meeting of the Standing Committee of the Ninth National People's Congress on February 28, 2001 and promulgated by Order No.45 of the President of the People's Republic of China on February 28, 2001)

Contents

Chapter IX Legal Liabilities

Article 73 Any drug manufacturer or distributor that, without obtaining Drug Manufacturing Certificate, Drug Distribution Certificate or Pharmaceutical Preparation Certificate for Medical Institution, manufactures or distributes drugs shall be banned, the drugs illegally produced or sold and the illegal gains therefrom shall be confiscated, and they shall also be fined not less than two times but not more than five times the value of the drugs (including the drugs sold and not sold, the same below). If a crime is constituted, criminal liabilities shall be investigated in accordance with law.

Article 74 Where counterfeit drugs are produced or sold, the drugs illegally produced or sold and the illegal gains shall be confiscated, and a fine not less than two times but not more than five times the value of the said drugs shall be imposed. The approval documents, if any, shall be withdrawn and an order shall be given to suspend production or business operation for rectification. If the circumstances are serious, the Drug Manufacturing Certificate, Drug Distribution Certificate or Pharmaceutical Preparation Certificate for Medical Institution shall be revoked. If a crime is constituted, criminal liabilities shall be investigated in accordance with law.

Article 75 Where substandard drugs are produced or sold, the drugs illegally produced or sold and the illegal gains shall be confiscated, and a fine not less than, but not more than three times, the value of the drugs shall also be imposed. If the circumstances are serious, an order shall be given to suspend production or business operation for rectification, or the drug approval documents shall be withdrawn and the Drug Manufacturing Certificate, the Drug Distribution Certificate, or the Pharmaceutical Preparation Certificate for Medical Institution shall be revoked. If a crime is constituted, criminal liabilities shall be investigated in accordance with law.

Chapter VI Control over Drug Packaging	Article 76 Where enterprises or other institutions are engaged in production or sale of counterfeit or substandard drugs, if the circumstances are serious, the persons directly in charge and the other persons directly responsible shall be prohibited from engaging in the drug production or distribution within 10 years.
Chapter VII Control over Drug Pricing and Advertising	
Chapter VIII Inspection of Drugs	The drug substances, excipients, packaging materials and manufacturing equipment specially used for producing counterfeit or substandard drugs by any producer shall be confiscated.
Chapter IX Legal Liabilities	Article 77 Anyone who knows or should know that the drugs are counterfeit or substandard drugs provides conveniences such as transportation, keeping or storage of the drugs, all the earnings therefrom shall be confiscated, and a fine not less than 50 per cent of, but not more than 3 times, the amount of the illegal earnings shall also be imposed. If a crime is constituted, criminal liabilities shall be investigated in accordance with law.
Chapter X Supplementary Provisions	
* Selected parts included here. A full version of the law is available at http://www.npc.gov.cn/englishnpc/Law/2007-12/13/content_1383969.htm	Article 78 The quality testing results provided by the drug testing institution shall be contained in the penalty notification regarding counterfeit and substandard drugs, except in cases specified in the provisions of Subparagraphs (1), (2), (5) and (6) of the third paragraph of Article 48 and the third paragraph of Article 49 of this Law.
	Article 79 Any drug manufacturer, drug distributor, institution for non-clinical safety study, or institution for drug clinical trial that does not implement the GMP, GSP, GLP or GCP according to regulations shall be given a disciplinary warning and shall be instructed to rectify within a time limit. If it fails to do so, it shall be instructed to suspend production or business operation or other work for rectification and shall also be fined not less than RMB 5,000 yuan but not more than 20,000 yuan. If the circumstances are serious, the Drug Manufacturing Certificate, Drug Distribution Certificate or the qualifications of the institution for drug clinical trial shall be annulled.
	Article 80 Any drug manufacturer, drug distributor or medical institution that, in violation of the provisions of Article 34 of this Law, purchases drugs from the enterprises without Drug Manufacturing Certificate or Drug Distribution Certificate shall be instructed to rectify, the drugs illegally purchased shall be confiscated, and it shall be fined not less than two times but not more than five times the value of the drugs purchased; the illegal gains, if any, shall be confiscated. If the circumstances are serious, the Drug Manufacturing Certificate, Drug Distribution Certificate, or the license for the medical

institution shall be revoked.

Article 81 If any enterprise that imports drugs to which import drug license has been granted fails to register, in accordance with the provisions of this Law, for the record with the drug regulatory department in the place where the port is located and drug importation is permitted, it shall be given a disciplinary warning and be instructed to rectify within a time limit; if it fails to do so, the import drug license shall be revoked.

Article 82 If anyone falsifies, alters, trades in, rents out or lends the license or drug approval documents, the illegal gains shall be confiscated and a fine not less than, but not more than three times, the amount of the illegal gains shall be imposed; if there are no illegal gains, a fine not less than 20,000 yuan but not more than 100,000 yuan shall be imposed. If the circumstances are serious, the Drug Manufacturing Certificate, Drug Distribution Certificate or Pharmaceutical Preparation Certificate for Medical Institution of the party that sells, rents out or lends it shall be revoked, or the drug approval documents shall be withdrawn. If a crime is constituted, criminal liabilities shall be investigated in accordance with law.

Article 83 If anyone, in violation of the provisions of this Law, obtains the Drug Manufacturing Certificate, Drug Distribution Certificate, Pharmaceutical Preparation Certificate for Medical Institutions, or drug approval documents by providing false certificates, documents and data, or samples, or by other fraudulent means, the said certificates shall be revoked and the documents shall be withdrawn, his applications for such certificates or approval documents shall be rejected within five years, and a fine not less than 10,000 yuan but not more than 30,000 yuan shall also be imposed.

Article 84 Any medical institution that sells its own dispensed pharmaceutical preparations on the market shall be instructed to rectify, the preparations for illegal sale shall be confiscated, and a fine not less than, but not more than three times, the value of the said preparations shall be imposed, and the illegal gains, if any, shall be confiscated.

Article 85 Any drug distributor that violates the provisions of Articles 18 and 19 of this Law shall be instructed to rectify and be given a disciplinary warning. If the circumstances are serious, the Drug Distribution Certificate shall be revoked.

Article 86 Drugs with labels or marks not in conformity with the provisions of Article 54 of this Law shall be treated as counterfeit or substandard drugs, and in addition, an instruction for rectification and a disciplinary warning shall be given. If the circumstances are serious, the approval documents for the drugs shall be withdrawn.

Article 87 Where a drug testing institution issues a false testing report, if it constitutes a crime, criminal liabilities shall be investigated in accordance with law; if it does not constitute a crime, the institution shall be instructed to rectify and be given a disciplinary warning, and also be fined not less than 30,000 yuan but not more than 50,000 yuan. The persons directly in charge and the other persons directly responsible shall, in accordance with law, be punished with demotion, dismissal, or expulsion and also be fined not more than 30,000 yuan. The illegal gains, if any, shall be confiscated. If the circumstances are serious, the institution shall be disqualified for testing. If the testing result issued by the drug testing institution is not true to fact and losses are thus occasioned, the institution shall bear corresponding liability of compensation for the losses.

Article 88 The administrative sanctions prescribed in Article 73 through Article 87 of this Law shall be determined by the drug regulatory departments at or above the county level according to the division of responsibility defined by the drug regulatory department under the State Council. Revocation of the Drug Manufacturing Certificate, Drug Distribution Certificate and Pharmaceutical Preparation Certificate for Medical Institution or withdrawal of the drug approval documents shall be determined by the department that issued the certificate or the approval documents.

Article 89 Any violation of the provisions of Article 55, 56 or 57 of this Law governing the control over drug pricing shall be punished pursuant to the provisions of the Pricing Law of the People's Republic of China.

Article 90 Drug manufacturers, drug distributors or medical institutions that offer or accept, in private, the rake-offs or other benefits in the course of purchasing and selling drugs or drug manufacturers, drug distributors or their agents that offer money or things of value or other benefits to leading members, drug purchasers, physicians, or other related persons of the medical institutions where their drugs are used shall be fined not less than 10,000 yuan but not more than 200,000 yuan by the administrative department for industry and commerce, and the illegal gains, if any, shall be confiscated. If the circumstances are serious, the said department shall revoke the business licenses of the drug manufacturers or drug distributors and inform the drug regulatory department of the matter, which shall revoke their Drug Manufacturing Certificate, or Drug Distribution Certificate. If a crime is constituted, criminal liabilities shall be investigated in accordance with law.

Article 91 Any leading members, purchasers or other related persons of drug manufacturers or distributors that, in the course of drug purchasing or selling, accept money or things of value or other benefits offered by other manufacturers, distributors or their agents shall be given sanctions according to law, and the illegal gains shall be confiscated. If a crime is constituted, criminal liabilities shall be investigated in accordance with law.

Leading members, drug purchasers, physicians or other related persons of medical institutions who accept money or things of value or other benefits offered by drug manufacturers, drug distributors or their agents shall be given sanctions by the administrative department for health or the institutions to which they belong, and the illegal gains shall be confiscated. With regard to licensed physicians who seriously violate laws, the administrative department for health shall revoke their licenses for medical practice. If a crime is constituted, criminal liabilities shall be investigated in accordance with law.

Article 92 Any violation of the provisions of this Law related to the control over drug advertising shall be punished pursuant to the provisions of the Advertisement Law of the People's Republic of China, the drug regulatory department that issues the advertisement approval number shall withdraw it and shall, within one year, reject any application for approval of advertising for the drug in question. If a crime is constituted, criminal liabilities shall be investigated in accordance with law.

Where a drug regulatory department does not perform its duty of drug advertisement examination in accordance with law and the advertisement approved for issuance contains false information or other content violating laws or administrative regulations, administrative sanctions shall, in accordance with law, be given to the persons directly in charge and the other persons directly responsible. If a crime is constituted, criminal liabilities shall be investigated in accordance with law.

Article 93 Drug manufacturers, drug distributors or medical institutions that violate the provisions of this Law and thus cause harm and losses to users of drugs shall bear the liability of compensation in accordance with law.

Article 94 Any drug regulatory department that violates the provisions of this Law and commits one of the following acts shall be instructed by the competent authority at the next higher level or the supervisory body to recall the certificates unlawfully issued or to withdraw the drug approval documents, and administrative sanctions shall be given to the persons directly in charge and the other persons directly responsible in accordance with law. If a crime is constituted, criminal liabilities shall be investigated in accordance with law:

(1) issuing the GMP or GSP certificates to the enterprises that do not comply with the corresponding requirements, failing to perform, in accordance with regulations, the duty of follow-up inspections in respect of the enterprises that have obtained the certificates, or failing to instruct, in accordance with law, the enterprises not complying with the requirements to rectify or withdraw their certificates;

(2) issuing the Drug Manufacturing Certificate, Drug Distribution Certificate or Pharmaceutical Preparation Certificate for Medical Institution to the enterprises or institutions not complying with the statutory requirements;

(3) issuing an Import Drug License to the drug not complying with the requirements for import; or

(4) granting approval for conducting a clinical trial, issuing a New Drug Certificate or a drug approval number, where the requirements for clinical trial or drug production are not fulfilled.

Article 95 If any drug regulatory department, drug testing institution established by the department or institution specially engaged in drug testing designated by the department is involved in drug production or distribution, it shall be instructed by the authority at the next higher level or the supervisory body to rectify, and the illegal gains, if any, shall be confiscated. If the circumstances are serious, administrative sanctions shall be given to the persons directly in charge and the other persons directly responsible in accordance with law.

Any staff member of the drug regulatory department, drug testing institution established by the department or institution specially engaged in drug testing designated by the department who is involved in drug production or distribution shall be given an administrative sanction in accordance with law.

Article 96 If any drug regulatory department or drug testing institution established or designated by the department, in violation of law, collects testing fees for supervision over drug testing shall be instructed by the relevant government department to return the fees, and administrative sanctions shall be given to the persons directly in charge and the other persons directly responsible in accordance with law. Any drug testing institution that collects testing fees in violation of law, if the circumstances are serious, shall be disqualified for drug testing.

Article 97 Drug regulatory departments shall, in accordance with law, perform their duties of supervision and inspection and shall see to it that the enterprises holding the Drug Manufacturing Certificate or Drug Distribution Certificate engage in drug production or drug distribution in accordance with the provisions of this Law. Where enterprises holding the Drug Manufacturing Certificate or Drug Distribution Certificate produce or sell counterfeit or substandard drugs, the legal liabilities of such enterprises shall be investigated and, in addition, the persons directly in charge and the other persons directly responsible of the drug regulatory departments who neglect their duty or commit dereliction of duty shall be given administrative sanctions in accordance with law. If a crime is constituted, criminal liabilities shall be investigated in accordance with law.

Article 98 The drug regulatory department shall instruct the drug regulatory department at a lower level to put right, within a time limit, the administrative action taken in violation of this Law, and it shall have the power to alter or annul the action which is not put right within the time limit.

Article 99 Anyone responsible for drug regulation who abuses his power, engages in malpractice for personal gain or neglects his duty, if it constitutes a crime, shall be investigated for criminal liabilities in accordance with law; if it is not serious enough to constitute a crime, he shall be given administrative sanctions in accordance with law. Article 100 Where a Drug Manufacturing Certificate or Drug Distribution Certificate is revoked in accordance with this Law, the drug regulatory department shall notify the administrative department for industry and commerce to alter or cancel the registration.

Article 101 The value of products mentioned in this Chapter shall be calculated on the basis of the marked prices of the drugs illegally produced or sold; where there is no marked price, the value shall be calculated according to the market prices of drugs of the same kind.

The Anti-Money Laundering Law of the People's Republic of China (Adopted at the Twenty-fourth Meeting of the Standing Committee of the	Chapter I General Provisions Article 2 ... anti-money laundering refers to the adoption of relevant measures according to the provisions of this Law to prevent any money laundering which is designed to cover up or conceal, by various means, the sources and nature of the criminal gains and proceeds derived from

Tenth National People's Congress of the People's Republic of China on October 31, 2006, is hereby promulgated and shall go into effect as of January 1, 2007)

Contents

Chapter I General Provisions

Chapter II Supervision over Anti-Money Laundering

Chapter III The Obligation of Financial Institutions to Fight Against Money Laundering

Chapter IV Anti-Money Laundering Investigation

Chapter V International Cooperation in Anti-Money Laundering

Chapter VI Legal Responsibility

Chapter VII Supplementary Provisions

* Selected parts included here. A full version of the law is available at http://www.npc.gov. cn/englishnpc/Law/2007- 12/13/content_1384114. htm;

drug-related crimes, crimes committed by organizations of the nature of criminal gangs, terrorist crimes, crimes of smuggling, graft and bribery, crimes of disrupting the order of financial management, crimes of financial fraud, etc.

Chapter VI Legal Responsibility

Article 30 Where a staff member of the administrative department in charge of anti-money laundering or of any other department or authority shouldering the duty of supervision over anti-money laundering according to law commits any of the following acts, he shall be given an administrative sanction according to law:

(1) in violation of relevant provisions, conducting inspection, investigation or adopting temporary freezing measures;

(2) divulging State secrets, business secrets or other persons' privacy which he comes to know in anti-money laundering;

(3) in violation of relevant provisions, imposing administrative penalties on relevant institutions or persons; or

(4) other acts committed when failing to perform his duties according to law.

Article 31 Where a financial institution commits one of the following acts, the administrative department in charge of anti-money laundering under the State Council or its authorized dispatched body at or above the level of a city divided into districts shall order it to rectify within a time limit; if the circumstances are serious, it shall propose that the financial regulatory body concerned order, according to law, the financial institution to give a disciplinary sanction to the director or senior manager who is directly in charge or any other person who is directly responsible:

(1) failing to establish an internal control system for anti-money laundering according to relevant provisions;

(2) failing to establish a special body for anti-money laundering or designate an internal division for anti-money laundering; or

(3) failing to conduct, among its employees, training in anti-money laundering as is required by relevant provisions.

Article 32 Where a financial institution commits one of the following acts, the administrative department in charge of anti-money laundering under the State Council or its dispatched body at or above the level of a city divided into districts shall order it to rectify within a time limit; if the circumstances are serious, a fine of not less than 200,000 yuan but not more than 500,000 yuan shall be imposed on the financial institution, and a fine of not less than 10,000 yuan but not more than 50,000 yuan shall be imposed on the director or senior manager who is directly in charge or any other person who is directly responsible:

(1) failing to perform the obligation of distinguishing its clients' identities, as is required by relevant provisions;

(2) failing to preserve the data of its clients' identities and records of transactions, as is required by relevant provisions;

(3) failing to submit report on transactions involving large sums of money or on dubious transactions, as is required by relevant provisions;

(4) making transactions with a client whose identity is unclear or opening an anonymous or pseudonymous account therefore;

(5) divulging any relevant information in violation of confidentiality rules;

(6) refusing to accept to or obstructing inspection of or investigation into money laundering; or

(7) refusing to provide data needed for investigation or intentionally providing false data.

Where a financial institution commits any of the aforesaid acts and thus leads to the consequence of money laundering, it shall be fined not less than 500,000 yuan but not more than 5,000,000 yuan, and the director or senior manager who is directly in charge or any other person who is directly responsible shall be fined not less than 50,000

	yuan but not more than 500,000 yuan; if the circumstances are especially serious, the administrative department in charge of anti-money laundering may propose that the financial regulatory body concerned order the financial institution to suspend business for rectification, or revoke its business license. With regard to the director or senior manager who is directly in charge of the financial institution or any other person who is directly responsible that finds himself in the circumstances mentioned in the preceding two paragraphs, the administrative department in charge of anti-money laundering may propose that the financial regulatory body concerned order, according to law, the financial institution to give a disciplinary sanction thereto or that it, in accordance with law, disqualify him for the post and prohibit him from working in the financial sector. Article 33 Where a person violates the provisions of this Law, which constitutes a crime, he shall be investigated for criminal responsibility according to law.
Amendment VI to the Revision of the Criminal Law of the People's Republic of China (Deliberated at the Twenty-second Meeting of the Standing Committee of the Tenth National People's Congress on June 29, 2006, promulgated and took effect on June 29, 2006) * Available at http://www.lawinfochina.com/law/display.asp?db=1&id=5300, retrieved on December 28, 2008.	Article 16: Article 191 Item 1 of the Criminal Law is amended as: "Whoever, while clearly knowing that the funds are proceeds illegally obtained from drug-related crimes, from crimes committed by mafias, or smugglers, or from terrorist crimes, crimes of graft and bribery, crimes of sabotaging financial management and order, or crimes of financial fraud, and gains derived therefrom, commits any of the following acts in order to cover up or conceal the source or nature of the funds shall, in addition to being confiscated of the said proceeds and gains, be sentenced to fixed-term imprisonment of no more than five years or criminal detention, and shall also, or shall only, be fined no less than 5% but no more than 20% of the amount of money laundered; if the circumstances are serious, he shall be sentenced to fixed-term imprisonment of no less than five years but no more than ten years, and shall also be fined no less than 5% but no more than 20% of the amount of money laundered: (I) providing fund accounts; (II) helping exchange property into cash or any financial negotiable instruments;

	(III) helping transfer capital through transferring accounts or any other form of settlement;
	(IV) helping remit funds to the outside of the territory of China;
	(V) covering up or concealing by any other means the source or nature of the illegally obtained proceeds and the gains derived therefrom."
	"Where an entity commits the crime as mentioned in the preceding paragraph, it shall be fined, and any of the persons who are directly in charge and the other persons who are directly responsible for the crime shall be sentenced to fixed-term imprisonment of no more than five years or criminal detention; if the circumstances are serious, any of them shall be sentenced to fixed-term imprisonment of no less than five years but no more than ten years."
Law of the People's Republic of China on Penalties for Administration of Public Security (Adopted at the Seventeenth Meeting of the Standing Committee of the Tenth National People's Congress on August 28, 2005) Contents Chapter I General Provisions Chapter II Types of Penalties and Their Application Chapter III Acts Against the Administration of Public Security and Penalties Section 1 Acts Disturbing Public Order and Penalties	Article 2 A person who disturbs public order, endangers public safety, infringes on the rights of person and property or hampers social administration, which is harmful to the society and which, according to the provisions of the Criminal Law of the People's Republic of China, constitutes a crime, shall be investigated for criminal responsibility according to law; and if such an act is not serious enough for criminal punishment, the public security organ shall impose on him a penalty for administration of public security according to this Law. Article 71 A person who commits one of the following acts shall be detained for not less than 10 days but not more than 15 days and may, in addition, be fined not more than 3,000 yuan; and if the circumstances are relatively minor, he shall be detained for not more than five days or be fined not more than 500 yuan: (1) illegally cultivating opium poppies of less than 500 plants or a small number of mother plants of other narcotic drugs; (2) illegally buying, selling, transporting, carrying or possessing a small quantity of the seeds or seedlings of the mother plants of narcotic drugs, such as the opium poppy, which have not been inactivated; or (3) illegally transporting, buying, selling, storing or using a small quantity of opium poppy shells.

Section 2 Acts Impairing Public Security and Penalties	A person who commits the act specified in Subparagraph (1) of the preceding paragraph uproots the plants, of his own accord, before they are ripe shall not be penalized.
Section 3 Acts Infringing upon Rights of the Person and of Property and Penalties	Article 72 A person who commits one of the following acts shall be detained for not less than 10 days but not more than 15 days and may, in addition, be fined not more than 2,000 yuan; and if the circumstances are relatively minor, he shall be detained for not more than five days or be fined not more than 500 yuan:
Section 4 Acts Impeding Social Administration and Penalties	(1) illegally possessing opium of less than 200 grams, heroin or methamphetamine of less than 10 grams or a small amount of other narcotic drugs;
Chapter IV Procedure of Penalties	(2) providing another person with narcotic drugs;
Section 1 Investigation	(3) ingesting or injecting narcotic drugs; or
Section 2 Decision	(4) coercing a medical worker to prescribe narcotic drugs or psychotropic substances or cheating the worker into doing the same.
Section 3 Execution	Article 73 A person who instigates, lures or cheats another person to or into drug ingestion or injection shall be detained for not less than 10 days but not more than 15 days and shall, in addition, be fined not less than 500 yuan but not more than 2,000 yuan.
Chapter V Law Enforcement Supervision	
Chapter VI Supplementary Provisions	
* Selected parts are included here. The full version of the law is available at http://www. npc.gov.cn/englishnpc/ Law/2007-12/13/content_ 1384114.htm	
Revision of the Criminal Law of the People's Republic of China	Section 7 Crimes of Smuggling, Trafficking in, Transporting and Manufacturing Narcotic Drugs
(Revised at the Fifth Session of the Eighth National People's Congress	Article 347 Whoever smuggles, traffics in, transports or manufactures narcotic drugs, regardless of the quantity involved, shall be investigated for criminal responsibility

on March 14, 1997, promulgated by Order No. 83 of the Chairman of the People's Republic of China on March 14, 1997, and effective as of October 1, 1997)

Contents

and given criminal punishment.

Whoever smuggles, traffics in, transports or manufactures narcotic drugs and falls under any of the following categories, shall be sentenced to fixed-term imprisonment of 15 years, life imprisonment or death and also to confiscation of property:

(1) persons who smuggle, traffic in, transport or manufacture opium of not less than 1,000 grams, heroin or methylaniline of not less than 50 grams or other narcotic drugs of large quantities;

(2) ringleaders of gangs engaged in smuggling, trafficking in, transporting or manufacturing narcotic drugs;

(3) persons who shield with arms the smuggling, trafficking in, transporting or manufacturing of narcotic drugs;

(4) persons who violently resist inspection, detention or arrest to a serious extent; or

(5) persons involved in organized international drug trafficking.

Whoever smuggles, traffics in, transports or manufactures opium of not less than 200 grams but less than 1,000 grams, or heroin or methylaniline of not less than 10 grams but less than 50 grams or any other narcotic drugs of relatively large quantities shall be sentenced to fixed-term imprisonment of not less than seven years and shall also be fined.

Whoever smuggles, traffics in, transports or manufactures opium of less than 200 grams, or heroin or methylaniline of less than 10 grams or any other narcotic drugs of small quantities shall be sentenced to fixed-term imprisonment of not more than three years, criminal detention or public surveillance and shall also be fined; if the circumstances are serious, he shall be sentenced to fixed-term imprisonment of not less than three years but not more than seven years and shall also be fined.

Where a unit commits any crime mentioned in the preceding three paragraphs, it shall be fined, and the persons who are directly in charge and the other persons

Section 5 The Death Penalty	who are directly responsible for the offence shall be punished in accordance with the provisions of the preceding three paragraphs respectively.
Section 6 Fines	Whoever makes use of minors or aids and abets them to smuggle, traffic in, transport or manufacture narcotic drugs or sells narcotic drugs to minors shall be given a heavier punishment.
Section 7 Deprivation of Political Rights	
Section 8 Confiscation of Property	With respect to persons who have repeatedly smuggled, trafficked in, transported or manufactured narcotic drugs and have not been dealt with, the quantity of narcotic drugs thus involved shall be computed cumulatively.
Chapter IV The Concrete Application of Punishments	Article 348 Whoever illegally possesses opium of not less than 1,000 grams, or heroin or methylaniline of not less than 50 grams, or any other narcotic drugs of large quantities shall be sentenced to fixed-term imprisonment of not less than seven years or life imprisonment and shall also be fined; whoever illegally possesses opium of not less than 200 grams but less than 1,000 grams, or heroin or methylaniline of not less than 10 grams but less than 50 grams or any other narcotic drugs of relatively large quantities shall be sentenced to fixed-term imprisonment of not more than three years, criminal detention or public surveillance and shall also be fined; if the circumstances are serious, he shall be sentenced to fixed-term imprisonment of not less than three years but not more than seven years and shall also be fined.
Section 1 Sentencing	
Section 2 Recidivists	
Section 3 Voluntary	
Surrender and Meritorious Performance	
Section 4 Combined Punishment for Several Crimes	Article 349 Whoever shields offenders engaged in smuggling, trafficking in, transporting or manufacturing of narcotic drugs or whoever harbors, transfers or covers up, for such offenders, narcotic drugs or their pecuniary and other gains from such criminal activities shall be sentenced to fixed-term imprisonment of not more than three years, criminal detention or public surveillance; if the circumstances are serious, he shall be sentenced to fixed-term imprisonment of not less than three years but not more than 10 years.
Section 5 Suspension of Sentence	
Section 6 Commutation of Punishment	
Section 7 Parole	Anti-drug officers or functionaries of a State organ who shield or cover up offenders engaged in smuggling, trafficking in, transporting or manufacturing of narcotic drugs shall be given a heavier punishment in accordance with the provisions of the preceding paragraph.
Section 8 Limitation	
Chapter V Other Provisions	
Part Two Specific Provisions	Conspirators to the crimes mentioned in the preceding two paragraphs shall be regarded as joint offenders in the crime of smuggling, trafficking in, transporting or manufacturing of narcotic drugs and punished as such.
Chapter I Crimes of	Article 350 Whoever, in violation of the regulations of

Endangering National Security

Chapter II Crimes of Endangering Public Security

Chapter III Crimes of Disrupting the Order of the Socialist Market Economy

Section 1 Crimes of Producing and Marketing Fake or Substandard Commodities

Section 2 Crimes of Smuggling

Section 3 Crimes of Disrupting the Order of Administration of Companies and Enterprises

Section 4 Crimes of Disrupting the Order of Financial Administration

Section 5 Crimes of Financial Fraud

Section 6 Crimes of Jeopardizing Administration of Tax Collection

Section 7 Crimes of Infringing on Intellectual Property Rights

Section 8 Crimes of Disrupting Market Order

the State, illegally transports or carries into or out of the territory of China acetic anhydride, ether, chloroform or any other raw material or elixir used in the manufacture of narcotic drugs or, in violation of the regulations of the State, illegally buys or sells the substances mentioned above shall be sentenced to fixed-term imprisonment of not more than three years, criminal detention or public surveillance and shall also be fined; if the amount involved is large, he shall be sentenced to fixed-term imprisonment of not less than three years but not more than 10 years and shall also be fined.

Whoever provides another person with the substances mentioned in the preceding paragraph, while clearly knowing that the person manufactures narcotic drugs, shall be regarded as a joint offender in the crime of manufacturing narcotic drugs and punished as such.

Where a unit commits any crime mentioned in the preceding two paragraphs, it shall be fined, and the persons who are directly in charge and the other persons who are directly responsible for the offence shall be punished in accordance with the provisions of the preceding two paragraphs.

Article 351 Whoever illegally cultivates mother plants of narcotic drugs, such as opium poppy and marijuana, shall be forced to uproot them. Whoever falls under any of the following categories shall be sentenced to fixed-term imprisonment of not more than five years, criminal detention or public surveillance and shall also be fined:

(1) cultivating opium poppy of not less than 500 plants but less than 3,000 plants or any mother plants of other narcotic drugs in relatively large quantities;

(2) cultivating any mother plants of narcotic drugs again after being dealt with by the public security organ; or

(3) resisting the uprooting of such mother plants.

Whoever illegally cultivates opium poppy of not less than 3,000 plants or any mother plants of other narcotic drugs in large quantities shall be sentenced to fixed-term imprisonment of not less than five years and shall also be fined or be sentenced to confiscation of property.

Persons who illegally cultivate opium poppy or any mother plants of other narcotic drugs but voluntarily uproot them before harvest may be exempted from punishment.

Article 352 Whoever illegally buys or sells, transports, carries or possesses a relatively large quantity of the seeds or seedlings of mother plants of narcotic drugs, such as opium poppy, which have not been inactivated, shall be sentenced to fixed-term imprisonment of not more than three years, criminal detention or public surveillance and

Chapter IV Crimes of Infringing upon Citizens' Right of the Person and Democratic Rights	shall also, or shall only, be fined.
	Article 353 Whoever lures, aids and abets, or cheats another person into drug ingestion or injection shall be sentenced to fixed-term imprisonment of not more than three years, criminal detention or public surveillance and shall also be fined; if the circumstances are serious, he shall be sentenced to fixed-term imprisonment of not less than three years but not more than seven years and shall also be fined.
Chapter V Crimes of Property Violation	
Chapter VI Crimes of Obstructing the Administration of Public Order	Whoever forces another person to ingest or inject narcotic drugs shall be sentenced to fixed-term imprisonment of not less than three years but not more than 10 years and shall also be fined.
Section 1 Crimes of Disturbing Pubic Order	Whoever lures, aids and abets or cheats a minor into drug ingestion or injection or forces a minor to ingest or inject narcotic drugs shall be given a heavier punishment.
Section 2 Crimes of Impairing Judicial Administration	Article 354 Whoever provides shelter for another person to ingest or inject narcotic drugs shall be sentenced to fixed-term imprisonment of not more than three years, criminal detention or public surveillance and shall also be fined.
Section 3 Crimes Against Control of National Border (Frontier)	Article 355 Persons allowed by law to engage in manufacture, transportation, administration or utilization of State-controlled narcotic and psychotropic substances who, in violation of the regulations of the State, provide narcotic and psychotropic substances that can make people addicted to their use and are controlled under
Section 4 Crimes Against Control of Cultural Relics	State regulations to persons who ingest or inject narcotic drugs shall be sentenced to fixed-term imprisonment of not more than three years or criminal detention and shall
Section 5 Crimes of Impairing Public Health	also be fined; if the circumstances are serious, he shall be sentenced to fixed-term imprisonment of not less than three years but not more than seven years and shall also be fined. If they provide offenders engaged in drug smuggling or
Section 6 Crimes of Impairing the Protection of Environment and Resources	trafficking with State-controlled narcotic and psychotropic substances that can make people addicted to their use and are controlled under State regulations, for the purpose of profit, provide narcotic and psychotropic substances to persons who ingest or inject narcotic drugs shall be convicted and punished in accordance with the provisions of Article 347 of this Law.
Section 7 Crimes of Smuggling, Trafficking in, Transporting and Manufacturing Narcotic Drugs	Where a unit commits the crime mentioned in the preceding paragraph, it shall be fined, and the persons who are directly in charge and the other persons who are directly responsible for the offence shall be punished in accordance with the provisions of the preceding paragraph.
Section 8 Crimes of Organizing, Forcing, Luring, Sheltering or Procuring Other Persons to	Article 356 Any person who was punished for the crime of smuggling, trafficking in, transporting, manufacturing or illegally possessing narcotic drugs commits again any

Engage in Prostitution	of the crimes mentioned in this Section shall be given a heavier punishment.
Section 9 Crimes of Producing, Selling, Disseminating Pornographic Materials	Article 357 The term "narcotic drugs" as used in this Law means opium, heroin, methylaniline(ice), morphine, marijuana, cocaine and other narcotic and psychotropic substances that can make people addicted to their use and are controlled under State regulations.
Chapter VII Crimes of Impairing the Interests of National Defense	The quantity of narcotic drugs smuggled, trafficked in, transported, manufactured or illegally possessed shall be calculated on the basis of the verified amount and shall not be converted according to its purity.
Chapter VIII Crimes of Embezzlement and Bribery	
Chapter IX Crimes of Dereliction of Duty	
Chapter X Crimes of Servicemen's Transgression of Duties	
Chapter XI Supplementary Provisions	
* Selected parts are included here. A full version of the law is available at http://www. npc.gov.cn/englishnpc/ Law/2007-12/13/content_ 1384075.htm	

Appendix 5

**Selected Administrative Regulations Regarding Narcotic Drugs
Passed after 1978**

The Regulation on the Punishment of Civil Servants of Administrative Organs (Adopted at the 173rd executive meeting of the State Council on April 4, 2007, promulgated and effective as of June 1, 2007) * A full version of the regulation is available at http://www.lawinfochina.com/law/display.asp?db=1&id=6023.	Article 31 (Those civil servants) who consume or inject narcotic drugs or organize, harbor, participate in prostitution, pimping, or other illicit sexual activities, shall be deprived of official positions or fired from the job. Chapter VII Legal Liabilities.
The Regulation on the Administration of Entertainment Venues (adopted at the 122nd executive meeting of the State Council on January 18, 2006, promulgated and took effective on March 1, 2006) * A full version of the regulation is available at http://www.lawinfochina.com/law/display.asp?db=1&id=4937	Article 30 An entertainment venue shall set up warning marks on prohibiting drugs, gambling, prostitution or going whoring as well as the marks on prohibiting or restricting minors from entering at the eye-catching sites of the halls, boxes and compartments of its business place. Such marks shall indicate the tip-off phone numbers of the public security organ and of the competent department for culture administration.
The Regulation on the Administration of Precursor Chemicals (Adopted at the 102nd executive meeting of the State Council on August	Chapter VII Legal Liabilities Article 38 Where an entity, in violation of the provisions of the present Regulations, engages in any production, distribution, purchase or transportation of precursor chemicals without license or filing relevant materials for

17th, 2005, promulgated and too k effect on November 1st, 2005)

* A full version of the regulation is available at http://www.lawinfochina.com/law/display.asp?db=1&id=4588.

record, forges application materials to cheat for the license of production, distribution, purchase or transportation, undertakes the production, distribution, purchase or transportation of precursor chemicals by using other's license or a forged, altered or invalid license, the public security organ shall confiscate the precursor chemicals illicitly produced, distributed, purchased or transported, the raw materials for illicit production of precursor chemicals and the equipments and tools for the illicit production, distribution, purchase or transportation of the precursor chemicals; and it shall impose a fine of not less than 10 times but not more than 20 times of the value of the precursor chemicals illicitly produced, distributed, purchased or transported. In case 20 times of such value is less than 10,000 yuan, the fine shall be 10,000 yuan. The relevant illicit gains, if any, shall be confiscated. If the violator has a business license, such business license shall be revoked by the administrative department for industry and commerce. If a crime is constituted, the relevant violator shall be investigated for criminal liabilities according to law.

As for an entity or individual that commits an irregular acts as prescribed in the preceding paragraph, the relevant competent administrative department may, within 3 years as of the day when administrative punishment is made, cease to accept its/his application for the license for production, distribution, purchase, transportation or import or export of precursor chemicals.

Article 39 Where an entity or individual, in violation of the provisions of the present Regulations, smuggles the precursor chemicals, the customs shall confiscate the precursor chemicals and the illicit gains, if any, and it shall impose an administrative sanction upon the violator in accordance with the customs laws and administrative regulations. If a crime is constituted, the relevant violator shall be investigated for criminal liabilities according to law.

Article 40 Where an entity, in violation of the provisions of the present Regulations, commits any of the following acts, the competent administrative department responsible for supervision and administration shall give it a warning and order it to make corrections within a prescribed time limit and impose a fine of not less than 10,000 yuan but not more than 50,000 yuan; and it may confiscate the precursor chemicals that are illicitly produced, distributed or purchased. If the violator fails to make corrections within the prescribed time limit, it shall be ordered to suspend its production and distribution for rectification within a prescribed time limit; and if the rectification is not made as required within the prescribed time limit, its relevant license shall be revoked:

(1) An entity that produces, distributes, purchases, transports or imports or exports the precursor chemicals fails to establish a safety management system as required;

(2) Lending its license or record-keeping certification to others;

(3) Producing, distributing or purchasing any precursor chemicals beyond the bound of licensed type and quantity;

(4) An entity that produces, distributes, purchases the precursor chemicals fails to record or to faithfully record the transaction information, or fails to keep the record of transaction as required or to timely and faithfully file the sales information for record with the public security organ and the relevant competent administrative departments;

(5) Failing to make a timely report when the precursor chemicals are lost, stolen or robbed, and thus causing serious consequences;

(6) Conducting transactions in cash or kind of any chemical liable to producing drugs other than those under the item of pharmaceuticals in Category I and those in Category III that may legally purchased by individuals;

(7) The product packaging or instructions of precursor chemicals does not comply with the provisions of the present Regulations; or

(8) An entity that produces, distributes, purchases the precursor chemicals fails to make annual report of its production, sales or inventory to the relevant competent administrative department and the public security organ faithful and timely.

Where an enterprise fails to timely alter its business scope or cancel its registration with the administrative department for industry and commerce after its business license for production and distribution of precursor chemicals is revoked pursuant to law, the precursor chemicals concerned shall be confiscated and a fine shall be imposed upon the enterprise according to the provisions of the preceding paragraph.

Article 41 Where the type, quantity, destination, owner, consignee or carrier of precursor chemicals in transportation is not in line with what is indicated in the transportation license or record-keeping certification for precursor chemicals, or where the type of the transportation license is improper or where the transportation personnel fail to carry with them the transportation license or record-keeping certification throughout the course of the transportation, the public security organ shall order the violator to cease the transportation for rectification, impose a fine of not less than 5,000 yuan to but not more than 50,000 yuan. If the violator has the qualifications for transportation of dangerous articles, the competent transportation department may disqualify it from transporting dangerous articles according to law.

Where an individual carries precursor chemicals at variance with the specified type or quantity, the precursor chemicals shall be confiscated and a fine of not less than 1,000 yuan but not more than 5,000 yuan shall be imposed upon the violator.

Article 42 Where an entity or individual that produces, distributes, purchases, transports or imports or exports precursor chemicals refuses to accept the supervision and inspection conducted by the relevant competent administrative department, the competent administrative department responsible for supervision and administration shall order it/him to make corrections and give a warning to the person-in-charge directly responsible and other personnel directly liable. If the circumstances are serious, a fine of not less than 10,000 yuan but not more than 50,000 yuan shall be imposed upon the entity, and a fine of not less than 1,000 yuan but not more than 5,000 yuan shall be imposed upon the person-in-charge directly responsible and other personnel directly liable. If a violation of the administration of public security is constituted, an administrative penalty for public security shall be imposed in accordance with the law. If a crime is constituted, the relevant violator shall be investigated for criminal liabilities according to law.

Article 43 Where a functionary of the competent administrative department in charge of precursor chemicals, in his/her administrative work, refuses to grant

<table>
<tr>
<td></td>
<td>license to those qualified or abusively grants license to those unqualified, fails to accept the materials for record according to law, or commits other illicit acts by abusing his power, neglecting his duty or practicing favoritism for selfish interests, he shall be given an administrative sanction according to law; and if a crime is constituted, the relevant violator shall be investigated for criminal liabilities according to law.</td>
</tr>
<tr>
<td>

Notice on Prohibiting Opium and Other Narcotic Drugs

(Issued by the State Council on August 27, 1981)

* Available at http://law. chinalawinfo.com/ newlaw2002/chl/index.asp, retrieved on December 30, 2008; translations are of the authors.
</td>
<td>

On February 24, 1950, after the Government Administration Council released the "Order on Prohibiting Opium", a national campaign to suppress opium and other narcotics was carried out. In just three years, the campaign made huge success and the drug problems left by the old society were completely gone. However, in recent years, due to a variety of reasons both domestically and internationally, private planting of opium poppies, manufacture, trafficking and use of opium and other drugs continued to take place in a small number of border areas and some places with history of drug problems, especially the smuggling of a large influx of opium from abroad to mainland which has become increasingly serious. In order to protect the health of the people, safeguard social order, and protect the construction of the four modernizations, the State Council reiterated that: for those who privately plant opium poppies and those who smoked opium, cultivation and consumption must be eradicated and stopped; (we shall) severely punish manufacture, trafficking, and smuggling of opium and other drugs according to law.

First, in provinces, municipalities and autonomous regions where drug epidemic exists, governmental officials, once received the notice, should quickly find out the situation, look for solutions, and take effective measures to organize public security, customs, civil affairs, health, medicine and industry and commerce administrations, and other sectors to seize the opportunity and work closely with them and do a good job to suppress drugs. At the same time, we have to educate the masses to consciously abide by the national drug prohibition laws and policies, mobilize and rely on the masses, and fight manufacture, trafficking, drug smuggling and private planting of opium poppies, and use of opium.

Second, to resolutely crack down on manufacture, trafficking, and smuggling of opium and other drugs. Public security departments should strengthen investigation on manufacture, trafficking and smuggling of opium and other drug-related cases. Public security, customs, border control and industrial and commercial administration departments in border regions shall, under the unified leadership of the local People's Government, strengthen their investigation of opium smuggling.
</td>
</tr>
</table>

Once opium and other drugs are found, they should be confiscated. Criminals who manufacture, traffic and smuggle opium and other drugs must be severely punished according to law. Once underground opium halls were found, they would be closed immediately.

For those who use opium and other drugs, it is public security, civil affairs, public health and other sector organizations that forced them to quit.

Third, with the exception of designated state farms who plant under strict supervision a small amount of opium poppies for medicine purpose, no other units or individuals are allowed to grow poppies. Unauthorized cultivation of opium poppy must be immediately eradicated, destroyed on the spot, and opium and seeds that have been harvested must be recovered. Private planting of opium poppies should be severely punished in the future.

Fourth, health, agriculture, medicine, chemical industry and other departments should earnestly implement regulations. Offenders are liable to seriously penalties; in serious cases, they should be punished according to law.

Fifth, opium, other narcotics and their seeds seized by public security, customs, frontier defense, industrial and commercial administration departments at all levels should be confiscated and turned over to Medicine Regulation Bureau in provinces, municipalities and autonomous regions, and then to the State Pharmaceutical Administration. No units and individuals are allowed to hide, split or embezzle opium, narcotics and their seeds. Offenders are liable to severe punishment.

The State Pharmaceutical Administration shall keep confiscated opium and other drugs in separate custody, and, after the price changed, hand them over to the Central Financial.

Please implement the above notice, in accordance with specific circumstances of the region.

Appendix 6

**Selected Judicial Interpretations Regarding Narcotic Drugs
Passed after 1978**

Notice of the Supreme People's Court, the Supreme People's Procuratorate and the Ministry of Public Security on Printing and Distributing the Opinions on Several Issues Concerning the Application of Law in Handling Drug-related Criminal Cases * Selected parts of the judicial interpretation are included here. A full version is available at http://www.lawinfochina. com/law/display. asp?db=1&id=6635	Second, issues with regard to the "subject knowledge" of drug-related criminal suspects or defendants "Knowingly" intent of smuggling, trafficking, transportation, or illegal possession of narcotics refers to that the perpetrator knew or should have known that the act is smuggling, trafficking, transportation, or illegal possession of narcotics violations. When one of the followings happens and the suspect or the defendant cannot make a reasonable explanation, 'knowingly' intent can be found (with the exception where there is evidence that the suspect or defendant was deceived): (A) while law enforcement officers in ports, airports, stations, and other checkpoints require the perpetrator declare items that he/she brought for other people or other suspected narcotics and inform the perpetrator his/her legal liabilities, the perpetrator does not truthfully declare so and drugs are seized; (B) the perpetrator evades customs inspections through for (D) the perpetrator's internal concealment of drugs; (E) the perpetrator carries or transports drugs for an unusually high rewards; (F) the perpetrator adopts highly covert means to carry and transport drugs; (G) the perpetrator uses highly covert means to transfer drugs, which is clearly contrary to the normal transfer of legitimate goods; (H) there is other sufficient evidence to prove that the perpetrator should have known.
Notice of the Supreme People's Court on Printing and Distributing Some Opinions of the Supreme People's Court about Providing Judicial Protection for the Construction of Socialist Harmonious Society	V. Combining Leniency with Severity, and Ensuring Social Stability 16. Accordance with the law, to crack down on serious crimes, safeguarding national security and maintaining social stability. The people's courts shall severely punish crimes of endangering national security, terrorist crimes and organized crimes; crimes of blasting, murder, robbery,

(No. 2 [2007] of the Supreme People's Court) * Available at http://www.lawinfochina.com/law/display.asp?db=1&id=5886.	and kidnapping that seriously endanger public security, crimes that seriously affect the security of the masses, major property crimes such as robbery and theft, drug-related crimes, kidnapping of women and children, and major crimes in production activities to protect social stability and peaceful lives of the masses; the people's courts shall severely punish, in accordance with the law, manufacture and sale of fake and shoddy goods to protect people's lives and health; punish smuggling, financial fraud, money laundering, illegal absorption of public deposits, counterfeit currency, import and export tax rebate fraud, forging VAT receipts, tax evasion and other crimes to safeguard the socialist economic market order; strictly punish corruption, bribery, dereliction of duty and other job-related crimes, and commercial bribery crime to promote anti – corruption movement. 17. To strengthen protection of human rights in criminal justice. The people's courts shall in accordance with the law respect the dignity of the accused, protect the defendant's legally entitled rights, fully listen to the views of the accused and their counsel, and ensure that the accused receive a legitimate, fair, and civilized trial; the people's court shall insist on the unity of the correctness of substantial justice and the accuracy of legal proceedings; not only insist on significance of evidence (not to rely on confession and make sure that the facts of the case are clear and the evidence is substantial) but also insist on the legality and principles of crime and punishment (to make sure that conviction is accurate, sentence is appropriate and an innocent person shall not be subject to criminal prosecution). 18. To render leniency when appropriate to minimize social confrontations. Attach importance to non-custodial sentences. For minor crimes, crimes with little subjective viciousness and personal dangerousness, and defendants who show remorse, plea guilty and obtain victims' acceptance, the people's courts shall, as much as possible, give them chance of rehabilitation, render more lenient sentence or reduce punishment, apply non-custodial sentences when conditions applicable such as probation, supervision or financial penalties, and coordinate with the work of Community Correction; the people's courts shall pay attention to the use of non-criminal punishment. For crimes that are trivial and do not require criminal punishment, the courts shall reprimand the defendant, demand repentance, apology and compensation for loss of the victim, or recommend that the defendant be dealt with through administrative penalty or other administrative means. The courts shall strictly implement "retaining the death penalty, and strictly controlling the death penalty"

<table>
<tr>
<td></td>
<td>policy; no death penalty with immediate execution shall be rendered normally in cases with statutory mitigating circumstances, or cases with lighter or mitigated punishment according to law; in cases where the crime was triggered because of marriage or family conflicts, neighborhood disputes arising from civil conflicts cases, or precipitated by victim's faulty behavior, and the defendant showed sincere repentance and took measures to compensate victim's losses, the death penalty with immediate execution should be used with caution.

19. To be actively involved in comprehensive management of social security. To Minors who commit crimes, the people's courts shall adhere to the policy of education and reformation, put teaching at the trial, combine punishment with treatment for a better effect, effectively prevent re-offenses, and promote their early return to society; the courts shall, in accordance with the law, take care of sentence commutations and parole cases; may expand the application of parole based on crime and behavior of the offenders (when they show repentance and do not constitute danger to society); promote transformation and rehabilitation of offenders; actively seek judicial recommendations for trial loopholes in public security and management; and combine trial work with legal education to comprehensively improve legal awareness in society as a whole.</td>
</tr>
<tr>
<td>**Notice by the Supreme People's Procuratorate on Strengthening Prosecution and Arrest of Drug-related Crimes**

(Issued on June 10, 1997)

* Available at http://law.chinalawinfo.com/newlaw2002/SLC/SLC.asp?Db=chl&Gid=18979</td>
<td>People's Procuratorates in provinces, autonomous regions and municipalities, the Military Prosecutor's Office:

Since the launching of a nationwide special anti-drug campaign in April this year, procuratorial organs at all levels, in accordance with the guidance of the central government and the requirement of the Supreme People's Procuratorate "April-10 notice", gave full play to the function and role of procuratorial organs, actively participated in the special task, and achieved certain progress . As a result, a large number of drug-related criminal cases were transferred to the procuratorial organs for arrests and prosecutions. In order to intensify crackdown on drug-related crimes and consolidate the effectiveness of the campaign, the Supreme People's Procuratorate made the following notice:

1. Procuratorial organs at all levels need to further enhance their understanding of the urgency and difficulty of fighting against drug-related crimes. Though combating drug-related crimes has achieved some success, the trend of drug-related crimes increase has not been reversed; in some places drug-related crimes are still rampant. Cracking down on drug-related crimes is a critical measure to contain the momentum</td>
</tr>
</table>

of the spread of drugs. Procuratorial organs must understand the significance of combating drug-related crimes from the perspectives of social stability, national prosperity, and national prosperity, and give full play to their functions and roles in the campaign.

2. To suspects whose arrests were approved by public security organs, the prosecution shall approve the arrest based on the spirit of severely punishing drug-related crimes, if there is evidence to prove the facts of drug-related crimes. For those who smuggle, traffic, transport and manufacture drugs (regardless of the amount of drugs), the prosecution shall approve the arrests to ensure smooth progress of investigations. The prosecution shall resolutely avoid weak links in approving arrests.

3. The prosecution shall take immediate action to review cases after public security organs transfer drug-related criminal cases. When the suspect's criminal facts have been investigated, evidence is sufficient, and the criminal behavior should be held criminally responsible, the prosecution shall promptly bring up prosecution. For drug smuggling, trafficking, transporting and manufacturing cases, regardless of the amount of drugs, the prosecution should be brought up.

4. For drug-related criminal cases, the prosecution shall resolutely implement the principle of severity and speed, handle the prosecution in accordance with the law, fulfill the function of legal supervision; render timely pursuit and prosecution in case of leakage capture and prosecution; bring up timely appeals in cases of wrongful verdicts to prevent and correct weak combat. In this special campaign, the prosecution shall strengthen ties with public security organs and courts and maintain contact and close coordination, solve problems in the interests of all concerned and in strict accordance with the law under the principle of co-ordination.

5. Procuratorial organs at the provincial level shall strengthen investigation and research, strengthen their guidance of this special campaign; timely report problems of law enforcement step by step to the Supreme People's Procuratorate.

Notice by the Supreme People's Court on Taking Care of Trials of Drug-related Crimes in Anti-Drug Campaign (Issued on April 25, 1997)*	People's courts in provinces, autonomous regions and municipalities, the PLA Military Court: The National Narcotics Control Commission decided to launch a nationwide campaign against drug-related crimes from April to September this year. This is a major move to contain the momentum of the spread of drug-related crimes. In order to do a good job in this special campaign, the Supreme People's Court issued a notice as follows:

Available at http://law. chinalawinfo.com/ newlaw2002/SLC/SLC. asp?Db=chl&Gid=18148

First, the current momentum of continuous rise of domestic drug-related crimes seriously endangered social stability and public security, and caused serious harm to national economic development and people's lives and property. In order to crack down on and effectively curb drug-related criminal activities, at the end of last year, the National Work Conference of Politics and Law made the issue of drug-related crimes a prominent task of the "strike hard" campaign in 1997. It was decided at the just-concluded national anti-drug work conference to launch a nationwide special anti-drug campaign. This decision will have a significant impact on safeguarding national, ethnical, and people's interests, maintaining long-term national stability, and prompting socialist material and cultural civilizations construction. People's courts at all levels should fully comprehend the severity of current drug proliferation problem and the long-term, arduous struggle against drugs, effectively deepen understanding of the necessity and importance of anti-drugs campaign, and carry out crackdown on drug-related crimes this year as a prominent task of the "strike-hard" campaign in terms of ideology, organization and action.

Second, people's courts at all levels, under the unified leadership and deployment of local Party committees, shall make specific arrangements in their own system and sectors of the anti-drug campaign; develop detailed implementation plans, and provide support in organizations, institutions, personnel and logistics to ensure effective and timely implementation of the campaign; principal responsible comrades of the court shall keep abreast of, understand, and check the trial work of drug-related cases in corresponding court system, and report in a timely manner to a higher court and the local party committee the progress of work as well as problems encountered. A higher court shall strengthen its guidance and supervision over the lower courts, and help resolve difficulties and problems encountered.

Third, people's courts at all levels shall, in the fight against drug-related criminal activities, strictly enforce the law, uphold the severity and speed policies of the "strike hard" campaign, and hold crimes of smuggling, trafficking, transporting and manufacturing (regardless of quantity) accountable in accordance with the law. While applying penalties for drug offenders, the courts shall step up strengthen of punishment, and render death sentences resolutely to heinous criminals in accordance with law. At the same time, the courts shall pay attention to the policy of combining strict implementation of punishment with leniency, and treat criminals who self surrendered with meritorious cases with leniency according to the law. In

	adjudicating drug cases, under the premise of ensuring the quality of handling cases, the courts shall improve the efficiency of handling cases, shorten the trial cycle, render fast-trial and fast resolutions, and timely punish criminals.
	Fourth, people's courts at all levels should, based on local characteristics of drug-related criminal activities, select typical cases with educational significance and hold public hearings and open verdict. The courts shall actively meet with the press and conduct legal education through news interviews, press conferences and case reports to strengthen the anti-drug campaign, strike the arrogance of criminal elements, educate and encourage the masses to actively participate campaigns against drug-related criminal activities.
	Fifth, people's courts at all levels shall establish a regular report system on drug-related cases. The High Court shall, on the 1st and the 15th days each month, brief to the Supreme People's Court on current status of the anti-drug campaign and important trials. Reports shall be sent to the First Criminal Tribunal. People's courts at all levels should designate a person who is responsible for liaison and communications matters.
	Please pass the spirit of this notice to party committees, and under the leadership of party committees seriously follow this notice. Status of implementation shall be reported to the Supreme People's Court.
Notice by the Supreme People's Court on Strictly Enforcement of the "Decision on Narcotics Control by the Standing Committee of the National People's Congress" and Severely Punishing Criminals (Issued on January 3, 1991) * Available at http://law.chinalawinfo.com/newlaw2002/SLC/SLC.asp?Db=chl&Gid=4935	"Decision" is an important legal weapon in our fight against drug-related crimes. Its promulgation and implementation indicates China's strong, consistent anti-drug policy and is bound to play an important role in combating drug-related crimes. In recent years, drug-related crimes have become increasingly serious. The number of cases increased, the quantity of drugs increased, and drug cases spread to more and more places. Drug-related crimes, which greatly harmed people's physical and mental health, led to the rise of drug use and addiction, and induced a variety of crimes that seriously endanger public security and smooth development of China's modernization. Therefore, to carry out anti-drug campaign is critical to the country's strength, the nation's prosperity, health and happiness of future generations, and the success of the reform and opening up of China's socialist cause. Cracking down on all drug-related criminal activities is a major event of common concern to the whole society, and a major task to the people's courts at all levels. For this purpose, the Supreme People's Court makes the following notice:

First, people's courts at all levels should be soberly aware of the current grim situation of drug-related crimes, and comprehend the significance of combating such crimes. At present, the courts should organize personnel to earnestly study the "Decision", and gain a profound understanding of the legislative spirit of the "Decision" and meanings of specific provisions in order to correctly apply the "decision" to drug cases.

Second, people's courts at all levels should conscientiously implement the "Decision"; in strict accordance with the Criminal Law and relevant provisions of the "Decision", conduct timely trials of drug-related cases. To criminals who smuggle, traffic, transport and manufacture dangerous drugs and illegally cultivate narcotic crops, the courts shall resolutely implement the principle of severe punishment according to law. People's courts located in areas with rampant drug-related crimes shall treat such cases as the current focus of criminal work, maintain close coordination with relevant organs and actively carry out the special campaign. To criminals whose circumstance of the crime is particularly serious, the courts shall severely punish them in accordance with the "Decision". For those who self-surrendered or reported and uncovered other drug-related crimes with meritorious performance, the courts shall render, according to the law, lighter sentences, reduce or waive penalties.

Third, hearing drug-related cases shall make sure that basic facts are clear, basic evidence is sufficient, pay attention to drug qualitative and quantitative identification, and ensure the quality of case handling. The courts shall correctly handle the "Decision" provisions on the composition of the amount standards of narcotics and the circumstances of the crime, and combine the drug type and the amount quantity with the circumstances of the crime and degree of dangerousness to ensure a comprehensive and accurate measure of sentencing. At the same time, it is necessary to correctly apply additional penalties such as fines and confiscation of property to punish criminals financially.

Fourth, people's courts at all levels should combine trials with education, and vigorously promote the "Decision." Especially in cases of drug-prone areas, the courts shall, based on local specific conditions, select some typical cases, widely publicize through public trials, the media and other forms, the "Decision" importance and its severity of cracking down on drug crimes, and educate the masses to consciously fight illegal criminal activities to deter criminals and to warm them to pull back from the brink and not to defy the law.

Fifth, the courts shall handle drug-related crimes that occurred after the promulgation of the "Decision" in accordance with the provisions of the "Decision"; for drug cases that happened before the promulgation of the "Decision", cases that occurred after promulgation but have not yet been tried or cases that are being processed, the courts shall handle the cases in accordance with the principles set forth in the Penal Code Article IX; for cases that occurred prior to promulgation and have been handled by people's courts in accordance with the law that at that time made legally effective judgments or rulings, no change is required.

Please seriously implement the above notice. If any questions, please timely report to the Supreme People's Court.

January 3, 1991

Glossary

Qianlong	乾隆
Ren	人
Shou	兽
Shunzhi	顺治
Sun Yat-sen (Sun Zhongshan)	孙中山
Taiping	太平
Tiananmen	天安门
Ti-mian	体面
Wang Jingwei	汪精卫
Wu wei	无为
Xianfeng	咸丰
Xiaoren	小人
Xuantong	宣统
Yao	药
Yitu diyang	以土抵洋
Yongzheng	雍正
Yuan	元
Yuan Shikai	袁世凯
Yujin yuzheng	寓禁于征
Zhao Ziyang	赵紫阳
Zan jianhou	斩监候
Zan lijue	斩立决

Bibliography

Aldrich, E. (1992), Illicit drug policy in China: What are the prospects for harm reduction? Master's thesis, Yale University.

Amnesty International, 2004, http://news.sina.com.cn/h/2007-11-29/105814413675.shtml.

An, R. (2003), *Miandui Dupin Nüxing Fanzui Zai Zengjia* [To face the increase of female drug offenses]. Retrieved July 10, 2007, from China Court website: http://Chinacourt.org.

Ansley, N. (1959), "International Efforts to Control Narcotics," *Journal of Criminal Law* 50:105–113.

Arbor, A. (1983), "Economic Trends, 1912-49," in J.K. Fairbank (ed.), *The Cambridge History of China, Volume 12, Republic China 1912-1939, Part 1*, 28–127. (London: Cambridge University Press).

Arnold, G. (2005), *The International Drugs Trade*. (London: Routledge).

Asbury, H. (1950), *The Great Illusion: An Informal History of Prohibition*. (New York: Doubleday).

Bailey, P.J. (2001), *China in the Twentieth Century*. (Oxford: Blackwell Publishing).

Bastid-Bruguiere, M. (1980), "Currents of Social Change," in J.K. Fairbank and K. Liu (eds), *The Cambridge History of China, Volume 11, Late Ching, 1800-1911, Part 2*, 535–602. (London: Cambridge University Press).

Baudrillard, J. (1998), *The Consumer Society: Myths and Structure*. (London: Sage).

Baum, R. (1992), "Political Stability in Post-Deng China: Problems and Prospects," *Asian Survey 32*(6): 491–505.

Baumler, A. (2000), "Opium Control versus Opium Suppression – the Origins of the 1935 Six-Year Plan to Eliminate Opium and Drugs," in T. Brook and B.T. Wakabayashi (eds), *Opium Regimes – China, Britain, and Japan, 1839-1952*, 270–291. (Berkeley: University of California Press).

Becker, H. (1963), *Outsiders: Studies in the Sociology of Deviance*. (New York: Free Press).

Becker, T. (1966), "A Survey of Hawaiian Judges: the Effect on Decisions of Judicial Role Variations," *American Political Science Review* 60: 677.

Beeching, J. (1976), *The Chinese Opium Wars*. (New York: Harcourt Brace Jovanovich).

Bello, D. (2000), "Opium in Xinjiang and Beyond," in T. Brook and B.T. Wakabayashi (eds), *Opium Regimes – China, Britain, and Japan, 1839-1952*, 127–151. (Berkeley: University of California Press).

Benedict, R. (1967), *The Chrysanthemum and the Sword*, 2nd Edition. (London: Routledge & Kegan Paul).

Bianco, L. (1986), "Peasant Movements," in J.K. Fairbank and A. Feuerwerker (eds), *The Cambridge History of China, Volume 13, Republican China 1912-1949*, 270–328. (Cambridge: Cambridge University Press).

Bianco, L. (2000), "The Responses of Opium Growers to Eradication Campaigns and the Poppy Tax, 1907-1949," in T. Brook and B.T. Wakabayashi (eds), *Opium Regimes – China, Britain, and Japan, 1839-1952*, 292–319. (Berkeley: University of California Press).

Black, D. (1976), *The Behavior of Law.* (New York: Academic Press).

Blocker, J.S. (1989), *American Temperance Movements: Cycles of Reform.* (Boston: Twayne Publishers).

Blue, G. (2000), "Opium for China: the British Connection," in T. Brook and B.T. Wakabayashi (eds), *Opium Regimes – China, Britain, and Japan, 1839-1952*, 31–54. (Berkeley: University of California Press).

Bodde, D. (1986), "The State and Empire of Chin," in D. Twitchett and M. Loewe (eds), *The Cambridge History of China: Volume 1, the Chin and Han Empires, 221 B.C. – A.D. 220*, 53–90. (Cambridge: Cambridge University Press).

Bonner, R.C. (1994), "The New Heroin Corridor-Drug Trafficking in China," in D. Altschiller (ed.), *China at the Crossroads*, 229–246. (New York: H.W. Wilson Co.).

Booth, M. (1998), *Opium: a History.* (New York: St. Martin's Press).

Bourdieu, P. (1984), *Distinction: A Social Critique of the Judgment of Taste.* (Cambridge: Harvard University Press).

Boyle, J.H. (1972), *China and Japan at War, 1937-1945: The Politics of Collaboration.* (Stanford: Stanford University Press).

Brook, T. (2000), "Opium and Collaboration in Central China, 1938-1940," in T. Brook and B.T. Wakabayashi (eds), *Opium Regimes – China, Britain, and Japan, 1839-1952*, 323–343. (Berkeley: University of California Press).

Brook, T. and B.T. Wakabayashi (2000), "Introduction: Opium's History in China," in T. Brook and B.T. Wakabayashi (eds), *Opium Regimes – China, Britain, and Japan, 1839-1952*, 1–30. (Berkeley: University of California Press).

Bureau of Justice Statistics, US Department of Justice.

Bureau of Narcotics and Dangerous Drugs. *Conference on the Challenges of Modern Society*, October 19–20, 1970.

Campbell, D. and H.L. Ross (1968), "The Connecticut Crack-Down on Speeding," *Law and Society Review* 3: 55.

Candlin, A. H. (1973), *Psycho-Chemical Warfare – The Chinese Communist Drug Offensive against the West.* (New Rochelle: Arlington House).

Carter, L.H. (1988), *Person in Law.* 3rd Edition. (Glenview: Scott, Foresman).

Chambliss, W.J. (1979), "On Lawmaking," *British Journal of Law and Society* 6(2): 149–171.

Chambliss, W.J. (1993), "The Political Economy of Opium and Heroin," in W.J. Chambliss and M.S. Zatz (eds), *Making Law: The State, the Law, and Structural Contradictions,* 65–86. (Bloomington: Indiana University Press).

Chambliss, W.J. and R. Seidman (1982), *Law, Order, and Power.* 2nd Edition. (Boston: Addison-Wesley).

Chambliss, W.J. and M.S. Zatz (1993), *Making Law: The State, the Law, and Structural Contradictions.* (Bloomington: Indiana University Press).

Chang, T. (2004), *China Always Says "No" to Narcotics.* (Beijing: Foreign Languages Press).

Chatterjee, S.K. (1981), *Legal Aspects of International Drug Control.* (The Hague: Martinus Nijhoff Publishers).

Chen, J. (1986), "The Communist Movement 1927-1937," in J. Fairbank and A. Feuerwerker (eds), *The Cambridge History of China: Volume 13, Republican China 1912-1949, Part 2,* 168–229. (Cambridge: Cambridge University Press).

Chen, J. (1995), *From Administrative Authorization to Private Law: a Comparative Perspective of the Developing Civil Law in the People's Republic of China.* (Boston: Martinus Nijhoff Publishers).

Chen, P.M. (1973), *Law and Justice: the Legal System in China 2400 B.C. to 1960 A.D.* (New York: Dunellen Publishing Company).

Chen, S. (1974), *Communist China and Drug Traffic.* (World Anti-Communist League).

Chen, X.L. (2002), *The New Horizon of Contemporary Criminal Law in China.* (Beijing: The Chinese University of Politics and Law Press).

Chen, Y. (1995), "The Blooming Poppy under the Red Sun: The Yan'an Way and the Opium Trade," in T. Saich and H. Van de Ven (eds), *New Perspectives on the Chinese Communist Revolution,* 263–298. (New York: M.E. Sharpe).

Chen, Z. and K. Huang (2007), "Drug Problems in China: Recent Trends, Countermeasures, and Challenges," *International Journal of Offender Therapy and Comparative Criminology* 51(1): 98–109.

Cherry, A. (2002), "China," in A. Cherry, M.E. Dillon and D. Rugh (eds), *Substance Abuse: a Global View,* 33–49. (Westport: Greenwood Press).

Cohen, P. (1978), "Christian Missions and Their Impact to 1900," in J.K. Fairbank (ed.), *The Cambridge History of China, Volume 10, Late Ch'ing, 1800-1911, Part 1,* 543–590. (London: Cambridge University Press).

Courtwright, D.T. (2001), *Forces of Habit – Drugs and the Making of the Modern World.* (Cambridge: Harvard University Press).

Curran, D.J. (1998), "Economic Development, the Floating Population and Crime," *Journal of Contemporary Criminal Justice* 14(3): 262-280.

De, M. (1936), "A Reflection on the Life of the Lower Classes in Shanghai," *Judu Yuekan,* 101: 36–38.

Deng, Z. (2002), "Drug Trafficking and Consumption in China: Case Studies from Two Cities in Guangdong Province," in Part 2, "Drug Trafficking, Criminal Organizations and Money Laundering," 85–109, of *Globalization, Drugs and Criminalization, Final Research Report on Brazil, China, India and Mexico.*

Dikotter, F., L. Laamann and Z. Xun (2002), "Narcotic Culture – A Social History of Drug Consumption in China," *British Journal of Criminology* 42: 317–336.

Douglas, M. (ed.) (1987), *Constructive Drinking: Perspectives on Drink from Anthropology.* (Cambridge: Cambridge University Press).

Drug Enforcement Administration (DEA) (2004), "Drug Intelligence Brief: China." Retrieved May 4, 2006 from http://www.fas.org/irp/agency/doj/dea/product/china0204.pdf#search="Drug%20intelligence%20brief%3A%20China.

Drug Enforcement Administration (DEA) (1996), *Drug Trafficking in the People's Republic of China and Hong Kong.* Washington: Drug Enforcement Administration, Strategic Intelligence Section, Europe, Asia, Africa Unit.

Dupont, A. (1999), "Transnational Crimes, Drugs and Security in East Asia," *Asian Survey* 39(3):433–455.

Durkheim, E. (1964), *The Division of Labor in Society.* (New York: Free Press). (Originally published in 1893).

Dutton, M. (1997), "The Basic Character of Crime in Contemporary China," *The China Quarterly* 149: 160–177.

Eastman, L.E. (1986a), "Nationalist China during the Nanking Decade 1927-1937," in J.K. Fairbank and A. Feuerwerker (eds), *The Cambridge History of China: Volume 13, Republican China 1912-1949, Part 2*, 116–167. (Cambridge: Cambridge University Press).

Eastman, L.E. (1986b), "Nationalist China during the Sino-Japanese War 1937-1945," in J.K. Fairbank and A. Feuerwerker (eds), *The Cambridge History of China: Volume 13, Republican China 1912-1949, Part 2*, 547–608. (Cambridge: Cambridge University Press).

Emmers, R. (2007), "International Regime-Building in ASEAN: Cooperation against the Illicit Trafficking and Abuse of Drugs," *Contemporary Southeast Asia*, 29(3): 506–525.

Epstein, E.J. (1991), *China's Legal Reforms: China Review, 9.1-9.38.* (Hong Kong: Chinese University Press).

Evan, W.M. (1965), "Law as an Instrument of Social Change," in A.W. Gouldner and S.M. Miller (eds), *Applied Sociology: Opportunities and Problems*, 285–293. (Newbury Park: Sage Publications).

Eykholt, M.S. (2000), "Resistance to Opium as a Social Evil in Wartime China," in T. Brook and B.T. Wakabayashi (eds), *Opium Regimes – China, Britain, and Japan, 1839-1952*, 360–379. (Berkeley: University of California Press).

Fairbank, J.K. (1978a), "Introduction: The Old Order," in J.K. Fairbank (ed.), *The Cambridge History of China, Volume 10, Late Ch'ing, 1800-1911, Part 1*, 1–34. (London: Cambridge University Press).

Fairbank, J.K. (1978b), "The Creation of the Treaty System," in J.K. Fairbank (ed.), *The Cambridge History of China, Volume 10, Late Ch'ing, 1800-1911, Part 1*, 213–263. (London: Cambridge University Press).

Fairbank, J.K. (ed.) (1978c), *The Cambridge History of China, Volume 10, Late Ching, 1800-1911, Part I.* (Cambridge: Cambridge University Press).

Fairbank, J.K. (1983), "Introduction: Maritime and Continental in China's History," in J.K. Fairbank (ed.), *The Cambridge History of China, Volume 12, Republic China 1912-1939, Part 1,* 1–27. (London: Cambridge University Press).

Fairbank, J.K. (1987), "The Reunification of China," in D. Twitchett and J.K. Fairbank (eds), *The Cambridge History of China, Vol. 14, The People's Republic, Part I: The Emergence of Revolutionary China 1949-1965,* 1–50 (London: Cambridge University Press).

Fairbank, J.K. and K.C. Liu (eds) (1980), *The Cambridge History of China, Volume 11, Late Ching, 1800-1911, Part 2.* (Cambridge: Cambridge University Press).

Fay, P.W. (1975), *The Opium War, 1840-1842.* (Chapel Hill: University of North Carolina Press).

Feuerwerker, A. (1980), "Economic Trends in the Late Ching Empire, 1870-1911," in J.K. Fairbank and K.C. Liu (eds), *The Cambridge History of China, Volume 11, Late Ching, 1800-1911, Part 2,* 1-69. (London: Cambridge University Press).

Feuerwerker, A. (1983), "The Foreign Presence in China," in J.K. Fairbank (ed.), *The Cambridge History of China, Volume 12, Republican China 1912-1949, Part I,* 128–208. (London: Cambridge University Press).

Forges, A.D. (2000), "Opium, Leisure, Shanghai: Urban Economies of Consumption," in T. Brook and B.T. Wakabayashi (eds), *Opium Regimes – China, Britain, and Japan, 1839-1952,* 167–188. (Berkeley: University of California Press).

Galanter, M. (1974), "Why the 'Haves' Come Out Ahead: Speculations on the Limits of Legal Change," *Law and Society Review* 9: 95.

Gaylord, M.S. and P. Levine (1997), "The Criminalization of Official Profiteering – Lawmaking in the People's Republic of China," *International Journal of the Sociology of Law* 25(2): 117-134.

Gentzler, J.M. (ed.). (1977), "Chinese Attitudes towards Foreigners," in *Changing China – Readings in the History of China from the Opium War to the Present,* 33–34. (New York: Praeger Publishers).

Ghodse, H. (ed.) (2008), *International Drug Control into the 21st Century.* (Aldershot: Ashgate).

Gil, V.E., M. Wang, A.F. Anderson and G.M. Lin. (1994), "Plum Blossoms and Pheasants: Prostitutes, Prostitution, and Social Control Measures in Contemporary China," *International Journal of Offender Therapy and Comparative Criminology* 38(4): 319–337.

Giles, M. and T. Walker (1975), "Judicial Policy Making and Southern School Segregation," *Journal of Politics* 37: 917.

Gove, W. (1975) (ed.), *The Labeling of Deviance: Evaluating a Perspective.* (New York: Wiley).

Grasso, J., J. Corrin and M. Kort. (2004), *Modernization and Revolution in China from the Opium Wars to World Power,* 3rd Edition. (Armonk: M.E. Sharpe).

Gross, H.J. (1988), "China's Special Economic Zone," *China Law Reporter* 4(4): 23–40.

Gui, W. (2005), "A Study of Female Drug Offenses," *Faxue Shiyong,* 7: 40–43.

Guo, T.X. (1993). *Zhongguo Sudu Zhan* [China's Anti-Narcotics War]. (Huacheng Chubanshe [Huacheng press]).

Guo, X. and W. Wang (2007), "Xingting Tingzhang Tan Nüxing Dupin Fanzui: Liuchengduo Nüxing Zhudong Canyu [Chief Judge of the Criminal Division Discusses Female Drug Offenses: Over 60 Percent of Female Offenders Actively Participated in Their Offenses]." Retrieved June 25, 2007 from China Court website: http://www.chinacourt.org/html/article/200706/25/253496.shtml.

Gusfield, J. (1963), *Symbolic Crusade: Status Politics and the American Temperance Movement*. (Chicago: University of Illinois Press).

Hanes, W.T. and F. Sanello (2002), *The Opium Wars: The Addiction of One Empire and the Corruption of Another*. (Naperville: Sourcebooks).

Hao, W. (1998), "A Study of Reasons of Increasing Female Juvenile Drug Use," *Qingshaonian Fanzui Yanjiu*, 4: 7–8.

Hao, Y. and E. Wang (1980), "Changing Chinese Views of Western Relations, 1840-95," in J.K. Fairbank and K.C. Liu (eds), *The Cambridge History of China, Volume 11, Late Ching, 1800-1911, Part 2*, 142–201 (London: Cambridge University Press).

He, X.D. and M. Fang (1998), *Zhongguo Jindu Da Shijiao [An Overview of China's Anti-Narcotics]*. (Beijing: Daxue Chubanshe [Beijing: Beijing University Press]).

Hoyt, E.P. (1989), *The Rise of the Chinese Republic – From the Last Emperor to Deng Xiaoping*. (New York: McGraw-Hill Publishing Company).

Hsu, I. (2000), *The Rise of Modern China*, 6th Edition. (New York: Oxford University Press).

Hu, S. (1953), *Imperialism and Chinese Politics*. (Beijing: Remin Publishing House).

Huang, S. (2000), "Characteristics of Female Drug Use and Selling and Their Harmful Effects," *Fanzui Yanjiu*, 4(6): 46–48.

Ichiko, C. (1980), "Political and Institutional Reform, 1901-11," in J.K. Fairbank and K.C. Liu (eds), *The Cambridge History of China, Volume 11, Late Ching, 1800-1911, Part 2*, 375–415. (London: Cambridge University Press).

Inciardi, J.A. (1986), *The War on Drugs: Heroin, Cocaine and Public Policy*. (Palo Alto: Mayfield).

Inciardi, J.A. (2002), (ed.), *The War on Drugs*. (Boston: Allyn and Bacon). *INCSR* (China), January 2003–June 2003.

Information Office of the State Council of the People's Republic of China (IOSC) (2000), "Narcotics Control in China," Retrieved May 1, 2006, from http://news.xinhuanet.com/zhengfu/2002-11/18/content_633171.htm.

International Narcotics Control Board (INCB) (1994), "Evaluation of the Effectiveness of the International Drug Control Treaties," *Supplement to the INCB Annual Report for 1994*. INCB website. Retrieved on May 11, 2008 from http://www.incb.org/incb/en/annual_report.html.

Ji, A. (1997), "Zhongguo Jindu Beiwanglu (Drug Prohibition in China)," *Zhengfu fazhi (Government Legal Control)* 6: 4–5.

Ji, L. (1998), "A Study of Female Drug Offenses in Yunnan Border Areas," *Faxue Ziazhi*, 3:25, 36.

Ji, L., Y. Wang, and T. Pang (1997), "A Study of Female Drug Offenses in Yunnan Border Areas," *Yunnan Faxue*, 4: 87–89.

Jian, B., X. Shao and H. Hu. (1981), *A Concise History of China*. (Beijing: Foreign Language Press).

Jiang, Q. and Q. Zhu (1996), *China's Anti-Narcotics History and Progress [Zhongguo jindu licheng]*. (Tianjin: Tianjin Education Press) [Tianjin: Tianjin jiaoyu chubanshe].

Jones, S.M. and P.A. Kuhn (1978), "Dynastic Decline and the Roots of Rebellion," in J.K. Fairbank (ed.), *The Cambridge History of China, Volume 10, Late Ching, 1800-1911, Part I*, 107–162. (London: Cambridge University Press).

Khan, A.R., K. Griffin, C. Riskin and R. Zhao (1992), "Household Income and Its Distribution in China," *China Quarterly*, 132: 1029–1061.

Kidder, R.L. (1983), *Connecting Law and Society: An Introduction to Research and Theory*. (Englewood Cliffs: Prentice-Hall).

Kobayashi, M. (2000a), "An Opium Tug-of-War: Japan versus the Wang Jingwei Regime," in T. Brook and B.T. Wakabayashi (eds.) (2000), *Opium Regimes – China, Britain, and Japan, 1839-1952*, 344–359. (Berkeley: University of California Press).

Kobayashi, M. (2000b), "Drug Operations by Resident Japanese in Tianjin," in T. Brook and B.T. Wakabayashi (eds), *Opium Regimes – China, Britain, and Japan, 1839-1952*, 152–166. (Berkeley: University of California Press).

Kritzer, H. (1979), "Federal Judges and Their Political Environment: The Influence of Public Opinion," *American Journal of Political Science* 23: 194.

Kuhn, P.A. (1978), "The Taiping Rebellion," in D. Twitchett and J.K. Fairbank (eds), *The Cambridge History of China, Volume 10, Late Ching, 1800-1911, Part I*, 264–317. (London: Cambridge University Press).

Kurlantzick, J. (2002), "China's Drug Problem and Looming HIV Epidemic," *World Policy Journal*, 19(2): 70–75.

Lee, H.W. (1963), *How Dry We Were: Prohibition Revisited*. (Englewood Cliffs: Prentice-Hall).

Leng, S. (1985), *Criminal Justice in Post-Mao China: Analysis and Documents*. (Albany: State University of New York Press).

Li, F., E. Luo and W. Chen (1995), *Drug Prohibition – Reality and Strategy – A Case Study of Guiyang City*. (Guizhou, China: Guizhou Education Publishing House).

Li, G. (1957), "Brief Account of Opium," in *Collection of Material on Modern History in China: The Opium Wars*. (Shanghai: Shanghai People's Publishing House).

Li, N., Y. Liu and X.W. Cao (1992), *Guomen Weishi: Zhongguo Jidu Jishi [Guards at Border: China's Anti-Narcotics Report]*. (Shanxi: Beiyue Wenyi Chubanshe [Shanxi: Beiyue Literature and Art Press].

Li, S. (1988), *Materia Medica*. (Beijing: Zhongguo Shudian). (Originally published in 1578).

Li, T. (1999), *Introduction to Medicine*. (Tianjin, China: Tianjin Science Publishing House). (Originally published in 1575).

Li, X. (1994), The Dragon Is Coming Back: A Descriptive Study of Illicit Drug Trafficking in China. Master's thesis, Southern Illinois University.

Li, X. and L. Yang (2004), "Female Drug Users' Social Attitude and Its Changes." *Sheke Zongheng*, 19(2), 35–36.

Li, X.M., Y. Zhou and B. Stanton (2002), "Illicit Drug Initiation among Institutionalized Drug Users in China," *Addiction* 97(5): 575–582.

Liang, B. (2005), "Severe Strike Campaign in Transitional China," *Journal of Criminal Justice*, 33(4), 387–399.

Liang, B. (2008), *The Changing Chinese Legal System, 1978-present: Centralization of Power and Rationalization of the Legal System*. (New York: Routledge).

Liang, B. and P. Lauderdale (2006), "China and Globalization – Economic & Legal Changes in the World System," *Journal of Developing Society* 22(2): 197-219.

Liang, B., H. Lu, and M. Taylor (2009), "Female Drug Abusers, Narcotics Offenders, and Legal Punishment in China," *Journal of Criminal Justice*, 37, 133–141.

Lin, J.Y., F. Cai and Z. Li (1996), *The China Miracle: Development Strategy and Economic Reform*. (Hong Kong: Chinese University Press).

Liu, K.C. and R.J. Smith (1980), "The Military Challenge; The North-West and the Coast," in J.K. Fairbank and K.C. Liu (eds), *The Cambridge History of China, Volume 11, Late Ching, 1800-1911, Part 2*, 202–273. (London: Cambridge University Press).

Lo, C.W. (1995), *China's Legal Awakening: Legal Theory and Criminal Justice in Deng's Era*. (Hong Kong: Hong Kong University Press).

Lu, H. and B. Liang (2008), "Legal Responses to Trafficking in Narcotics and Other Narcotic Offenses in China," *Journal of International Criminal Justice Review* 18: 212–228.

Lu, H. and T.D. Miethe (2007a), *China's Death Penalty – History, Law and Contemporary Practices*. (New York, NY: Routledge).

Lu, H. and T.D. Miethe (2007b), "Provincial Laws on the Protection of Women in China: A Partial Test of Black's Theory," *International Journal of Offender Therapy and Comparative Criminology* 51(1): 25–39

Ma, B. (1994), *A History of Chinese Medical Culture*. (Shanghai: Shanghai People's Publishing House).

Ma, M. (1998), *Historical Material on the History of Narcotics in China*. (Tianjin: Tianjin People's Publishing House).

Madancy, J.A. (2000), "Poppies, Patriotism, and the Public Sphere – Nationalism and State Leadership in the Anti-Opium Crusade in the Fujian, 1906-1916", in T.B. and B.T. Wakabayashi (eds), *Opium Regimes – China, Britain, and Japan, 1839-1952*, 228–247. (Berkeley: University of California Press).

Mao, J. (1999), *Zhongguo Jiujue Dupin [China Says "No" to Drugs]*. (Shenyang: Liaoning Renmin Chubanshe [Shenyang Liaoning People's Press]).

Mao, Y. and X.M. Wang (2002) (eds), *Zhongguo Zhian Anjian Yanjiu [A Study of Selected Criminal Cases in the People's Republic of China]*. (Wuhan, Hubei Province: Hubei Kexue Jishu Chubanshe. [Henan: Hubei Science and Technology Press]).

Martin, B. (1996), *The Shanghai Green Gang: Politics and Organized Crime 1919-1937*. (Berkeley: University of California Press).

Mathaus, M. (1989), "Residence Control in Present-Day China," *Asian Affairs*, 20, 184–194.

Maurer-Fazio, M., T.G. Rawski and W. Zhang (1999), "Inequality in the Rewards for Holding Up Half the Sky: Gender Wage Gaps in China's Urban Labour Market, 1988-1994," *The China Journal* 41: 55–88.

McAllister, W.B. (2000), Drug Diplomacy in the Twentieth Century: An International History. (London: Routledge).

McCoy, A.W. (1973), *The Politics of Heroin in Southeast Asia*. (New York: Harper-Collins).

McCoy, A.W. (2004), "The Stimulus of Prohibition: A Critical History of the Global Narcotics Trade," in Michael K Steinberg, Joseph J. Hobbs and Kent Mathewson (eds), *Dangerous Harvest: Drug Plants and the Transformation of Indigenous Landscapes*, 24–111. (New York: Oxford University Press).

McCoy, C. B., et al. (1997), "No Pain, No Gain, Establishing the Kunming Drug Rehabilitation Center," *Journal of Drug Issues*, 27(1): 73 85.

McMahon, K. (2002), *The Fall of the God of Money: Opium Smoking in Nineteenth-Century China*. (Lanham: Rowman & Littlefield Publishers, Inc.).

Merrill, F.T. (1942), *Japan and the Opium Menace*. (New York: OPR/FPA).

Mosher, C. and S. Akins (2007), *Drugs and Drug Policy: The Control Consciousness Alteration*. (Thousand Oaks: Sage).

Navarro, P. (2007), *The Coming China Wars: Where They Will Be Fought and How They Can Be Won*. (Upper Saddle River: FT Press).

Newman, R.K. (1995), "Opium Smoking in Late Imperial China – A Reconsideration," *Modern Asian Studies* 29(4): 765–794.

Nonet, P. and P. Selznick (1978), *Law and Society in Transition: Toward a Responsive Law*. (New York: Octagon Books).

Packer, H. (1968), *The Limits of the Criminal Sanction*. (Stanford: Stanford University Press).

Pan J. (2002), "Theories of Ethnic Identity and the Making of Yi Identity in China," in C.X. Wei and X. Liu (eds), *Exploring Nationalisms of China – Themes and Conflicts*, 187–218. (Westport: Greenwood Press).

Patric, G. (1957), "The Impact of a Court Decision: Aftermath of the McCollum Case," *Journal of Public Law*, 6: 455.

Peng, F. (ed.) (2006), *Themed Collections of Narcotics Crimes*. (Beijing: China People's Public Security Publishing House).

The *People's Daily*, April 12, 2001.

The *People's Daily*, August 24, 2001; Zhou, 1999; "China Always Says 'No' to Narcotics," 2004.

The *People's Daily*, February 14, 2006.

Platt, A. (1969), *The Child Savers: The Invention of Delinquency.* (Chicago: University of Chicago Press).

Polacheck, J.M. (1992), *The Inner Opium War.* (Cambridge: Harvard University).

Qi, L. and J. Hu (2004), *China's Anti-Narcotics History* [*Zhongguo jindu shi*]. (Gansu: Gansu People's Press). [Gansu renmin chubanshe].

Qi, S. (1959), *A Combined Volume of Huang Juezi's and Xu Naijin's Memorials.* (Beijing: Zhonghua Shuju).

Qiu X. Commissioner of the National Bureau of Statistics of China (NBSC), posted at www.legalinfo.gov.cn (October 2, 2006).

Quinney, R. (1977). *Class State and Crime – On Theory and Practice of Criminal Justice.* (New York: David McKay).

Rankin, M.B., J.K. Fairbank and A. Feuerwerker. (1986), "Introduction: Perspectives on Modern China's History," in J.K. Fairbank and A. Feuerwerker (eds), *The Cambridge History of China: Volume 13, Republican China 1912-1949, Part 2*, 1–73. (Cambridge: Cambridge University Press).

Reins, T.D. (1991), "Reform, Nationalism and Internationalism: The Opium Suppression Movement in China and the Anglo-American Influence, 1900-1908," *Modern Asian Studies*, 25(1), 101–142.

Rojek, D.G. (2001), "Chinese Social Control: From Shaming and Reintegration to 'Getting Rich Is Glorious,' in J. Liu, L. Zhang and S.F. Messner, *Crime and Social Control in a Changing China*, 89–104. (Westport: Greenwood).

Ross, H.L. (1976), "The Neutralization of Severe Penalties," *Law and Society Review*, 10: 403.

Ruan, H. (2007), "A Case Study of the Female Drug-Related Crime," *Yunnan Minzu Daxue Xuebao*, 24:1, 49–53.

Scobell, A. (1990), "The Death Penalty in Post-Mao China," *China Quarterly* 123: 503–20.

Selden, M. (1985), "Income Inequality" in W. L. Parish (ed.), *Chinese Rural Development: The Great Transformation*, 193–218. (Armonk: M.E. Sharpe, Inc).

Sheridan, J.E. (1975), *China in Disintegration – The Republican Era in Chinese History, 1912-1949.* (London: The Free Press).

Sheridan, J.E. (1983), "The Warlord Era: Politics and Militarism under the Peking Government, 1916-28," in J.K. Fairbank (ed.), *The Cambridge History of China, Volume 12, Republican China 1912-1949, Part I*, 284–321. (Cambridge: Cambridge University Press).

Shirk, S.L. (1994), *How China Opened Its Door.* (Washington: The Bookings Institution).

Slack, E.R. (2000), "The National Anti-Opium Association and the Guomingdang State, 1924-1937," in T. Brook and B.T. Wakabayashi (eds), *Opium Regimes*

– *China, Britain, and Japan, 1839-1952,* 248–269. (Berkeley: University of California Press).

Slack, E.R. (2001), *Opium, State, and Society – China's Narco-Economy and the Guomindang, 1924-1937.* (Honolulu: University of Hawaii Press).

Slyke, L.V. (1986), "The Chinese Communist Movement during the Sino-Japanese War 1937-1945," in J.K. Fairbank and A. Feuerwerker (eds), *Cambridge History of China: Volume 13, Republican China 1912-1949, Part 2,* 609–722. (Cambridge: Cambridge University Press).

Solinger, D.J. (1999), *Contesting Citizenship in Urban China: Peasant Migrants, the State, and the Logic of the Market.* (Berkeley: University of California Press).

Somers, R.M. (1979), "The End of the Tang," in D. Twitchett (ed.), *The Cambridge History of China: Volume 3, Sui and Tang China,* 589–906. (Cambridge: Cambridge University Press).

Song, X. (1999) (ed.), *A Critical Translation of the Muslim Materia Medica,* Volume 2. (Beijing, Zhonghua Shuju).

Spence, J.D. (1975), "Opium Smoking in Ching China," in F. Wakeman, Jr. and C. Grant (eds), *Conflict and Control in Late Imperial China,* 143–173. (Berkeley: University of California Press).

Steinberg, M.K., J.J. Hobbs and K. Mathewson (eds) (2004), *Dangerous Harvest: Drug Plants and the Transformation of Indigenous Landscapes.* (New York: Oxford University Press).

Stelle, C.C. (1981), *Americans and the China Opium Trade in the Nineteenth Century.* (New York: Arno Press).

Su, Z. (1997), *Chinese Narcotics History [Zhongguo dupin shi].* (Shanghai: Shanghai People's Press) [Shanghai: Shanghai renmin chubanshe].

Su, Z. and C. Zhao (1998), *Treaties of War on Drugs.* (Beijing: China Democracy and Law Publishing House).

Sun, J. (1996), *Scattered Essays.* (Shanghai: Shanghai Shudian). (Originally published in 1925).

Swanström, N. and Y. He (2006), *China's War on Narcotics: Two Perspectives.* Central Asia-Caucasus Institute & Silk Road Studies Program.

Teng, S. and J.K. Fairbank (1954), *China's Response to the West: A Documentary Survey 1839-1923.* (Cambridge: Harvard University Press).

Timberlake, J.H. (1963), *Prohibition and the Progressive Movement, 1900-1920.* (Cambridge: Harvard University Press).

Tobias, J.J. (1968), *Crime and Industrial Society in the Nineteenth Century.* (New York: Schocken Books).

Trocki, C.A. (2000), "Drugs, Taxes, and Chinese Capitalism in Southeast Asia," in T. Brook and B. T. Wakabayashi (eds), *Opium Regimes – China, Britain, and Japan, 1839-1952,* 79–104. (Berkeley: University of California Press).

Twitchett, D. (1979), "Introduction," in D. Twitchett (ed.), *The Cambridge History of China, Volume 3, Sui and Tang China, Part I,* 589–906. (Cambridge: Cambridge University Press).

Twitchett, D. and J.K. Fairbank (1978), *The Cambridge History of China, Volume 10, Late Ching, 1800-1911, Part I*. (London: Cambridge University Press).

Van Den Berge, P.L. (1967), "Dialectic and Functionalism: Toward a Synthesis," in N. Demerath and R.A. Peterson (eds), *System Change and Conflict: A Reader on Contemporary Sociological Theory and the Debate Over Functionalism*, 294–310. (New York: Free Press).

United Nations Office on Drugs and Crime (UNODC) (2007). *2007 World Drug Report.*

Wakeman, F. (1978), "The Canton Trade and the Opium War," in J.K. Fairbank (ed.), *The Cambridge History of China, Volume 10, Late Ching, 1800-1911, Part I*, 163–212. (London: Cambridge University Press).

Wakeman, F. (1988), "Policing Modern Shanghai," *China Quarterly*, 115: 408–440.

Wakeman, F. (1995), *Policing Shanghai, 1927-1937*. (Berkeley: University of California Press).

Wang, H. (1996), Transnational Networks and International Capital Flows: Foreign Direct Investment in China. (Unpublished doctoral dissertation, Princeton University).

Wang, L. (2000), *Chinese Tea Culture*. (Beijing: Foreign Languages Press).

Wang, X. (2002), "China Learning to Stand Up: Nationalism in the Formative Years of the People's Republic of China," in C. X. Wei and X. Liu (eds), *Exploring Nationalisms of China – Themes and Conflicts*, 77–100. (Westport: Greenwood Press).

Wang, Y. and R. Shi (2005), "Investigation of Female Drug Use in Zhejiang," *Zhejiang Gongshang Daxue Xuebao* 5: 51–55.

Wang, Y. and Q. Zhou (2005), "A Study of Female Drug Use in Zhejiang Province," *Gong'an Xuekan—Zhejiang Gong'an Gaodeng Zhuanke Xuexiao Xiaobao* 2: 88–90.

Wang, Z., P. Chen, and P. Xie (1999), *History and Development of Traditional Chinese Medicine*. (Beijing: Science Press).

Wen, J.H. and Q. Zhong (2007), "An'yuan Qu Fayuan Fenxi Dangqian Nüxing Dupin Fanzui Chengxian Liüda Tuchu Xianxiang [An Analysis by the People's Court in An'yuan District Showing Six Features of Female Drug Offenses]." Retrieved July 10, 2007, from the *Discipline and Inspection Committee of An'yuan District, Jiangxi Province, People's Republic of China*, http://www.ayqf.gov.cn.

Whyte, M. K. and W.L. Parish (1984), *Urban Life in Contemporary China*. (Chicago: The University of Chicago Press).

Wong, J.Y. (1998). *Deadly Dreams: Opium, Imperialism, and the Arrow War (1856-1860) in China*. (New York: Cambridge University Press).

Wong, R.B. (2000), "Opium and Modern Chinese State-Making," in T. Brook and B.T. Wakabayashi (eds), *Opium Regimes – China, Britain, and Japan, 1839-1952*, 189–211. (Berkeley: University of California Press).

World Bank (1992), *China: Strategies for Reducing Poverty in the 1990s.* (Washington: The World Bank).

World Bank (1997), *China 2020: Development Challenges in the New Century.* (Washington: The World Bank).

Wright, Mary C. (ed.) (1968), *China in Revolution: The First Phase 1900-1913.* (New Haven: Yale University Press).

Wu, Z.Y. et al. (1996), "Risk Factors for Initiation of Drug Use Among Young Males in Southwest China," *Addiction* 91(11): 1975–1985.

Wyman, J. (2000), "Opium and the State in Late-Qing Sichuan," in T. Brook and B.T. Wakabayashi (eds), *Opium Regimes – China, Britain, and Japan, 1839-1952*, 212–227. (Berkeley: University of California Press).

Xiao, Z. (2002), "Nationalism in Chinese Popular Culture: A Case Study of the Opium War," in C.X. Wei and X. Liu (eds), *Exploring Nationalisms of China – Themes and Conflicts,* 41–56. (Westport: Greenwood Press).

Xie, R. (1995), "A Study of Reasons of Female Drug Use," *Lanzhou Xuekan* 3: 57–58.

Xu, Y. (2007), "Qinhuai Dajindu (Drug Prohibitions in Qinhuai)," *Wenshi Jinghua (Culture and History Digest)* 204(5): 29–32.

Yan, X. (1992), Regulation of Foreign Investment in Chinese Law. (Unpublished LLM thesis, McGill University, Canada).

Yang, G. (1981), *A Biography of Lin Zexu.* (Beijing: Renmin Publishing House).

Yao, J. (2001), "A Study of Female Drug Use," *Qingshaonian Fanzui Wenti* 6: 47–51.

Yao, Z. and Xue, L. (eds) (2004), Jindu Da Shijiao: Zhongguo Jindu Lishi Gaikuang [The Vision of Narcotics Control: a Brief History of China's Narcotics Control]. (Beijing: Zhongguo Renmin Gong'an Daxue Chubanshe [Beijing: Chinese People's Public Security University Press]).

Young, A.N. (1971), *China's National-Building Effort, 1927-1937: The Financial and Economic Record.* (Stanford: Hoover Institution Press).

Yu, E. (1934), *The Changing History of Opium Prohibition in China.* (Beijing, China: Zhonghua Shuju).

Yuan, T. (1995), *A History of Smoking in China.* (Beijing: Shangwu Yinshuguan).

Zatz, M. and J. McDonald (1993), "Structural Contradictions and Ideological Consistency: Changes in the Form and Content of Cuban Criminal Law," in W. Chambliss and M. Zatz (eds), *Making Law: The State, the Law, and Structural Contradictions*, 127–167. (Bloomington: Indiana University Press).

Zhang, Z. (2004), *The Theory and Practice of the Suspended Death Penalty System in China.* (Wuhan: Wuhan University Publishing House).

Zhao, B. (1993), *A Study on Narcotic Drugs.* (Beijing: People's University of China Publishing House).

Zhao, B.Z. and Z.G. Yu (1998), *Dupin Fanzui [Drug-Related Crimes].* (Beijing: Zhongguo Renmin Gongan Daxue Chubanshe [Beijing: The People's Public Security Press of China]).

Zhao, C. and S. Liang (1998) (eds), *Encyclopedia of Narcotics Prohibition*. (Beijing: China Democracy and Law Publishing House).

Zhao, D. (1997), "Decline of Political Control in Chinese Universities and the Rise of the 1989 Chinese Student Movement," *Sociological Perspectives* 40(2): 159–182.

Zhao, X, and Zhang, T (eds) (2004), *Jindu Da Shijiao: Dupin De Zhonglei He Weihai* [*The Vision of Narcotics Control: Narcotics Typology, Danger and Harm*]. (Beijing: Zhongguo Renmin Gong'an Daxue Chubanshe [Beijing: Chinese People's Public Security University Press]).

Zheng, Y. (1935), "A Study on the Trade Balance in the Recent Decade in China," *Social Science Journal* 4: 4.

Zheng, Y. (2005), *The Social Life of Opium in China*. (Cambridge: Cambridge University Press).

Zhou, Y. (2000), "Nationalism, Identity, and State-Building – The Antidrug Crusade in the People's Republic, 1949-1952," in T. Brook and B.T. Wakabayashi (eds), *Opium Regimes – China, Britain, and Japan, 1839-1952*, 380–403. (Berkeley: University of California Press).

Zhou, Y.M. (1999), *Anti-Drug Crusades in Twentieth-Century China: Nationalism, History and State Building*. (Lanham: Rowman & Littlefield Publishers, Inc).

Zhou, Y.M. (2000a), *China's Anti-Drug Campaign in the Reform Era*. (Singapore: Singapore University Press).

Zhou, Y.M. (2000b), "Nationalism, Identity, and State-Building: The Anti-Drug Crusade in the People's Republic, 1949-1952," in T. Brook and B.T. Wakabayashi (eds), *Opium Regimes: China, Britain, and Japan, 1839-1952*, 380–403. (Berkeley: University of California Press).

Zhou, Y.M. (2004), "Suppressing Opium and 'Reforming' Minorities: Antidrug Campaigns in Ethnic Communities in the Early People's Republic of China," in M.K. Steinberg, J.J. Hobbs and K. Mathewson (eds), *Dangerous Harvest: Drug Plants and the Transformation of Indigenous Landscapes*, 232–245. (New York: Oxford University Press).

Zhu, R. (2002), "Wu-Wei, Lao-Zi, Zhuang-Zi and the Aesthetic Judgment," *Asian Philosophy* 12(1): 53–63.

Index

247